MADMEN
OF
HISTORY

MADMEN OF HISTORY

OF

HISTORY

by Donald D. Hook

DORSET PRESS
New York

First published 1976

This edition published by
Dorset Press,
a division of
Marboro Books Corporation,
by arrangement with
Donald D. Hook
1986 Dorset Press

ISBN 0-88029-112-5
(Formerly ISBN 0-8246-0202-1)

Printed in the United States of America
M 9 8 7 6 5 4 3 2 1

Table of Contents

Preface

A fairly broad definition of madness has been taken as the basis for this book. There are examples of clinical madness, legal insanity, and temporary derangement, but for the most part the characters are studies in over-dedication to an ideal or to a political objective. Some have drastically altered the course of history by their acts, and some have merely changed the flow of the times. Each character has left his peculiar imprint on the history of mankind.

The book is divided into three parts: Despots; Assassins; and Hangmen, Henchmen and Mystics. So many rulers could have qualified for the first category that it was decided to limit the selection to the most outstanding of the past five centuries. As for assassins, there was no dearth of candidates, but the author did feel it important to treat all the assassins of American Presidents. Turner and Mishima were presented as evidence that madness is not the exclusive province of the white race. And Charlotte Corday was included in order to demonstrate that madness is not peculiar to the male sex.

Madmen of History is history, not fiction, although now and then, liberty has been taken to dramatize a character or an event. What better way to become acquainted with history than through biography?

I wish to express my appreciation to my friend and colleague, Professor Lothar Kahn, for his many suggestions and his special help with the chapter on Robespierre. For reading and criticizing the chapter on Nat Turner, I am indebted to Mr. Thomas A. Champ, history instructor at Trinity College. To my wife goes a big vote of thanks for her professional assistance in gathering sources and for her patience and interest in hearing and reacting to each chapter.

Donald D. Hook

PART I: Despots

1. Ivan the Terrible

"If you do this wicked thing, you will have a wicked son; your states will become prey to terrors and tears; rivers of blood will flow; the heads of the mighty will fall; your cities will be devoured by flames."

Thus spoke the patriarch of Jerusalem to Grand Duke Vasili III of Russia. Vasili was about to send his barren wife, Salome, off to a nunnery so that he might marry a Lithuanian beauty by the name of Helena. Desperately hoping for a male heir, and heedless of the patriarch's warning, Vasili married Helena. Four years later, in 1530, she bore him a son. In this child, who was named Ivan, the patriarch's prophecy would be fulfilled.

Seventeen years later, on the occasion of Ivan's coronation as czar and autocrat of all Russia, another cleric, Metropolitan Makary of Moscow, invoked the following blessing of God: "May Ivan's throne flourish even as the throne of David! May his throne be ever a throne of righteousness! May he turn a terrible face to those who rebel against his power; but a smiling face to those who are his faithful subjects!"

The actions of Ivan, as czar, were to bring a new meaning to the word "terrible."

When Ivan was three, his father died. Immediately, a struggle for power ensued. His father's brothers considered themselves next in line, but also claiming control were the boyars—the blue-bloods of the aristocracy. Both sides expected little opposition from Helena, for after all, she was a mere woman—and a foreigner at that.

But they were mistaken. An imaginative and energetic woman, Helena obtained the support of her uncle, Michael Glinsky, and her lover, Prince Obolensky. The church, rallying around her and Ivan, and her younger son Yuri, demanded that everyone swear allegiance to them.

After five years of rule, Helena suddenly died. Although the cause of death is not certain, some claim she was poisoned. During this period, Michael Glinsky also died, after having been thrown into prison. Of the entire immediate family, only eight-year-old Ivan and little Yuri remained. It was at this point in his life that Ivan received a basic training in cruelty that became the hallmark of his long reign.

Thrust into the middle of a vicious struggle for power between the two most important boyar families, the Shuiskys and the Belskys, little Ivan was treated more like a servant's child than royalty. He was underfed, underclothed, ridiculed, and subjected to frequent beatings. This treatment molded his attitude towards life: life was brutal, even for many among the privileged. He concluded that the only way to survive was to be brutal; to inflict greater torture on others than they could inflict on him.

As a youngster, Ivan was powerless to act on his feelings. But he was storing up his resentment, waiting for the day and for the opportunity to avenge himself of the wrong that had been done to him.

Ivan was patient. He found relief from frustration in solitude. Often, alone in his room, he brooded and wallowed in self-pity. The games that he played were an outlet through which he could give fuller expression to his bitterness.

Not surprisingly, these games took a sadistic turn. From time to time, Ivan, either alone or with other children, rounded up a number of dogs and either enticed or carried them up to the top of the Kremlin walls or to the top of a nearby tower. He then dropped them to the pavement below—a distance of 100 feet or more. Ivan then scurried down the steps and, with great glee, examined the brutal mess he had created.

In another game, he mounted a horse and plunged headlong, and at great speed, into the middle of a crowd of unsuspecting people walking peacefully down the street. Those who did not escape his path quickly enough were maimed or killed. Complaints against the young prince were never lodged for fear of retaliation. As a consequence, Ivan learned very early in life how to take advantage of his royal status, and how fear and awe could be made to work for him.

When not brooding or playing games, Ivan was reading. His selection of books was not varied. In addition to the breviary and psalter, there were several history books with which he spent his time. Ivan had an excellent memory, and learned countless prayers and psalms by heart. He also studied the lives of many ancient rulers and began to identify his problems with theirs.

Ivan's reading, more than any other childhood activity, was instrumental in making him a powerful force against the boyars. After reading that the ancient rulers of Byzantium considered themselves czars and direct descendants of Augustus Caesar, he was determined that he would resurrect that title in all its majesty. Consequently, at age 16—in 1546—Ivan summoned the boyars and church leaders to the Cathedral of the Assumption where he made two announcements.

First, he announced that he would begin a search for a wife from among the noble Russian families. Second, he intended to be crowned czar of Russia prior to his wedding.

Privately, the first piece of news was greeted with enthusiasm by the aristocracy. Since most were related to the czar by marriage, this would be helpful in gaining favors and exercising one's influence. But the ramifications of the second announcement were not at all clear.

In January of 1547, a large crowd alternately stood and knelt at a ceremony lasting more than four hours. They listened as the church hierarchy intoned the ancient coronation liturgy. Seventeen-year-old Ivan was now czar and autocrat of all Russia.

Ivan lost no time in beginning the search for a wife. Official notices were posted in and around Moscow ordering all boyar families to register their eligible daughters with the proper authorities. Failure to bring one's daughter to the registration center would incur the czar's great "disfavor."

Meanwhile, preparations were being made for the arrival of the girls at the Kremlin. A huge dormitory was set up in one wing of the czar's living quarters. Several of the larger rooms were converted into smaller chambers, each containing 12 beds. A few of the great hallways were also partitioned. Ivan, apparently, expected to choose from a very large number of young women.

The precise number of girls who did eventually assemble in the Kremlin is not known. Estimates ranged from 500 to 2,000. Whatever the number, Ivan was satisfied, and he immediately set the elimination process in motion.

Helping him were physicians, midwives, priests and legal counselors. A girl had to be a virgin; she had to be devoted to the church; and she had to be free of any political involvement. Backgrounds were scrupulously checked. Not less carefully examined was each girl's body. Within two weeks, the original number had been narrowed down to approximately 200. By the end of the third week, only 10 eligible girls remained.

By and large, the experience had not been an unpleasant one for the girls. Even though all came from aristocratic families, most of them had never before been "a guest" at the Kremlin. They were served sumptuous meals, were entertained royally, and were even instructed in dress and good manners. It was like attending a short, intensive course at a finishing school or spending two or three weeks at an elegant resort.

Aside from the doctors' thorough examinations, the girls had to contend only with minor annoyances. Ivan himself often quizzed them on their knowledge of the Bible, and corrected their table manners. Occasionally he would poke one of them to ascertain whether she was filled out in the right places. From time to time, he would observe the girls through a crack in the wall as they dressed. Late at night, he often walked through their sleeping quarters and checked each girl to see if she slept quietly or snored. Everything had to be just right.

One day, less than a month after the start of the process, Ivan reached his decision. The ten finalists were dining together. Ivan entered the dining hall and took a seat at the table. Midway through the meal, he reached into his pocket and extracted a handkerchief and a ring, and offered them to the girl seated next to him. Her name was Anastasia Zahkarina-Koshkina. The other girls were immediately thanked and showered with gifts and dismissed.

Although not the prettiest of girls, Anastasia was one of the sweetest, wisest and most virtuous. Her marriage to Ivan took place on February 3, 1547. She was a perfect mate. No other person had ever had such a calming influence on him. Had she lived longer, there might never have been an Ivan the "Terrible." He loved her deeply, and when she died, his latent madness manifested itself in all its fury, unbridled and uncontained.

For the first five years of his marriage, except for two minor battlefield encounters with the Kazan Tatars, Ivan remained in the Kremlin, where he carried on state business in a reasonably responsible way. On two occasions, however, his cruel streak emerged.

On the first such occasion, Ivan was annoyed and angry because a delegation from the city of Pskov had come to complain about a governmental affair. They had interrupted his vacation with Anastasia, and he became furious. First, each one was stripped naked and forced to lie on the ground. Then, Ivan personally poured vodka over them, and set their hair afire.

The second occasion occured shortly after the great fire of

Moscow in 1547. A mob stormed the Kremlin and threatened the royal family. Ivan responded by having his guards execute the leaders immediately and in full view of the mob. Frightened, the crowd rapidly dispersed. Ivan never forgot the effectiveness of his swift action, and he used this method many times in later years.

Despite these moments of excitement, Ivan, at the age of 22, found that he was usually bored. He reviewed his accomplishments during his five years as czar and decided they were meager in comparison to those of his grandfather, Ivan the Great, and even to those of his father, Vasili. In his years of reading, he had acquired a vision of himself as a conquering hero of such magnitude that none could equal. In view of the fact that he was basically somewhat cowardly, this was indeed a strange self-conception.

But an opportunity soon presented itself that could lead to fame on the battlefield. The year was 1552. The Tatars of Kazan, a city located near the confluence of two rivers, the Sviaga and the Volga, had been a source of trouble for Ivan for some time. In their raids, they had once penetrated as far as the Kremlin walls. But Ivan forced them back, and by now they were weakened and worn out by the numerous retaliatory lightning raids. The Kazan Tatars, it now seemed to Ivan, were ripe for the taking. As he prepared for a final onslaught, the Tatars began to make peace overtures. Ivan was not fooled. He felt it was a ruse. He was sure they were merely stalling for time so that they might enlist the support of the Crimean Tatars.

Luck was with Ivan. His forces accidentally encountered an army of Crimean Tatars on their way to Kazan, and he routed it. This was Ivan's first major military victory. Elated, his army was ordered to march on Kazan. Czar Ivan himself would lead the troops into battle!

In the summer of 1552, Ivan accompanied the large but motley army toward Kazan. Composed largely of undisciplined conscripts, the army would have been wiped out had it not been for its size, and the incredible stamina of its troops.

Ivan's first offensive against the city led nowhere. Thinking the city to be empty, the Russians made several test attacks on the fortress in the center of town. At first there was no response, but, suddenly, 10,000 Tatar troops swarmed out of their hiding places and attacked the Russians. In panic, the czar's men fled. Had the Tatars continued their pursuit, they might well have achieved a victory.

But there were no less than four times as many Russians as

Tatars, and in less than two days Ivan and his generals had regrouped their retreating men, and marched them back to attack the fortress once again. This time the Tatars did not come forward to face the Russians on open terrain.

Throughout the remainder of the summer, and into early fall, Russian troops harassed the occupants of the Kazan fortress. Finally, with the cold of winter on its way, Ivan and his advisers decided on October 2nd as the day on which they would launch a major offensive.

The day dawned. All preparations had been made; the troops were ready to advance. But Ivan was nowhere to be found! When his whereabouts was discovered, he was in his tent praying with a priest. "Hurry," his generals said, "we await your order to attack."

Thirty minutes passed. Another messenger was sent to Ivan with a note from the deputy commander, General Vorotinsky, requesting permission to attack. When still another half-hour elapsed without an answer from the czar, Vorotinsky took matters into his own hands and began the assault.

The priest and Ivan were in the midst of a chant when a tremendous explosion caused the front wall of the fortress to collapse. The priest stopped chanting and looked at Ivan, fully expecting him to discontinue his prayers and to join the battle. But no, Ivan continued to pray. Only after the walls had been breached and columns of troops flooded the fortress, attacking Tatars right and left, did Ivan cease his devotions. With a final kiss for the icon of his patron saint, St. Sergius, Ivan asked for the priest's blessing, mounted his horse, and rode off toward the fortress "to suffer for the true faith," as he had earlier explained to the priest. Never one to endanger himself, Ivan was relieved that the battle was almost over. All that was left for him to do was to order that the Russian flag be raised to the top of the tallest tower in town.

The successful siege earned Ivan the title, "The Conquering Czar." He was on his way to becoming an epic hero.

The return to Moscow was slow. The czar stopped in towns and villages to enjoy the adulation of the people. It seemed as if the Russians had suddenly become aware of their country's power.

One day, outside the city of Vladimir, a messenger arrived from Moscow to tell Ivan that Anastasia had just given birth to a son. Ivan was overjoyed, and made plans to leave immediately for Moscow. His wife had already borne him one child—a girl named Anna—but she had died soon after birth. Even if she had lived, the czar would have wanted a male heir to carry on his name.

The end of 1552 was now at hand. Ivan had been czar for nearly six years. He had been a reasonably good ruler, considering the times, and considering the record of some of his contemporaries: Henry VIII in England, Philip II in Spain, among others.

In March of 1553, Ivan became desperately ill. He and those around him were convinced that death was near. Knowing that the boyars were making plans to regain their power, Ivan became even more concerned with establishing the hereditary right of succession.

He trusted no one, always searching for hidden motives. He was convinced that all his associates and advisers were traitors. This distrust, as it manifested itself in Ivan's later years, can only be described as paranoia. The persecution complex which had begun in childhood as a result of the machinations of power-hungry boyars, was now deepening. This may have contributed to Ivan's worsening illness. The true nature of his illness is pure conjecture. Perhaps it was the plague. An epidemic was raging just north of Moscow.

Ivan summoned a number of prominent boyars to his bedroom, and asked for their support and loyalty. He requested that in the event of his death they recognize and pledge their allegiance to Dmitri, his infant son, as the next czar. As a symbol of their loyalty, he asked that they kiss the cross. No one would do so.

Even on his sickbed, Ivan was a frightening man. Burning up with fever, he shouted violently at the boyars for their treachery. Within two days, he had, either by force or by persuasion, convinced a majority of the highest-ranking boyars to accept Dmitri as his successor. But Ivan swore to himself that he would never forget the disloyalty of the boyars. He swore, too, that he would make an extensive pilgrimage if God would permit him to live.

Within three days, Ivan was up and about, and making plans for the pilgrimage. Several of his advisers, among them a monk named Maxim, advised that he not waste time on a religious mission, and urged him instead to attack the Tatars again. Some segments of the khanate (the region ruled by the Khan) had become rebellious.

But Ivan would not listen—even after Maxim prophesied that little Dmitri would die if the pilgrimage were carried out. On this trip Dmitri did indeed die, a victim of exposure to the cold, damp, early spring weather, and Anastasia contracted an illness that was to leave her sickly for the rest of her life.

Ivan's life had also started to crumble, but it wasn't until August 7, 1560, when Anastasia died, that it became totally uncontrolled.

The czar was overwhelmed with grief, and for months after the funeral would sit in complete silence for hours on end. Entire days would sometimes pass with Ivan refusing to see anyone. If approached, he would scream invectives and physically attack the visitor. He pulled the hair out of his beard by the handfuls, banged his head against the walls and floor and furniture in full view of the boyars. He smashed vases, chairs—anything in sight. At night, he would sit by an open window, howling like a dog as he hurled out objects reminding him of Anastasia. By morning, his mood would take a strange turn. He would order young virgins sent to him, make them strip naked, and ravish them.

"You poisoned her!" Ivan screamed at Prince Andrei Kurbsky. He was to make this same accusation after the death of his other wives, but there was no evidence to support the contention.

He continued to blame Kurbsky for Anastasia's death. In a letter, written in 1577, Ivan said: "And why did you separate me from my wife? If only you had not taken from me my young wife."

Ivan could not accept his personal tragedy. He could not live with the thought that God had not intervened on his behalf and kept Anastasia alive. After all, in his many pilgrimages and prayers he had served God; how could God forsake him? Seeing treachery everywhere, he suspected even God of perfidy!

Ivan's overwhelming grief over the death of Anastasia was an indication of his deep love for her. No other woman was ever able to fill the void created by her loss. Her devotion to him, her patience and long-suffering, were forces that kept his destructive tendencies in check.

Aside from Anastasia, two other people served to help curb Ivan's aggressive nature. But they were to disappear from Ivan's life within months of Anastasia's death. His two closest advisers —the priest Sylvester, and a former minor government official and later Ivan's chamberlain, Alexei Adashev—both fell into disfavor because of their refusal, in 1553, to take oath of allegiance to Dmitri. Ivan never again trusted either, although he did continue to make use of their services.

After Anastasia's death, Ivan began to intensify his persecution of the boyars, causing many to flee to distant parts of Russia or Poland. He also intensified his efforts to extend his territory. Sylvester and Adashev cautioned restraint in both instances. Ivan was infuriated at the unacceptable advice.

It is strange that Sylvester and Adashev should have advised *against* the removal of boyars from high government places. After all, neither of them was of noble background. Sylvester, although a cleric, had been completely unknown before his association with Ivan. Adashev, although very intelligent and exceptionally gentle and compassionate, came from a poor and insignificant family. Ivan had raised him from the status of chamberlain to minister and adviser. Sylvester's and Adashev's resistance to Ivan's tactics probably was nothing more than a reflection of their human concerns—concerns that were incomprehensible to Ivan.

Sylvester and Adashev misunderstood the nature of their relationship with Ivan. They hoped that through their friendship with him, they could help control and regulate Ivan's lust for power and territory. But Ivan had never been truly intimate with anyone but Anastasia. He never forgot that both Sylvester and Adashev had been less than enthusiastic about his marriage to Anastasia. Further, Ivan, by his very nature, could not be intimate with anyone of lesser stature than himself. Sylvester and Adashev were humans; but Ivan was convinced, in the inner recesses of his strange mind, that he was more than a mere mortal. He was but one rung below God—a kind of intermediary between God and man.

Even with this high estimate of his own worth, he was, like many other madmen of history, plagued by an awareness of his own sinfulness which required that he carry out the most extreme forms of penance and self-torture. His cruelty to others was a form of self-punishment as well. As the "greatest of men" he, in his own mind, had the authority to administer and receive punishment in the name of all, so that his soul and the souls of others might be purged of sinfulness. In Ivan, sadism and masochism were one.

In later years, the blade and the gibbet were the reward of those who incurred his wrath. But, in his treatment of Sylvester and Adashev, Ivan was much more gentle. Sylvester was banished to a distant monastery where he passed the remainder of his days in disgrace. Adashev was imprisoned and, in all likelihood, committed suicide. Ivan often referred to that "treacherous, idiot priest Sylvester" and that "dog Adashev" whom he "had lifted off the dunghill." With the removal of Sylvester and

Adashev everyone became more circumspect.

Before Anastasia's body had spent one year with Mother Earth, Ivan married a woman possessed of many of the same traits as he. She was a princess from Circassia, a tribal nation located along the shores of the Black Sea. Uncommonly attractive, with long, black tresses and flashing eyes, the princess had little to offer besides her beauty, and an understanding that her role was to be that of a submissive wife. Maria, as she was baptized just before the marriage, was unable to read or write— but she knew how to handle Ivan. Known as the "wild Circassian," she never advised him or rebuked him for his violent ways. She let him behave as he pleased.

When Anastasia was alive, Ivan was a faithful man. Now he filled his harem with young girls from all over the empire. Nightly, he took his pick from among a score or more of teenaged virgins. When he had run through the group once or twice, he replaced them with others. Maria never objected, for she knew intuitively that it would have been futile to do so. Besides, for the most part Ivan ignored her.

The point had come when Ivan no longer heeded anyone's advice. Suspicious to a psychotic degree, he saw enemies lurking everywhere. Not only did he imagine the political threat of the boyars to be growing, but he was convinced that his life was in danger. To protect himself, he carried with him a long, spiked stick. At the slightest provocation, he would gore anyone who angered him. And, for 17 years, the paranoid Ivan carried the iron-pointed staff with him.

Ivan's brother, Yuri, was moderately retarded. He could be of no help to Ivan, but Ivan loved him and provided for him and his wife Ulyana. When Yuri died unexpectedly in 1563, not long after Ivan had lost an infant son, Ivan was distraught. He ordered a regal funeral, proclaimed an official period of mourning, and offered all manner of assistance to Ulyana. She thanked him but expressed a resolve to take the veil. Despite his own religiosity, Ivan could not comprehend Ulyana's desire to lead the spartan life offered by a convent. He insisted that she lead her life in a style befitting a czar's sister-in-law. But Ulyana steadfastly refused his offers of money and luxuries. Ivan became infuriated over her independent spirit and promptly had her executed.

Ivan could not tolerate being thwarted on any level. He seized control of every situation; his word had to be law.

Ivan now turned his perverted mind to the boyars who, from the very beginning, he had considered a threat to his rule. He was determined to rid the world of them so that he might become an absolute despot. His means of achieving this end was diabolical.

Shortly before the Christmas of 1564, without any announcement, Ivan loaded his family and many of his prized belongings into sleighs, left the Kremlin, and headed north. When word got back to Moscow that he had passed his favorite pilgrimage spot, Trinity Monastery, without stopping, people questioned his destination.

In several days, the party reached the town of Alexandrov. There, the sleighs were unloaded, and it appeared as if the czar intended to set up headquarters for an indefinite length of time. The citizens of Moscow were confused, and they were concerned that the czar might be planning not to return.

The boyars were also worried. Even more than Ivan, they feared and distrusted the Russian people. Lacking the power to rule, they decided to "play" for time, and dispatched a delegation to Alexandrov to ascertain the czar's plans. As the delegation was about to leave, a message addressed to the Russian people arrived from Ivan. The message accused the boyars of plotting his overthrow. He told also of real and imagined thefts of property and land, and requested the support of the populace. He assured the common people of his love for them, and spoke of his sorrow at having had to desert them. God had led him "into the wilderness," he explained.

A great hue and cry was raised. The Russians wanted their czar to return to Moscow. Accordingly, a group consisting of older clergy and high officials departed for Alexandrov in January.

Ivan received the emissaries indifferently. He looked haggard and unkempt. On their knees, the members of the delegation pleaded with Ivan to return home. He listened carefully, and indicated that he would consider returning if he could expect their full support in eliminating his enemies by whatever means he thought necessary. The group agreed instantly. In fact, some stated their willingness to personally participate in the massacre.

Ivan was elated, but he masked his joy. Dramatic genius that he was, he stayed in Alexandrov for another month before leaving for Moscow. By the time he reached the city gates, in February 1565, all Moscow was in a state of great excitement and expectation. Banners waved, dancers whirled in the streets, women cried with joy, and people prostrated themselves in the snow before their "Little Father."

The next day Ivan met with the highest officials of the land and extracted a formal promise that they would not interfere with his future actions. He was to be revered as the absolute ruler of Russia. Further, the Council had to agree that he could banish or execute anyone at will. The leaders agreed to both conditions; and Ivan announced he had permanently returned. He had gambled everything—and won.

Why had he gone to such lengths?

Firstly, Ivan felt that his power was eroding. Through their intrigues, he was convinced that the boyars were intent upon destroying the rule of the czar.

Secondly, he feared that his life was at stake. For years he had been the captive of horrible nightmares in which he saw himself as being poisoned, cut and quartered, or impaled. The mental torture had become too much for him.

Ivan found relief from political worries and concern for his personal safety in the strange *coup d'état* that he had concocted and accomplished. His dreams, fantasies, and hallucinations served as his guide. The establishment of absolute despotism was perhaps the most courageous act of his life, and the cruelties carried out in the name of the newly established Oprichnina were certainly among the most cowardly and dastardly acts of his life.

The term Oprichnina meant a separatist state within a state. Ivan set up the Oprichnina like a royal court, complete with guards, retainers, clerks, and judges, as well as carefully chosen, loyal boyars. These people known as Oprichniki were settled in certain key parts of Moscow by evicting the previous inhabitants. Ivan then duplicated the Moscow arrangement in other cities and communities scattered throughout Russia. Those Oprichniki then proceeded to expel as many people as they wished from their assigned areas.

Often, people were "resettled" in wastelands or forests or, literally, in snowbanks. Some groups were successful in developing the land, but thousands of others died in the attempt. Expelled along with these people were boyars disloyal to the czar. By means of this "sorting-out process," as Ivan himself called it, the czar was able to dissipate the power of the boyars.

Within five years, the map of Russia took on a most peculiar appearance. Instead of clearly marked national boundaries, there were dots of concentrated czarist power—those areas held by the Oprichniki—interspersed with larger districts of a rural or less consequential nature, called the *Zemshchina*, into which the dispossessed had been herded. The country had become two, and steadily the power of the Oprichniki grew.

Ivan's actions were based on his fear of treasonous activity and assassination. His Oprichniki were fully empowered to dispossess, maim, or kill, as they saw fit, in order to bring the people into line. Although the expropriated were filled with resentment toward Ivan and the Oprichnina, the masses of people generally felt better disposed toward the czar than to their former boyar masters. In a sense, it was a class struggle in operation—and the czar had taken the side of the common man. Ivan must have known this; in fact, he was smart enough to have conceived of the Oprichnina as a major propaganda tool.

But the Oprichnina was more than that. It was an elitist organization frightfully similar to those of modern times. Complete with a ritual and a distinctive black uniform, it attracted those malcontents, rapists, murderers, and sadists who were seeking official sanction to carry out their nefarious acts.

On the whole, the members of the Oprichnina were young. Ivan loved to mix with them at their rowdy meetings. The experience temporarily restored his own youth. With great gusto, he drank and caroused with his henchmen.

Yet, he was still their chief. This fact became immediately clear if anyone incurred Ivan's suspicion of disloyalty. A careless remark in Ivan's presence could lead to a personal goring by the czar himself.

The people lived, understandably, in dread of a visit by the Oprichniki. Often, without any reason whatsoever, black-uniformed men on black horses would dash up to a dwelling in the dark of night, roust everyone from their sleep and drive them from their homes. They would hack men to pieces, rape women, and seize property for themselves. All this was done in the name of the czar—as a safeguard against treason!

From this time on, because of the vicious acts carried out by the Oprichnina, the czar was christened with a new title: "Ivan the Terrible."

Ivan's private life was every bit as terrible as his public life —and perhaps worse.

His favorite retreat was a monastery located about 100 miles from Moscow, near the city of Alexandrov. There, Ivan, together with a large contingent of Oprichniki, would sometimes spend months on end, either conducting or attending endless religious services, without foregoing the baser pleasures of life.

His day would begin at four o'clock in the morning. Playing the role of abbot, he and his sons would ring the bells to summon everyone to morning prayer. After the service, which would last until seven o'clock, breakfast was served, followed by the Divine Liturgy at eight, which, if not abbreviated, lasted until almost noon. During the midday meal Ivan often read aloud from the Bible or another religious tract. The brothers listened while they ate.

Part of the afternoon was unstructured, but there were always chores to be performed, manuscripts to be read, and private intercessions to be made. At eight o'clock in the evening, a vesper service was held; at midnight everyone appeared once more in church for the last prayers of the day. Despite the exhausting daily routine, Ivan invariably had difficulty falling asleep. It was reported that three blind men, all excellent narrators, awaited him in his room each night and told him stories until he fell asleep.

Such a regimen left little time for pleasure. But it did not mean that one had to forego pleasure completely. It simply meant that one had to use the allotted time for pleasure to its fullest.

Ivan engaged in every form of entertainment available at the monastery. Aside from the conventional gorging of oneself with food or drinking oneself into a state of insensibility, having sexual relations with women was a favorite pastime. Young orphan boys were also available for those who wished to indulge in homosexuality. If none of this appealed—or if something else were needed to round out an evening—one could descend to the monastery dungeons and watch the torture of prisoners.

Ivan particularly enjoyed watching people being stretched on the rack or mercilessly cut with the knout. Occasionally, he would take a swipe with the knout himself. All this was necessary, Ivan insisted "to get at the truth."

Bears have long been considered sources of entertainment in Russia. Ivan sometimes rid himself of a gloomy mood by ordering a bear brought into the monastery refectory to amuse him after supper. The bears had been trained to perform tricks, but if Ivan was feeling especially out of sorts, he would order that a man be pitted against the beast. The bears "won" so often that Ivan started providing the bears' human opponents with spears. If the man won, he was pardoned of his crime. "I am a man of compassion," the czar explained.

Sometimes, Ivan had bears turned loose in the monastery courtyard to attack any passer-by. At other times, he released them in the courtyard for the purpose of deciding a matter of guilt. He once offered freedom to a group of priests accused of treason if they could survive such an encounter. Ivan watched while six of the men were clawed, chewed, and squeezed lifeless. The seventh survived—although severely mauled—and Ivan, faithful to his word, set him free.

Women were not exempt from Ivan's playful torture sessions. He would dispatch a squad of Oprichniki to a neighboring village to seize a dozen or so young girls and bring them to the monastery. They would then be forced to strip, stark naked, and run around the courtyard while sharpshooters aimed to kill them. Ivan considered it excellent target practice and a most amusing sport. He always laughed heartily as the girls desperately tried to hide in the bushes or scale the walls.

But somewhere in the dark recesses of the soul of this iniquitous man there lurked a sense of guilt, for after some murderous deed or a night of debauchery, he could be heard intoning the most pathetic prayers for forgiveness as he kept banging his head on the floor until his forehead was lumped with bruises. He once characterized himself as "a stinking dog living in drunkenness, adultery, murder and brigandage."

During the years 1560 through 1570, terror reigned throughout Russia. Hardly anyone was safe anywhere. The Oprichniki had quickly increased in numbers from the original 1,000 to more than 6,000. They had infiltrated practically every business and every influential house. The highways and byways were under their surveillance. Unsuspecting boyars, traveling from one town to another, were accosted, accused of treason against the czar, and were summarily knocked in the head, drowned, or hung by the heels.

Ivan saw treason in every action, movement and gesture. He saw it in individuals; he saw it in entire communities. But often, after he had ordered large numbers of people executed, he would assuage his guilt by having prayers recited for their souls. On one occasion, he sent a list of 3,470 names to the Monastery of St. Cyril.

But none of Ivan's offenses against mankind can compare with the massacre of Novgorod in the year 1570.

Like Kiev, Novgorod was an older city than Moscow. The inhabitants had always considered themselves superior to the people of the relatively new capital. For centuries, Novgorod had been extending itself and claiming district after district as its own. The people's confidence, self-reliance, and downright egotism were reflected in their motto: "Who has power against God and Great Novgorod?"

Ivan considered the Novgorodians dangerous, and he resolved to eliminate them. The city exhibited traces of democratic government which were extremely repugnant to an autocrat like Ivan. He saw it aligned, in spirit, more with the Western world than with the rest of Russia. In fact, there was speculation that Novgorod was planning an alliance with King Sigismund's Poland.

Ivan's troops arrived in Novgorod during the first part of January. Ivan himself, together with a force of Oprichniki, went wild during the journey, razing villages and towns. "Our task is secret," said Ivan. "We mustn't leave anyone to talk about it."

The vanguard had aroused abundant fears in the hearts of the people of Novgorod. All activity ceased. By order of Ivan's army, no one could leave town. Life stood still—as if the populace awaited the arrival of its executioner.

In the third week of January, Ivan the Terrible arrived in Novgorod. He was met by the archbishop, who offered his blessing. Ivan refused it, but accepted the prelate's invitation to dinner that evening. It was a short dinner. In the middle of the meal, Ivan had the archbishop seized and carried off to a dungeon.

The next morning, the massacre began. It continued for more than five weeks. On an average day, 1,000 persons were killed. (Mass murders of such proportions were not to be committed again until the coming of Hitler.)

Horrible as the means of execution were, they were ingenious. Seated high above the crowd, on a specially built platform, Ivan and his son observed the cruelty in its finest detail.

Several of the horrors were devices Ivan had designed himself. One was a frying pan—large enough to hold a man. As the first man began to sizzle and jump about, glee shone on Ivan's face.

Another was the impaling stick, one of Ivan's favorites. A person would be stripped, lifted up, and then lowered onto a 6-foot-high, heavily greased, pointed shaft. After an hour or so, the weight of the person's body would have caused the shaft to ram its way up to the lungs or heart.

The implementation of individual torture was time-consuming, and Ivan was growing bored; so he ordered sleighloads of people to be bound and pushed into the icy Volkhov River. If anybody broke his bonds, he was quickly put to death by the Oprichniki stationed along the bank.

In time, Ivan wearied of death. Rounding up the few survivors, he instructed them quite dispassionately to "be thankful and to pray for victory over all enemies of the czar." With that, he left for Pskov where the terrified inhabitants awaited him.

But Ivan decided to spare Pskov. The people expressed their gratitude by blessing him and kneeling for days in the snow outside his tent.

There was no welcome for Ivan in Moscow. In fear and trembling, people stayed in their homes. They sensed violence.

Ivan's paranoia had, by now, become so great that he even suspected many of the top Oprichnina officials of treason. He lost no time in arresting them and making a public spectacle of their execution.

Men worked for days erecting gibbets, shafts, and whipping posts. Cauldrons were filled with boiling water. When the citizens did not flock in mass to witness the happenings, Ivan flew into a ferocious rage.

Many of the highest ranking Oprichniki were sliced into pieces or dropped into boiling water and peeled before the eyes of all. Occasionally, an unenthusiastic spectator was singled out and garroted on the spot. The carnage was frightful.

Ivan himself was frightful. Haggard, unwashed, eyes and teeth flashing, he was the picture of madness. It is incredible that the people did not seize him and tear him limb from limb.

Over the next 10 years, Ivan's rule continued through periods of widespread famine, pestilence and unrest. He took wife after wife. The first three died from disease, although Ivan was convinced that the boyars had poisoned them. Two he banished. Little is known about the fates of the other two.

His two sons, Ivan and Fyodor, lived with him in the Kremlin. The czarevitch, the spitting image of his father, was his favorite. It was to be Ivan's ultimate earthly punishment that he should kill his own son.

The murder was almost an accident. Ivan, who like most madmen had a prudish side, criticized his son's wife for the way in which she was dressed while pregnant. The czarevitch took exception to his father's remarks, and a violent argument ensued, in the course of which Ivan ran the point of his ever-present stick through the young man's temple. Ever since, artists have attempted to portray the extent of the father's grief as he gathered the mortally wounded boy in his arms.

Young Ivan lived another five days, but the father's remorse and horror were all the greater because he had to witnesss his son's slow and painful death. The czar's days and nights were crammed with self-accusations, accompanied by endless howling and head-banging.

The fury of Ivan the Terrible's madness had now reached its peak. The end was dramatic, and came on the night of

March 28, 1584. Ivan was lying in bed, playing chess with his regent, Boris Godounov. As he moved the king, legend has it, a surge of pain passed through him and he collapsed on the pillow.

The Metropolitan was summoned immediately and, as prearranged, he tonsured Ivan, dubbing him Monk Jonah. Reaching for the cowl held out by the Metropolitan, Ivan's hand struck the king on the chessboard, knocking it over. Ivan gasped his last.

All eyes turned toward the weak-minded Fyodor who was standing by the bed. He would be the next ruler of Russia.

2. Alexander VI

The Borgia family was responsible for three-quarters of a century of intrigue, greed, licentiousness and murder. At the center of this notoriety stood Alexander VI. He has been variously maligned, praised and tolerated, but possibly never fully understood. He was an administrative genius who used his talent for personal gain. He loved his family, but with an intensity that blinded him to their evil ways. He was the Vicar of Christ on earth, but his life reflected none of Jesus's humility and purity of heart and body.

Alexander and his progeny have always been a source of shame for the Roman Catholic Church, and a wide variety of "excuses" have been employed to offset the harsh criticism of the papacy brought on by the unsavory behavior of Alexander. The Church has placed extraordinary emphasis on the excellence of Alexander's administrative accomplishments. His conduct has been explained purely in terms of the evil times in which he lived. Because he functioned as both a spiritual and temporal head of state, the Church has sometimes labelled him "just another man." As a last resort, his name was once removed from the list of popes.

The story of the Borgias begins not in Italy, but in Spain. Alexander was born Rodrigo Borja in Jativa on January 1, 1431. He was one of six children of Isabel and Jofré de Borja y Doms. Jofré was a man of substance and learning, a country gentleman from an old patrician Aragonese family with important connections at the royal court. Isabel was her husband's cousin on the Borja side, and so Rodrigo was possessed of a double dose of that peculiar virus that was to infect even the next generation.

Rodrigo was an intelligent and studious boy. At first, he received instruction from a well-known local tutor, but later, in 1441, after his father had died, the family moved to Valencia, where the opportunities for intellectual growth were greater.

With the passage of time, Rodrigo reached a high level of scholastic achievement. He also became adept in the use of weaponry. Handy with a dagger and a crack shot with a pistol, Rodrigo never missed a chance to go hunting. In mock battles with other youngsters, he invariably took command, mapping out tactics and strategies that amazed even the adults.

In a very short time, Rodrigo believed himself to be superior to any of his friends. His success in his studies made him arrogant; his skill with lethal weapons made him an almost tyrannical character. He was cocksure in matters of religion and morality, which led him to bigotry. On one occasion, it is alleged, he cold-bloodedly disemboweled a 12-year-old boy for having used "some indecent words" in his presence.

At about this time, Rodrigo's uncle, Alonso de Borja was receiving his scarlet robes and cardinal's hat from Pope Nicholas V in Rome. Alonso had come to Rome in the service of the King of Aragon after many years of service to him in Spain, first as adviser and legal assistant, then as Bishop of Valencia. With his clerical status, Spanish nationality, and close association with Alfonso of Aragon, who now held Naples in his feudal system, he was invaluable to the pope as a go-between.

Alonso did not forget his relatives back home on the peninsula. Two of his four sisters were married and had given birth. Of these sisters, Isabel was his favorite. Of her children, Rodrigo stood at the top of the list. Alonso wrote his nephew often, advising him about the proper course of study, and lavishing gifts upon him. It was not long before Alonso had convinced his nephew, Rodrigo, to embark upon an ecclesiastical career. This was the road to status, wealth and power.

Alonso presented such a glowing account of his young nephew's capabilities that Nicholas V issued a papal bull in 1445 in which he stated his readiness to grant the boy ecclesiastical benefices within the chapter of Valencia. His decision was based, Pope Nicholas went on to say, upon numerous reports of Rodrigo's exemplary life and great virtue. Needless to say, the bull was viewed by the Valencian clergy with acute resentment, for to them the 14-year-old boy was no more than an upstart. They, like many others, wondered why only the good reports had reached the ears of the pope.

In late March, 1449, Rodrigo, now a strapping 18-year-old, set sail for Rome. He lived with his uncle in Rome for the next four years. He studied at one of the best schools in the city, steeped himself in Rome's cultural life, and witnessed, or took part in, many civic, ecclesiastical and royal functions. He also witnessed the horrors of the plague of 1450.

Among other things, he learned that there are at least two kinds of people: the powerful and everybody else. This became particularly clear to him when he saw the entire papal court travel to distant points—including foreign countries—when the plague struck. The pope himself ran from castle to castle, finally barricading himself in one at Fabriano, and threatening anybody from Rome who came within seven miles of him with excommunication and loss of title and land.

In June of 1453 Rodrigo departed for Bologna. For the next two years he studied canon law at the university. He might have stayed on for another year—he was doing well scholastically and Bologna was a gay and carefree town filled with fun and pleasant opportunities—but an event took place that was to propel the Borgias (who by now had Italianized their name) to the pinnacle of power.

In the wee hours of the morning of March 25, 1455, Pope Nicholas breathed his last. Immediately, as always, the pope's favorites, clutching their possessions, went into hiding. Simultaneously, various factions began preparations for the upcoming fight for their choice of a successor. Other persons, some with an axe to grind, appeared on the scene. Rodrigo, too, lost no time in leaving Bologna and returning to Rome.

Of all the cardinals, Alonso Borgia seemed at first to be the least likely candidate for the papacy. At 77 years of age, he was in poor health—and he was a Spaniard. He himself never gave thought to the possibility of being elected. But, in the final analysis, it was all these negative points—precisely, his age and infirmity—which led to his selection as the successor to Nicholas V.

For days the conclave had been split in their choice of a candidate. Suddenly, they saw in Alonso a chance to temporarily resolve the impasse. They would elect him, and he would live just long enough for one group to emerge and assert its dominance.

But Alonso, now known as Callistus III, fooled them. Quite unexpectedly this ailing old man became hale and hearty, and the newly-elected pope started making grandiose plans for a crusade. Rodrigo, and his brother Pedro, were always at his side. Callistus showered favors on both of them, but for Rodrigo he had something special — a cardinal's hat. This he bestowed upon his nephew who was only 25 years of age.

To the astonishment of all, Callistus reigned for three years. During this time he never abandoned his idea of a massive, final crusade to crush Islam, but in his last days, he became sour and disillusioned when his envoys kept returning from foreign lands without support for his cause. Scarcely a soul could be found who agreed with Callistus III's objective.

In contrast to his scholarly predecessor, Callistus was not favored by the people. For Callistus, books and works of art were no more than frivolities. Without hesitation, he sold jewel-encrusted tomes, and fine paintings, for a fraction of their value. By many, he was considered a typical, barbaric Spaniard.

Upon Callistus' death, his relatives thought it wise to make a fast retreat from prominence. Disguised, and in the dark of night, the two most prominent relations, Pedro and Rodrigo, left Rome. Pedro died of a fever while trying to make his way back to Spain. Rodrigo, of sturdier stuff, turned around after several weeks, and made his way back to Rome. This took courage. To the Romans, Spaniards were a smelly, ignorant, arrogant, barbarous lot who lived like pigs. To Spaniards, Italians were a weak-kneed, disorganized, pampered people that could be conquered and molded. Rodrigo held the latter belief and he intended to prove its validity. But he had to bide his time.

The election of his uncle's successor was undoubtedly the most important event to take place in the lifetime of young Cardinal Borgia. At 27, he was much too young to be a candidate himself, but, as for all the cardinals, alliances were of great importance. Each cardinal tried to determine who was likely to get majority support; and then spoke out forcefully at a time when that support was crucial. Borgia sensed a trend, and threw his weight behind Aeneas Silvius Piccolomini, Bishop of Siena. Being vice-chancellor, Borgia's position would influence the outcome.

It was a wise choice. Not only was Piccolomini the most astute and experienced member of the House of Cardinals, but he possessed the highly esteemed virtue of rewarding loyalty. Borgia retained his position as vice-chancellor, a key post at the Vatican.

Pius II, the name taken by Piccolomini, became very fond of Borgia. The pope was an inveterate traveler, and everywhere he went, Borgia was his companion. So similar were their tastes for plain food, hard beds, and deep discussions that in many ways they were like father and son.

But Pope Pius and Cardinal Borgia differed when it came to women. If the former had a pronounced weakness along that line, we know little about it. Borgia learned very soon that Pius would not tolerate scandal.

During the period of 1460, while the pope was relaxing at Spa Petriolo, Borgia attended a marathon baptismal feast in Siena at which he acquitted himself with such sexual ardor that word of his behavior got back to the old man. Less out of anger toward Borgia than concern for the image of the Church, Pius dispatched a long and highly critical missive to his protégé. The pope was very specific in his condemnation, referring not only to the "shameful acts" but "the indecent words associated with them."

Somehow, Borgia had managed to incarcerate a number of the loveliest young women of Siena on the estate of wealthy Giovanni de Bichis. For a two-week period, he enjoyed these women "in various positions." Apparently, the women did not object to their incarceration. Nor, it seems, did their husbands.

This was the first documented "sexcapade" connected with Borgia. Despite the pope's admonition to practice the utmost discretion, the cardinal was unable to conform. Incident after incident followed, resulting in the birth of four illegitimate children between the years of 1463 and 1471.

Pope Pius died in 1464. Borgia, who had been very sick, nevertheless attended the conclave. His long-time friend, Pietro Barbo, was elected Pope Paul II. Once again, evidence exists that Borgia, rather than the Holy Spirit, influenced the outcome of the election.

During Paul's seven-year reign, Borgia prospered. In 1468, he was finally ordained as priest (he had been a cardinal and bishop)—a sequence no longer possible—and held the bishopric at Albano for eight years. He was careful not to alienate those in power, for he now had his eye on the greatest prize of all—the papal tiara.

Paul died quite suddenly in 1471. As the story goes, he died of apoplexy while sitting, bareheaded, under a hot sun and stuffing himself with food. His successor called himself Sixtus IV. Again, Borgia was instrumental in determining the election of the pope. For this service, as before, he was amply rewarded.

Among his rewards was his appointment as Cardinal-Legate to Spain. From the spring of 1472, until September 1473, Borgia did his best to smooth out differences between the ruling houses of Castile and Aragon, and to gain manpower and equipment for a new crusade against the Turkish Empire. He was most successful in his task, and the pope was tremendously pleased. What displeased Sixtus, however, were the innumerable communications from prelates and ambassadors relating to Borgia's personal conduct in Spain. Everywhere he went, the cardinal lined his own pockets with money and jewels received as donations for the crusade. By the time he had returned to Rome, he was looked upon as vain, and self-seeking, and rather condescending toward his fellow-countrymen. Lastly, as before, the cardinal left a trail of young women on whom his amorous passions were bestowed.

During the interregnum between the death of Sixtus on August 12th, and the election of Innocent VIII on August 29, 1484, the deceased pope's kinsmen and close associates took to the security of their homes and castles, guarding their money and jewels from would-be plunderers. Rodrigo barricaded himself in his palazzo behind a wall of guards and bristling cannon.

When the thieves, rabbler-rousers, and opportunists began to disband, Rodrigo and the other cardinals came out of hiding and attended to the business of electing a pope.

Deciding it was time to throw off the mask of humble servant, Rodrigo worked to have himself elected to the highest office. To accomplish this, he decided to shift his loyalty from the powerful Colonna family to the equally influential Orsinis. This was a dire error in judgment, for it led everyone to conclude—and quite correctly—that he was a devious, power-hungry, and self-serving man. An equally wily cardinal, Giuliano della Rovere, outwitted Rodrigo, and succeeded in getting his candidate elected: Giovanni Battista Cibo. Cibo reigned for eight long years. They were endless years for Borgia.

When Cibo, who ruled under the name of Innocent, died in the summer of 1492, Borgia was ready. For years, he had patiently curried support for his election and was now prepared to meet della Rovere's opposition. However, after four days of haggling, Borgia found it necessary to resort to bribes and promises of favors to assure his election. At 61 years of age, Borgia succeeded in attaining his goal. He was the new pope, and he was ecstatic.

And so was the populace. The people were not ecstatic because they loved their new pope for his fine personal qualities, or because they revered him as a holy man, but because he was precisely the kind of leader that could meet the needs of the moment. Avaricious, unscrupulous, and forceful, he was a ruler who could withstand the encroachments of the equally greedy princes whose lands surrounded and threatened Rome. Italy had been in a constant state of anarchy; the Italians—Christian doctrine notwithstanding—could not conceive of a humble, self-effacing, Christlike pope as their leader. Borgia, now Alexander VI, possessed the qualities they sought.

Whereas Cardinal Rodrigo Borgia had lived like a prince, Pope Alexander VI lived like a king. And so did his family—which consisted of four children and their mother; the pope's teenaged mistress; and swarms of obscure relatives. And it was

Alexander's family—his children, in particular—that was to bring about his ruination.

Two of the four children, Cesare and Lucrezia, emerge as two of the most wicked persons in European history. The other two, Giovanni and Goffredo—often known by their Spanish names of Juan and Joffre—were nonentities by comparison. Juan's murder (probably instigated or carried out by Cesare) was his only claim to fame.

The mother of these children was Vannozza Catanei. Little is known of her background, but her letters to Alexander show her to have been a woman of some breeding. He made her the mother of his second group of children because he loved her. But, he wanted to legitimize their children. Therefore, he permitted her—even urged her—to marry four different men. Each husband, in turn, conveniently stepped out of the picture and left the field open to Borgia. Even more unexplainable was Alexander's decision to take the children away from Vannozza (the woman he supposedly loved), in 1483, when the youngest was nine months of age, and to give them to his cousin, Adriana da Mila, to raise. Borgia allowed Vannozza to visit them often, and he provided well for her—even after becoming pope.

Years later, when Alexander wanted to present Cesare with a cardinal's hat, and found it necessary to establish his son's legitimacy, he published two paternity documents—one public and one private. They contradicted each other, but Cesare received his hat regardless. (The web which Alexander purposely wove around his family to protect them, and to advance his own interests, has never been adquately untangled.)

While still a cardinal, in 1489, Alexander "acquired" the other important member of his family, Giulia Farnese. Giulia, a gorgeous 16-year-old, had already actually been married, in a sumptuous ceremony at the Borgia palace, to Orsino Orsini, a member of that famous and powerful family with whom Borgia had fought and then allied himself. But Orsini, like Vannozza's husbands, absented himself and relinquished his beautiful child bride to His Excellency, 58-year-old Cardinal Borgia.

The power that this teenaged beauty wielded over Alexander is a legend unto itself. Bewitched by her, Alexander would plunge into fits of raving jealousy when Giulia would temporarily withhold her favors or (on infrequent occasions) return to her legal husband.

On one occasion, in the fall of 1494, he threatened her with excommunication and eternal damnation if she did not return to him immediately. At the time, the forces of Charles VIII of

France were advancing on Rome in their push through Italy toward Naples and Jerusalem. They intended, on the way, to seize Rome and to reform the papacy.

Alexander was beset with countless military problems, but the domestic problem of maintaining Giulia's affection occupied him far more. She was visiting in Capodimonte, and was about to depart for her husband's residence in Bassanello, when she received instructions from the pope. She was warned in no uncertain terms, on official stationery embossed with the *Chi Rho* symbol of Jesus Christ, to return to Rome. On the way back, she and her party were captured by the French and held hostage. Everybody but Alexander thought the incident amusing. He paid 3000 ducats for the release of the ladies. The French were not aware that they could have made a better deal; Alexander would have gladly paid 20 times that amount to get Giulia back.

When the French escort delivered the women to the Roman gates, Alexander was waiting, attired as a Spanish don in a black cloak, velvet boots and frilly shirt, and armed with sword and dagger. Even at the age of 63, His Holiness was an imposing man.

Although Alexander paid little or no attention to criticism aimed at him personally, he bristled when members of his family were attacked.

One such attack took place when Juan attended a reception at the Sforza palace and amused himself by poking fun at the dress of several of the guests. Somewhat inebriated, and not particularly watchful of his words, he called one man a "pig." The guest replied by accusing Juan of being a "priest's bastard." Rather than handling the matter on his own, Juan reported the incident to his father. Alexander, who was especially fond of Juan, dispatched a group of soldiers to the palace in search of the offender. When they located him, he was summarily arrested and hanged on the pope's orders.

When a member of his own family was the offender, the pope ordinarily found it easy to ignore the matter. However, when both the victim and the criminal were his own sons, he found himself thrust into a difficult dilemma.

On the night of June 14, 1497, Cesare and Juan attended a small party at their mother's house. At midnight, the two brothers, in the company of their cousin, Cardinal Juan Borgia-Lanzo, and a few family friends, left for their quarters. Juan was not seen again until two days later, when his body was washed up on the bank of the Tiber, terribly mutilated, his hands tied behind his back.

The pope was beside himself with grief, and launched an immediate investigation. All of Juan's suspected enemies were investigated—and exonerated. Cesare, who was rightful heir to Juan's secular honors, and who must have been extremely jealous of his brother's various dukedoms, was the most likely suspect and the one whom history has accused. But he was never questioned by Alexander, who not only wanted to protect the family name, but also greatly feared Cesare. Alexander briefly considered his son Joffre as a suspect, but even in the deepest moments of desperation he could not have seriously thought the bland, colorless Joffre capable of murder.

Alexander's relationship with his daughter Lucrezia has never been clear, except for his persistent protectiveness. On December 22, 1497, Lucrezia's three-year marriage to Giovanni Sforza was annulled on the grounds that it had never been consummated. Despite the fact that Lucrezia had been married once before, Alexander had her declared a "virgin still intact" so that her opportunities for marrying an important and politically powerful man would not be diminished. Sforza had fallen into disfavor because of his part in precipitating the French invasion of Italy, which nearly toppled Alexander from his papal throne. Consequently, although Sforza was offended and embarrassed by the declaration, he was powerless before Alexander, and eventually signed a paper stating that he had never had intercourse with Lucrezia. He accused the pope of wanting Lucrezia for himself. Lucrezia was pleased with the outcome.

But she did not do as her father had expected; she did not marry a man of substance and the right political persuasion. Instead, grieving over the death of her brother Juan, she entered the convent of San Sisto. Sex, however, interfered with religion, and in a short time she began a love affair with Pedro Calderón, a courier who carried messages between the convent and the Vatican.

On February 14, 1498, Calderón's body, together with that of the convent maid who had arranged the trysts, came floating down the river. According to a later report, Calderón had sought safety in the Vatican, but was discovered by Cesare, who chased him wildly, sword in hand, through halls and chambers and literally into Pope Alexander's arms. There, Cesare stabbed Calderón repeatedly, until his blood spurted over the pope.

Protective as always, the pope ordered the body dumped into the Tiber. When Lucrezia gave birth to a baby boy one month later, he set about legitimatizing the child. In a public bull, he claimed that the child was the offspring of Cesare and an unknown spinster; in a private bull, he claimed he was the father. It was of the utmost importance to him that the child be kept within the bosom of the family. But why he named himself as the father cannot be readily explained. Since he also refused to name the mother—asserting only that she was an unknown spinster—it was rumored that he had committed incest with his daughter. Alexander never denied this accusation.

Johannes Burchard was the Vatican Master of Ceremonies. His duties included keeping official records of all church ceremonies and other important happenings. He was known for his meticulousness. Burchard refers only to the fact that Calderón's body was found floating in the Tiber. Yet, history has given more credence to Cesare's killing of Calderón than to another incident recorded in some detail in Burchard's diary.

It is alleged that Cesare gave a party for his father and sister on the night of October 30, 1501. The entertainment during the first part of the evening consisted of observing horses and donkeys copulate. During the latter part, 50 female guests, described as "honest whores," stripped and danced naked, and then participated with the guests in a number of highly imaginative perversions. Considering the accuracy of other entries in Burchard's diary, it is difficult to discredit both stories completely.

By the first years of the 16th century, the Borgias had reached the peak of their power and wealth. The people lived in abject fear of the family—with good reason. To be an enemy of the Borgias meant imminent death.

On February 22, 1503, Cardinal Orsini passed away in the Vatican. Burchard wrote in his diary that he did not want to know "more than necessary." He did not attend the cardinal's funeral. Had he done so, he would have seen the bloated features, highly indicative of poisoning.

During the spring of the same year, Cardinal Giovanni Michiel vomited himself to death. He had just had a meal with the pope. His wealth, estimated at nearly 200,000 ducats, soon found its way into the coffers of the Vatican.

But on August 12th, the tables were turned. The evening prior, Alexander and Cesare had been guests at the home of Cardinal Adriano da Corneto. They had apparently conspired to poison the cardinal and a number of his guests, but either through carelessness or maliciousness, the chief steward gave the poisoned wine to the pope and his son. Within a short time they returned to the Vatican, violently ill. Cesare eventually recovered but, after a week of high fever and vomiting, the pope succumbed on the evening of August 18, 1503. Some historians have regarded the story as apocryphal and have attributed Alexander's death to either malaria or another fever. In any event, Alexander VI's death spelled the end of a most corrupt and evil reign, unprecedented in the annals of the papacy.

Alexander's remains were washed and robed by order of Burchard, and laid out on a simple table. Toward evening, servants came and stuffed the pope into an undersized coffin and clamped his mitre carelessly on his head. The corpse was bloated and black; and the tongue filled the open mouth. It emitted a revolting stench. Not a cardinal, not a single soul came to view the body.

3. Robespierre

The world recalls Robespierre more vividly than any other leader of the French Revolution. In popular memory, this little man with the high forehead and pallid complexion lives on as one of the most cruel executioners of all times. Between the winter of 1793 and the summer of 1794, before and during the Reign of Terror, he approved death by guillotine for more than 6,000 men and women.

This man, who neither smoked, drank nor consorted with women, has often been pictured as a figure bending over long lists of names, and scribbling *oui* next to most and *non* next to others. Those in the first group would die that very day; the others had earned a reprieve. He is also remembered as one who enjoyed the sound of tumbrils as they carted away his victims to the Place de la Révolution.

It was on this square—known today as the Place de la Concorde—that the guillotine had been erected and demanded its daily quota. The decapitation machine had been used in 1789, at the suggestion of Dr. Guillotin, a physician interested, oddly enough, in making executions more merciful.

The name of Robespierre, more than that of its inventor, is closely linked to the guillotine. For, through this instrument, Robespierre speedily and efficiently removed the enemies of France and the enemies of the revolution. The trouble was that Robespierre was a pathologically suspicious man, who saw enemies when there were none and whose sick imagination worked overtime. At the height of his power, which extended from the end of 1793 until his death in July of 1794, Robespierre considered anyone an enemy whose concept of the revolution differed from his. The same applied to anyone who criticized him or, if in a position of leadership, was found deficient in "virtue."

Toward these men and women—some of them his closest friends—Robespierre showed neither mercy nor compassion. Without hesitation, he submitted their names to the Revolutionary Tribunal he had helped create. From there it was but a short step to the death machine.

Robespierre was, at one time, a sincere and idealistic man.

But, in the last year of his life, he was convinced that he had a monopoly on truth, patriotism and virtue. He became completely obsessed with his idealism. A personal paranoia became the guide to all his actions. As a result, France became a nation of suspicious people, of mass accusers, of mass paranoia; and of widespread hysteria and sadism. One of Robespierre's biographers has pointed out that he suffered from many delusions, but the most terrible of all was that of considering himself virtuous. In those final weeks before his death at the age of 35, Robespierre went so far as to execute people who, in his considered judgment, were immoral. He was the sole judge and jury.

Yet, Robespierre's activities were not all evil. As late as 1792, three years after the outbreak of the French Revolution, he was known as a prime champion of the neglected and downtrodden; as one who spoke up for the lower classes; as one who demanded rights for Protestants, Jews, peasants, actors and actresses. Perhaps more clearly than most, he saw the revolution as a sharp break with accepted tradition and the society that created that tradition. It was the people—not the king—who were to be sovereign. The priests and noblemen were not to rule; the general will of the people was to prevail. Robespierre was fond of the expression, "the general will", which he had been taught by Jean-Jacques Rousseau, the philosopher whom he most admired.

But who were the *people*? Who represented the general will? Were they the merchants, the businessmen, the middle-class citizens who had first supported the revolution against the absolute monarchy of Louis XVI? Was it the clergy and nobility? Robespierre's attitude was revealed as the revolution progressed. By the 1790s, he made it clear that the *people* were the broad masses. All those who had lived in deprivation were the people. The time had come to consider *their* needs.

Thus, even among revolutionary leaders, Robespierre was regarded as a progressive. He was also thought of, in those earlier days of revolution, as a man of simplicity, of character and intelligence. In fact, these were the qualities that had been observed in him since childhood. But there was one other characteristic about him that stood out: he was strange, different, complex.

Of all that was strange, different and complex about the man, several facets were most significant. These were his aloofness, his intellectual rigidity, his hypochondria, his compulsive need for order, and, above all, his strict demand for virtue.

Maximilien François Marie Isidore Robespierre was born in

1758, in Arras, 120 miles north of Paris. His mother died when he was seven. His father, disconsolate over the loss of his wife, abandoned his law practice and his young children, and wandered off alone to travel over the face of Europe.

As a consequence, the family fell apart. Maximilien, the oldest son, and his brother, Augustin, were cared for by their maternal grandfather, a brewer also residing in Arras. Maximilien's teachers, all priests, were opposed to his being apprenticed as a brewer to his grandfather. Maximilien, they felt, was much too gifted a student. They intervened with the bishop and got a scholarship for him at the famed *college* Louis-le-Grand in Paris.

Robespierre was only 17 when he met his king. King Louis XVI, himself only 21 at the time, was passing through Paris on his return from his coronation in Rheims. The king paid a courtesy call at the Parisian college because it bore the name of an illustrious ancestor. Being the best pupil in the school, Robespierre was chosen to read a speech before the king, affirming the school's loyalty and devotion.

The royal coach drew up to the front portal of the school, but because of inclement weather, the monarch chose to remain inside his carriage. Robespierre, standing in a drenching rain, proceeded stoically to read his water-soaked manuscript. The king grew impatient, and at the moment Robespierre finished his Latin oration, the king's coach pulled away. Robespierre was insulted; the king had barely acknowledged his presence.

As a student, Robespierre kept to himself a great deal. He did not enjoy physical activity, and dancing and the pursuit of the opposite sex were activities from which he shied away. He was a loner, and in his solitude, Robespierre devoured his beloved Rousseau, reading and rereading his works. He adored Rousseau's *The New Heloise*—the hymn to nature and her beauties. He admired the master's *Emile*—the education of a young man according to the principles of nature. But, above all, he was entranced by Rousseau's *Social Contract*, a justification of revolution and a call for the acceptance of the principle of human equality.

By 1781, Maximilien de Robespierre was a member of the bar. To practice law, he returned to his native Arras. His puritanical morality quickly secured for him the approval of the provincial town. But, despite this acceptance, Robespierre was only moderately successful as an attorney. Fortunately for him, the bishop helped advance Maximilien's career by appointing him—at the age of 25—as a judge of his seignorial court. But when Maximilien was called upon to sentence a man to death, the future executioner of thousands preferred to resign his judge-ship, rather than take such action.

From time to time, Robespierre was called upon to address groups of friends and fellow attorneys. With plenty of spare time on his hands, he devoted himself to improving his oratorical skills. Audiences would listen and, on the whole, comment favor-ably. Yet his speeches were often long and pedantic.

As a lawyer, Robespierre attracted attention only once or twice. He defended a wealthy fellow lawyer, whose lightning conductor, then a novelty, had been labeled by neighbors as a public menace. Robespierre drew on the latest scientific evidence and won his case with impassioned arguments about the need for progress. In another well-known case, he fought against arbi-trary imprisonment.

In the fall of 1788, news from Paris electrified Robespierre. The king had convoked the States General, the nearly forgotten parliamentary body which had not met for 175 years.

Robespierre offered himself as a candidate. As he election-eered, he spoke ardently about a more just future, greater equa-lity, the need to remove oppressors. But, rather ominously, and foreshadowing the future, he also began to allude to conspira-cies, and to a country in danger. Three years later, with vast power in his hands, he was to use the same arguments to put thousands to death.

In offering his candidacy for the States General, Robespierre urged the election of incorruptible men. Although he was not yet called—as he was in later years—the Incorruptible, he looked upon himself as incorruptible and virtuous. He considered him-self morally superior to most mortals. Most people of Arras had to admit that the description of Robespierre as one who was incorruptible did fit the man.

Robespierre was elected a deputy and, in May of 1789, went to Versailles. Thomas Carlyle, who detested him, described Ro-bespierre in these unflattering terms: "The meanest of the six hundred deputies [was] an anxious, slight, ineffectual-looking man ... in spectacles; his eyes ... troubled, careful; with up-turned face, snuffing dimly the uncertain future time..." Yet, there was little evidence then that Robespierre was, or could become, "the meanest of men."

At the States General, Robespierre represented the Third Estate: middle-class businessmen who were weary of the domi-nance of the First and Second Estates—that is, the clergy and aristocracy. The Third Estate alone paid taxes, and they cla-mored for more power. But from the first, it was clear that these demands were overly mild, Much more had to be expected and fought for.

Yet, on the whole, Maximilien de Robespierre did not say much in 1789 or even 1790. His reluctance to become too active was partly a realization of his political inexperience. A second reason was that Robespierre was a hypochondriac who often absented himself from the debates and deliberations.

Another factor that kept him aloof was his lack of courage. Not being truly competitive by nature, Robespierre was often uncomfortable in the public arena. Oratory was more his style than bold, direct, face-to-face confrontation. Stress caused by the fear of competition produced his many psychosomatic symptoms. These, in turn, provided him with an escape from the rough environment in which he was forced to operate. Thus, Robespierre was absent during such momentous events as the storming of the Bastille or the March on Versailles following the king's forced return from attempted flight.

But Robespierre made sure he was present on occasion when his oratory could help shape public policy. Count Mirabeau, leader of the Assembly, listened to Robespierre and pronounced him a remarkable young man, "visibly sincere, one who believed all he said." Robespierre, however, was less charitable in his appraisal of Mirabeau: "Mirabeau's position will be destroyed by the evil effects of his morals," he said. Within another two years, such "immoral leaders" would have their heads severed from their bodies.

One contributing factor to Robespierre's ascent to the top was his control of the revolutionary Jacobin clubs which he helped mold into the first powerful modern party in history. Established in 1789 as a Society of Friends of the Constitution, at first it did little more than discuss the issues of the day.

Robespierre began to attend meetings of the Paris Jacobin Club shortly after the Assembly moved to Paris in October of 1789. Because he had little else to do in the evening—the pleasures of the flesh holding no interest for him—Robespierre spent a good deal of time at the Club. Here, not in the Assembly, he began to slowly acquire the reputation which was in a few short years to carry him to high places. He helped increase the membership of the Paris Club to over 3,000, and he succeeded in winning the support, within France, of over 1,200 other clubs or related societies.

The Jacobins were radicalized greatly after the king's forced return from attempted exile in 1791. They now opposed the monarchy, and demanded the king's death. Between 1792 and 1794, when the Assembly transformed itself into the National Convention, the Jacobins, under Robespierre, acquired their greatest power. Few actions could be taken by the Convention without the prior approval of the Jacobins—or the Mountain, as they were sometimes called.

Robespierre thought at first that the Jacobins' chief role was to educate the people. After the king's flight, he added another function: they were also to watch out for enemies. They were to keep their eyes open and report anyone who was less patriotic, less virtuous, less committed to the revolution than they were. Dissenting citizens had to be denounced. Robespierre's unconscious aim was to make the Jacobin clubs a great police force.

The purpose of this police force was to guard against the enemies of France, mostly the "enemy within." At one time, Robespierre called the Paris Club the "Tribunal of Public Conscience." When Robespierre assumed supreme power, toward the end of 1793, anyone not in good standing with the Jacobins could find himself in deep trouble.

Robespierre once called himself "the most mistrusting of citizens." Driven by their leader's distrust and suspicion, the Jacobins proceeded to "purify" their clubs. Like the Bolsheviks a century or more later, they purged themselves of members bold enough to express an independent thought, or foolish enough to create that impression. The Cherbourg Club underwent several purges under the direction of a Paris emissary. Upon this cleansing of blood, a "certificate of civic virtue" was presented to the club whose membership had been cut in half during the process of "purification." In Lyon, there was a virtual bloodbath.

Robespierre's obsession with enemies reached alarming proportions. He saw enemies everywhere. Even so-called "leaders of the revolution" could not be trusted. The betrayal by General Dumouriez on the field of battle became the reason for new cries for vigilance and the ruthless prosecution of monarchists, aristocrats, anti-patriots and traitors. From Robespierre and his Jacobins the cry went forth: Trust no one; be watchful; inform on all enemies of the revolution. Protect the gains of the revolution!

France became a nation of informers.

The hysteria was such that the prisons were filling faster than they could be emptied. The governing body of France, the Convention, delegated vast responsibilities to a Committee of Public Safety, with Robespierre as its most prominent member. The Committee uncovered new enemies, real and imaginary. A special Revolutionary Tribunal had to be established to speed the process of justice. But speeding up justice meant that normal judicial procedures had to be suspended. In 1793, the Law of Suspects was passed, which was designed to apprehend and punish as expeditiously as possible all those denounced, whether the accusation had a basis in fact or not. Justice became a mockery. Some called it legalized murder.

In 1792, Louis Capet, formerly known as His Majesty Louis XVI, was found guilty of treason, and the following year he was beheaded. His widow, Marie Antoinette, followed him to the scaffold a short time later. Aristocrats were eliminated by the knife, even if they sympathized with the Revolution.

Even the Girondists were not spared. Robespierre and his Committee and tribunal thought they (the Girondists) were not zealous enough. Their desire for a more deliberate exercise of justice was considered obstructionist and detrimental to the revolution. Robespierre did not shed a tear when many of his friends among the Girondists were carted away to their rendezvous with the knife wielded by Samson, the executioner. One of these friends of Robespierre was the intelligent Mme. Roland, whose salon he had been visiting for years.

This was no longer the Robespierre who found it impossible to sentence a man to die. This was not the Robespierre who had once opposed the death penalty in all cases except national treason. This was the man gone mad; the man who had become the chief recruiter for the guillotine. Girondist François Buzot, Mme. Roland's lover, openly called Robespierre a murderer, and then fled to the provinces, unwilling to live in a world governed by Robespierre and his guillotine.

The Robespierre who, in 1793, together with his fellow revolutionary Georges Danton, controlled the Convention, the Committe of Public Safety and the Revolutionary Tribunal, had become insensitive to justice, to law, to the shedding of blood, and to human suffering. He seemed to recognize only the cold abstractions of Revolution, Nation, and Virtue. The individual counted for nothing.

When the king was hauled before revolutionary justice, Robespierre demanded the royal head "without defense, without debate." The greatest of all criminals "cannot be judged—he is already condemned." Robespierre sat calmly in his humble chamber at the house of Duplay, the carpenter, when the rumbling tumbril carried the king to his destiny. The Duplays drew the curtain so that their famous roomer would not be disturbed. They need not have concerned themselves, for in Robespierre—the Just, the Virtuous, the Incorruptible—the ideal and principle had finally triumphed over compassion and human concerns.

Robespierre saw his mission clearly. "Our destiny is to found the empire of wisdom, justice, and virtue." He had no qualms about the means. "We shall only attain this destiny through wise laws, and such can only be constructed on the ruin of the incorrigible enemies of liberty." To emphasize his point of view, he told his Jacobin supporters that "liberty cannot be established unless the heads of scoundrels fall."

When a group of women, frightened by the unlawful detention of their men under the Law of Suspects, appeared before Robespierre, he called them to "higher values." *"Women,"* he declaimed. "What holy and dear ideas that word calls up. *Wives!* What sweet memories such a name recalls to representatives of the nation who are founding liberty on all the virtues. But are not these women and wives also citizens, and does not that rank lay on them duties higher than those of their domestic life?" This appeal that patriotic duty be placed above womanly concern for husbands and sons fell on unreceptive ears.

To insure that no enemy would escape detection, Robespierre introduced new types of crimes subject to punishment. For the old *lèse-majesté*—insults to the king—he now substituted *lèse-nation,* crimes against the nation. In practice, this became *lèse*-Robespierre—crimes against the Incorruptible. He could now say publicly what he had been saying only among close Jacobin friends: "I declare that I shall fight to the death against the agents of this horrible conspiracy. . ." But what conspiracy? Most often, there was none, except in Robespierre's demented mind.

Robespierre heard rumblings accusing him of spilling too much blood; that he was terrifying the people; that government of law had given way to government of the knife. Robespierre rejected the allegations. He claimed that he did only what was necessary for the best interests of all, and that he was just and merciful.

Some of Robespierre's associates had tried to persuade him that the use of the guillotine was inhuman. They told him about the procedure in every grisly detail: how the executioners' assistants prepared their "clients" for their final moment; how the shirt collar of the victim was cut open; and how the victim's hair was clipped and his hands tied behind his back. They informed Maximilien of all this horror because they thought he was ignorant of the gory details, and that if he knew he would stop the executions.

He did know, and it made him sick. His psychogenic symptoms became more severe than ever before. He vomited often. He had stomach cramps daily. He was plagued by constipation. But he insisted that the terror was necessary. "The Terror is nothing else save Justice," he proclaimed, "prompt, severe, inflexible. It is therefore an emanation of Virtue."

Though he knew of the horrors, and they repulsed him, he insisted on hearing about them. He knew he was doing no wrong —traitors of the sacred revolution needed to be liquidated. He would shoulder the responsibility before France, posterity and the Supreme Being. If irregularities occurred, even injustices, it could not be helped. The cause was greater than any individual. And if the stories aggravated his ailments, that was his burden to bear.

And so, in the new year of 1794, the death carts kept rumbling onto the cobbled square more frequently than even before, and more heads rolled into Samson's basket. Bloodthirsty crowds at the Place de la Révolution clearly outnumbered the revolutionists. Their hurrahs drowned out the weeping of relatives and friends of the victims.

But there were also the curiosity-seekers—spectators with nothing much else to do. Refreshments were sold not only in the courtroom of the Revolutionary Tribunal, but also in the vicinity of the guillotine itself. Spectators sipped lemonade while the condemned raved incoherently about wives and children, or fought the executioner as he clipped their hair or opened their collar. The mixed crowd of onlookers shouted excitedly as bleeding, decapitated bodies were hauled away.

Robespierre remained outwardly unaffected by the stories of horror. They told him of Marshal de Mouchy, one of the king's great soldiers—a man in his eighties—and of his wife, who had not even been legally arrested. The trial had proceeded despite this error, and the decrepit octogenarians were sent to the guillotine. He learned of the many women who declared themselves falsely pregnant, just so that they could live another day—until the physician discovered their lies. He heard of mothers who begged the executioner to cut off a lock of their hair and give it to their children as a remembrance. He was told about hundreds of children crowding the orphanages of Paris because their parents had been beheaded by Samson's blade.

Maximilien listened with neither joy nor remorse. To him, these acts were necessary. The revolution required that its foes be destroyed. The cost was high; but it had to be paid. He was more convinced than ever of the justice of his actions.

Meanwhile, the great executioner Maximilien de Robespierre led so exemplary a life that it was hard to think of him as a fanatic and a killer. It appeared to be a life of total dedication, not wasted on any kind of personal pleasures. While walking his dog in the park, his prime pleasure in life seemed to be nothing more than stopping occasionally to play with children.

Though he was now, with Georges Danton, the co-leader of France, he continued to live at the house of Duplay, the carpenter. When the Duplays went out of their way to provide him with comfort and loving attention, he reminded them sternly that he was only *citizen* Robespierre. His mode of living was not the kind expected of the dictator of France.

At the Duplay home, at least one of the three daughters was known to be in love with him. Robespierre was urged by his friends to marry, to become more sociable. "I shall never marry," he declared. Yet the many letters of admiration he received from women did give him pleasure.

In 1794, Robespierre's health was growing worse as his problems became greater. Confined for the most part to this home and bed, he made few public appearances. He was not at peace with himself—the threat from the enemies of France always in the forefront of his mind. He knew no sleep; he knew no rest.

It was the vision of lurking foes that kept him awake nights, not the vision of headless bodies buried in a common trench. It was concern that the new society might not be based on virtue, and it was of no concern to him that the killings on the Place de la Révolution were the very antithesis of virtue.

In early 1794, Robespierre became convinced that two allies were plotting against him. One was Camille Desmoulins, as close a personal friend as Robespierre ever had; the other, Georges Danton, his long-time associate and co-leader in the revolutionary councils.

Desmoulins had been an admirer of Robespierre since their school days together at Louis-le-Grand. He had always paid tribute to Robespierre's tenacity, brilliance, and idealism. Desmoulins was witty, clever, cheerful, enthusiastic—all of which Maximilien was not. In Maximilien, Camille had sometimes confided his most intimate thoughts.

Thus, he had told him of his passion for the beautiful Lucile Duplessis whom Camille soon married in a ceremony attended, and officially witnessed, by Robespierre. As an editor and journalist, Camille had found Maximilien's speeches electrifying.

In the early phases of the revolution, Camille Desmoulins had passionately urged revolt against the abusive royal authority. But in time—like Danton, his close friend—some of this revolutionary ardor had been cooled because of the cruelties and bloodletting. It was beyond Camille's comprehension that denouncing the guillotine should itself become a "guillotinable" offense! He had recently become the editor of *Le Vieux Cordelier,* named after a powerful revolutionary club he had founded with Danton.

In the first three issues of *Le Vieux Cordelier,* Desmoulins had obliquely, yet unmistakably, expressed doubts about some policies of the regime, especially the Terror. Robespierre, who had only recently defended freedom of the press as an instrument against tyrants, had at first encouraged the critiques. Suddenly, he refused to receive his old friend. "I am lost," Camille was heard to mumble as he blanched.

Indeed, he was. Robespierre had been stung by the criticisms. He was also fearful of a Desmoulins-Danton alliance in opposition to the terror. Above all, Robespierre had been piqued by his friend's doubts that a republic based on virtue was a meaningful possibility.

An order for Desmoulins' arrest was issued, with Robespierre's signature affixed to it. Maximilien turned a deaf ear to Lucile Desmoulins' pleadings: "Have you forgotten, Robespierre," the soon-to-be-widowed Lucile wrote to him, "the ties which bind you to Camille, ties that he can never recall without the deepest emotion?"

On April 5, 1794, one month after his arrest, Camille was executed. Lucile herself followed her husband to the guillotine within a few days after his death. Revolutionary *justice* had become more efficient. "The Revolutionary Tribunal," Robespierre had announced, "must be as active as crime itself, and conclude every case within twenty-four hours."

When Lucile's mother learned what had happened to Camille, and that Lucile's fate had been sealed, she dispatched a horrified note to Robespierre. "It is not enough for you to have murdered your best friend," she wrote. "You must have his wife's blood as well! Your monster, Fourier-Tinville [the public prosecutor], has just ordered Lucile to be taken to the scaffold. In less than two hours' time she will be dead. If you aren't a human tiger, if Camille's blood hasn't driven you mad, if you are still able to remember the happy evenings you once spent before our fire fondling our Horace [the Desmoulins' child], spare an innocent victim. If not, then hurry and take us all—Horace, myself and my other daughter Adele. Hurry and tear us apart with your claws that still drip with Camille's blood—hurry, hurry so that we can all sleep in the same grave."

The mother's anguished appeal was ignored.

Like Robespierre, Danton was a lawyer and a revolutionary leader of comparable stature. Danton had made the mistake of retiring periodically from public life to enjoy life in the provinces. He had resigned several offices, including his seat on the Revolutionary Tribunal—a fatal error.

Danton enjoyed life to the fullest. He loved women, wine, song—in about that order. Recently, he had told the puritanical Robespierre just how much he enjoyed his nighttime activities with his much younger wife. Robespierre had listened with distaste. Danton was also often in need of money—which, in Robespierre's eyes, was the first step to corruptibility.

Robespierre was aware of these shortcomings in "virtue." If he deplored them, he did not let on. In fact, Maximilien actually had defended Danton against those enemies who would "destroy the best patriot in the country."

In February of 1793, Danton's first wife died. In a letter, Maximilien consoled his "devoted friend" whom he would "love unto death." Their political collaboration had been so friendly and harmonious.

But then Danton—human, gregarious, easy-going, charming—had developed misgivings about the continuing terror. He returned from the provinces, and Robespierre sensed danger. In a private comment, Danton remarked that the innocent were being executed along with the guilty. "Who told you that a single innocent person has perished?" was Maximilien's sharp response.

Whether Danton's doubts about the continued killing instilled guilt in Robespierre, or merely emphasized the need to get rid of Danton who was now a dangerous rival, is hard to determine. It is certain, however, that Danton was wearied by continuing executions, and could not accept Robespierre's easy dismissal of the terror; he could not condone the excesses. He had become disenchanted with the France he had helped to create.

Told that he might be in danger, Danton responded, "I would rather be guillotined than guillotine..." This was the remark of a man bent on suicide, and capable of any action.

Robespierre recognized the threat and moved swiftly. Aware that Danton's supporters were as numerous as his own, and that Danton might solicit their help, Robespierre quickly ordered Danton's arrest. Maximilien sat at the Duplays', sweating and trembling. But Danton did not ask for help.

Danton did request the right to address the Tribunal. Ever distrustful, Robespierre turned him down. Using patriotic doubletalk; and employing words like treason, foreign plots, etc., Maximilien piously maintained that all prisoners—like all citizens—had to be treated alike.

Danton's death has been described many times and has become the subject of plays and novels. As the cart of the condemned passed the Duplays' house, its shutters tightly closed, Danton shouted, "Vile Robespierre... You will follow me. Your house will be leveled and the ground where it stood sowed with salt."

Later, the larger-than-life Danton said: "If I could leave my legs to Couthon [Robespierre's close ally] and my virility to Robespierre, things might still go on." Danton obviously had his own ideas as to why Robespierre led such a sexually puritanical life.

At the Place de la Révolution, Danton engaged a fellow victim in conversation. Samson grew impatient, for he had other heads to sever. Danton turned on the executioner, called him a wretch, and said he would not be able to keep their heads from meeting in the basket. Asking Samson not to forget to hold up his magnificent severed head for inspection, Danton submitted to the inevitable.

Maximilien, who had become the undisputed leader after Danton's death, wrote, in March 1794, the following: "As for me, I was the friend of Pétion (a Girondist leader): when he was unmasked, I abandoned him. I also had some intimacy with Roland; he was a traitor and I denounced him. Danton wished to take the place of these men; he is in my eyes the enemy of the country."

That Robespierre was now on the very threshold of insanity —equating himself fully with virtue, scourging those less virtuous than himself, aspiring to a form of saintliness—is evidenced by his restoration of a Supreme Being.

The revolution had gone far toward atheism, and Robespierre considered atheism the philosophy of aristocrats. Virtue could not be attained without a God figure. To be sure, the God whom Robespierre wanted to see re-established was not the conventional God, but a God made in the likeness of Maximilien de Robespierre.

Robespierre in his final month organized a Festival of the Supreme Being. Neatly, yet simply attired as always, he led a procession carrying a hideous cardboard statue of atheism. In a solemn ceremony, he took a torch from an acolyte and set fire to the statue. "The Universe seems assembled here," he said solemnly. "O Nature, how sublime, how beautiful is thy power.

How all tyrants must pale at the thought of this Festival."

Apparently, Robespierre did not think of himself as an oppressor and tyrant. Now, more than ever, the man who had inaugurated the worship of the Supreme Being saw himself as a saintly man.

The champion of virtue was more distressed than ever by the absence of that quality in others. Between April and July, his final months, he began to send people to the guillotine for simple acts of immorality. Robespierre's new religiosity seemed childish and ludicrous in light of the extreme cruelties of which he was guilty. Those still in leadership positions were terrified by the turn of events. None was innocent of what Robespierre now considered "serious crimes." He did not suspect that his own followers now felt threatened and that they might prove even more formidable plotters than the Girondists and the other idealists he had already guillotined.

Paris in the very hot summer of 1794 was terrified by continuing executions. In the words of a contemporary, "From the stupefied expression on people's faces, you would have said that it was a city desolated by a plague. The laughter of a few cannibals alone interrupted the deadly silence which surrounded you."

The cycle of fanaticism, enthusiasm, and moral austerity was entering a new phase of calm, repose, and laxness. The days of Robespierre were numbered. Though he prided himself on his intuition and superior insight, both failed him on those fateful days of July 26th, July 27th and July 28th.

On July 26th, Robespierre delivered an especially long and boring oration before the Convention. Paradoxically, he made an urgent appeal for termination of the terror. He also called for punishment—for those members of the Convention who had engaged in excessive harshness.

The next day's debate was noisy and disorganized. It bordered on the chaotic. When Robespierre announced that he knew how to restore order to the discussion, there were shouts of "tyrant" from everywhere. As Robespierre rose to address the Convention once more, he was overwhelmed by the hostility of the members.

Robespierre was not prepared to cope with this situation. His opposition was vocal—and angry. Fears which had haunted him since childhood—fears of murderers, brigands, criminals, traitors—had suddenly overwhelmed him.

Robespierre's stomach tightened. His whole being shook. His voice cracked. He could fight no more.

Robespierre's power over the mob evaporated within minutes. The Convention ordered his arrest. Shortly after the arrest was made he was shot through the jaw. (The assailant was never found; some have claimed that it was a suicide attempt.)

He was carried on a stretcher and forced to wait while a filthy bandage was applied to the painful wound. As people passed him, they spat at the still breathing, fallen dictator.

After a mock trial that lasted 16 hours, Robespierre, humiliated and in pain, was carried to the scaffold. Just before his own decapitation, he had to witness the guillotining of his closest allies—the brilliant, rigid Saint-Juste, the crippled but loyal Couthon, and his own brother, Augustin de Robespierre.

With Robespierre's death came the end of the reign of terror in France. Constitutional government was returned to the people. But, soon the Napoleonic era would create its own trauma and madness.

4.Mussolini

Mussolini's father named him Benito Amilcare Andrea: Benito after the 19th century Mexican liberator and revolutionary, Benito Juárez; Amilcare after a local anarchist, Amilcare Cipriani; and Andrea after the Socialist, Andrea Costa. Mussolini styled himself *Il Duce*—which means the same thing as *der Führer*.

In the beginning, Hitler imitated Mussolini—his conception of the ideal dictator. Later, when he attained a position of power, he looked upon his Mediterranean cohort as a military bungler and a political liability.

Mussolini admired and feared Hitler. His admiration grew out of a sense of awe for Hitler's superior military ability; his fear, from the conviction that in any contest with him, Hitler would win.

Benito was born on July 29, 1883 in a tiny, dilapidated village called Dovia, located near Predappio in the northeastern sector of Italy. Here, Benito grew up with a brother, Arnaldo, and a sister, Edvige. It was not a particularly happy childhood, for the necessities of life were in short supply.

Benito's father, Alessandro, was a blacksmith. He pounded away at his anvil on the ground floor of a three-story house from early morning till early afternoon; and then he started his drinking. Added to this was Alessandro's weakness for women, a passtime in which many of his peers indulged and which was not considered immoral. Alessandro, it appears, was a model for his son, for Benito at a later age became an expert in both areas: drinking and women. According to his wife, Benito never again got drunk in her presence, after a particularly bad night in 1911 when he went berserk and wrecked their apartment. But various women played a part in his life till the very end.

Mother Rosa ran a little school on the second floor of their house and earned more—though it amounted to little—than her husband the blacksmith. Better educated and better dispositioned than Alessandro, Rosa was admired by Benito.

The difficulties of life and the abject poverty in which the Mussolinis lived drove Alessandro into the camp of the socialists.

Benito admired his father for his fiery socialist views, but he also feared him. Alessandro was determined to make a man of Benito, and he often physically assaulted him in an attempt to "toughen" him. Benito was taught never to accept defeat, even in the face of overwhelming odds.

Once, after a bully had beaten up seven-year-old Benito, Alessandro sent his son back to settle the score. Benito was afraid at first, but he was more afraid of his father, and so he armed himself with a pointed rock, and set out in search of his tormentor. This time the bully did not fare as well: with several deep gashes about the head, he went home screaming. Benito was pleased with his victory, and thereafter did not hesitate to assert himself even when confronted by a number of assailants simultaneously.

When Benito was nine, his mother decided that it would be beneficial for him to continue his schooling elsewhere. She had taught him all she was capable of, and Benito was bright enough, she felt, to profit from study at a higher level. She mentioned to Alessandro a school run by the Salesian Fathers at Faenza, but he opposed the idea of his son's being under the influence of priests. The old man was an avowed atheist who publicly harangued against the Church so vehemently that his wife, who was devout and even-tempered, was constantly embarrassed. She persisted in trying to convince Alessandro of the desirability of Benito's attending the school at Faenza. Eventually, he consented.

It wasn't long before the priests discovered that Benito's presence in their midst was a total liability. The boy fought with everybody in school, with the children in town, and even with the teachers. He had grown fond of knives, and became quite adept at handling them. Not only did he employ them for his own defense, but also to initiate attacks against his schoolmates. After stabbing a boy in the arm with a penknife, Benito was summoned to the headmaster's office. Benito did not like the dressing-down and flogging he received, so he picked up a large inkwell from the desk and hurled it at the priest, splattering his face with ink. The result: immediate expulsion.

His mother was mortified by his behavior, but his father thought it exemplary. Benito was sent to the Giosuè Carducci school in Forlimpopoli where, very soon after being admitted, he stabbed another pupil and was summarily expelled. After an impassioned plea by his mother, and a promise from Benito that he would mend his ways, the school readmitted him as a day student.

The officials at the Carducci school were not very hopeful that Benito's behavior would improve, but surprisingly it did and, at the age of 18, Benito graduated from the Instituto Magistrale with a teaching certificate.

The first employment he held was at an elementary school in the decrepit village of Gualteri on the Po River. No complaint about his teaching was ever lodged, but everybody—from school authorities to the citizens of Gualteri—objected to his loose and rowdy life. When he wasn't drunk, he was making inflammatory speeches. When he wasn't brawling in a tavern, he was cavorting from one girl's bed to the next. Drinking, brawling, speechmaking, and whoring—he was a chip off the old block!

But Benito had a special quirk. The first girl he desired, who was not a prostitute, he raped. The first girl who angered him, he stabbed. Little wonder then that he was relieved of his teaching position only a few months after he had been engaged.

For the greater part of the next three years Benito Mussolini worked as a common laborer in many different parts of Switzerland. Expelled from various cities and jailed a dozen times, he was regarded as a low-brow rabble-rouser and first-class nuisance.

In the summer of 1903, he was tossed into prison in Berne for advocating violence towards a group of workers. When he had served his two-week sentence, he went to Geneva under an expulsion order. There he stirred up more violence among striking workers, was imprisoned and later expelled upon his release.

It was at about this time that Mussolini received word from Italy that he had been sentenced, in absentia, to a one year prison sentence for failing to report for military service. He caught the next train for Zurich.

In Zurich, he was received with enthusiasm by resident and visiting socialists. During his extended contact with these revolutionaries, he became acquainted with Lenin and Trotsky and took as his mentor an aging, hunchbacked woman, Angelika Balabanoff, who was the acknowledged leader of the exiled plotters.

When King Victor Emmanuel III announced an amnesty for all draft dodgers who were now willing to serve in the military, Mussolini decided to return to Italy. He joined the tenth Bersaglieri Regiment, and completed his service obligation on time and without incident.

Upon receipt of his discharge, Mussolini accepted a teaching position at the elementary school in Caneva, but his fierce nature and his debauchery quickly became the talk of the town.

This time he did not wait to be fired—he quit. When he left Geneva he suffered from an ulcerated stomach, syphilis, and a number of other ills acquired during this "year of moral deterioration," as he himself later called it. These ailments plagued him all the days of his life.

Mussolini's mother died; and in the summer of 1908 Benito sought out his father who was living in Forlì. There, he operated a small inn. Alessandro had taken into his home a young widow named Guidi as a common-law wife, together with her three daughters. Benito was attracted to the plump, blonde 16-year-old daughter, Rachele, whom he had known casually since she was seven, and he decided that he wanted to marry her.

Rachele returned Benito's love, but Alessandro Mussolini and Rachele's mother were vehemently against the marriage. Benito reacted violently. He threatened to kill himself and Rachele. Alessandro relented, and granted his permission.

Benito, however, didn't bother to marry Rachele. Like his father, he took her into his house and shared his bed with her. Religion, custom, tradition, morals meant nothing to Mussolini. On December 16, 1915, while a soldier, he finally married her so that she and their children would collect his pension in the event of his death. One of his numerous lovers, an Austrian named Ida Dalser, had been styling herself as Mrs. Mussolini, and threatened to make trouble.

Soon Mussolini began the publication of a newspaper espousing socialistic views. His talent came to the attention of prominent socialists, and he was asked to speak and write for various other publications. His oratory was so admired, and his journalistic skills so valued, that in 1912 he was offered the editorship of the socialist organ, *Avanti!* Benito accepted.

When the war broke out in 1914, Mussolini, whose fame as an editor had now begun to spread, took an anti-violence stance. This was indeed a strange position for a man with his history. But, in fact, this had been his posture in 1911 when Italy annexed Tripoli; and he also espoused this belief in 1913 when he ran unsuccessfully ran for a seat in the National Socialist Congress.

It did not take Mussolini long to sense which way the wind was blowing, and he quickly rethought his position and aligned himself with social revolutionary forces under the banner of incipient fascism. Financed by a wealthy publisher, he founded the paper *Il Popolo d'Italia,* and preached a curious mixture of nationalism and socialism.

The old-line socialists were quick to recognize the impurity of the broth and, at a meeting in Milan, which turned into a shouting match, he was driven out of the party with the words "traitor," "cutthroat," "hireling," "bum." Mussolini, his anvil jaw jutting forward in hysterical rage, spewed back worse epithets at his opponents.

Inspired by his own cry of *Viva l'Italia,* Mussolini again joined the Bersaglieri, fought, and was severely wounded in battle. When he returned from the conflict, his anti-capitalist ideas remained, but his commitment to a strong nationalist movement was even greater. In addition, he now believed that a dictator was required to promote and to enact his ideas. He nominated himself.

Much like Hitler some years later, out of a band of misfits—dischargees, grumbling socialists, anarchists, nutty bombthrowers, and bums—he created, by 1919, a unified group that rallied under the banner of fascism. He saw his revolutionaries bound together as tightly as the bundle of fasces carried by the ancient Roman lictors as their symbol of authority. He did not overlook the axe in the fascist symbol either, as he urged his band to employ vicious means of coercion in directing others into their ranks.

His targets were all those who disagreed with him and his methods, although the victims were usually hard-line socialists. Mussolini's black-shirted fascists, carrying their provocative flag with a white skull on a black background, would break up meetings with clubs and pistols. Speakers for the opposition were sometimes corralled and doses of castor oil were poured down their throats. At night, gigantic parades were staged in major cities: pistols were fired; songs were sung; and bombs and grenades were exploded at random.

On occasion, important socialist and religious leaders received special treatment, and found themselves the victims of back-alley assaults. When the Archbishop of Milan was vehement in his criticism of Mussolini for his violent tactics, Mussolini personally wrapped a time bomb in a ten lira note, and asked a passing stranger on the street to deliver it to His Excellency. The man did so but, luckily for the archbishop, the bomb was a dud. This same archbishop later was to permit his would-be assassin to kiss his foot when as Pope Pius XI he undertook to establish a Lateran Concordat between fascism and Roman Catholicism.

For Mussolini, Italy's many ills could be cured only by authoritarianism. And *he* was the supreme authority.

But his motives were not altruistic. He had no real love for people or country. His motivation was an insatiable thirst for power and absolute control. In fact, he was always scornful of Italians, and considered them weak and cowardly.

By 1921 Mussolini was known throughout Italy. He and 34 other fascists were elected in that year to the Chamber of Deputies, and they immediately began to wield tremendous political and military power. The following year, a nationwide strike was called by the socialists and other leftist groups, and Mussolini threatened to march on Rome and overthrow the government if the government didn't prevent the strike. The king capitulated in the face of Mussolini's 25,000 troops heading towards Rome, and Benito was appointed premier.

During the victory march through the streets of Rome, the people shouted themselves hoarse with joy. Mussolini, they believed, would solve all their problems!

At first, not only to the people of Italy, but to many people throughout the world, Benito was a savior. Quickly forgotten were the riots and beatings initiated by his fascist followers. All that was remembered were the swishy uniforms and rhythmic bands that paraded before them. And now, of course, the savior was admired for what appeared to be his ability to form a stable government, and an alliance between Church and State.

A problem that the Italians failed to recognize was the unstable nature of Mussolini himself. He was an egotist whose every move was calculated to further his own gain. He had no sense of loyalty to his country or his constituency. Instead, he subscribed wholeheartedly to the advice given him by Professor Vilfredo Pareto, under whom he had studied briefly at the University of Lausanne: "Go with every turn in the road."

The first act of any dictator, upon assuming power, is to eliminate the enemy. Mussolini followed the pattern, and undertook the task with enthusiasm. But the intensity of his enthusiasm bordered on the barbaric. He put his notorious Black shirts on the Army payroll and established a secret service; and then dispatched them both to do his dirty work. Innocent people were knifed in their beds—at home and in hospitals. People were stabbed and shot in the streets. Others were dumped in rivers, flung down steps and out of windows. These infamous acts were perpetrated on anyone suspected of disloyalty. For merely reading an anti-fascist newspaper, one could be dosed with castor oil (there was something unmistakably Freudian about this favorite torture technique of Mussolini's), ruined financially, or thrown into a smelly, dank prison. The whole process gave *Il Duce* immense satisfaction.

"The people should thank me for getting rid of the trash," he muttered. And then he added, and the people echoed, as was the custom: *Il Duce ha sempre ragione!* ("The Duce is always right!")

One particular enemy was hard to eliminate because of his prominence. His name was Giacomo Matteotti, and he was an outspoken socialist deputy who left no stone unturned to expose the prime minister as a murderer, ballot-box stuffer, and crooked dealer. He made his accusation to Mussolini's face during a session of the Chamber of Deputies. It was clearly an act of suicide, for the next day *Il Popolo,* the government's smear sheet, wrote that it would not be surprising if Matteotti suddenly acquired a fractured skull.

Matteotti kept up his hammer-blow criticism of *Il Duce* throughout the first part of 1924. Then, one night in June, he was kidnaped as he was walking down the street, by five professional ruffians. Matteotti, no coward, had to be repeatedly slugged and clubbed before he entered the waiting car. He continued to fight his assailants so valiantly during the ride out of town that the infuriated kidnapers stabbed him to death.

After burying him in the woods at Quartarella, they returned to Mussolini with Matteotti's clothes and identification papers as evidence of his elimination. Mussolini was not pleased. He feared the effect that Matteotti's murder might have on his own national and international reputation. He severely upbraided his men for their stupidity. When they protested that he had spoken of "fracturing Matteotti's skull," Mussolini flew into a towering rage, insisting that that did not mean to kill him!

When Matteotti's death became public knowledge, the criticism started pouring in. Bitter Italians scrawled epithets directed at Mussolini on walls and windows: *Assassino* was the favorite word. Foreign newspapers condemned him in editorials. The criticism was intense. Mussolini began quaking in his jack boots.

"Italy was mine," he whined, "and now I've lost her." He started to bite his fingernails, to cry easily, and to be forgetful. He was so nervous, and so lacking in self-control, that he would slam his head against the wall with a force that would cause him to scream from pain.

In desperation, Mussolini started arresting some of his own followers, accusing them of complicity in Matteotti's murder. When one of them, Cesare Rossi, party secretary and boss of the dreaded Cheka secret police force, threatened to expose the truth, Mussolini backed off and changed tactics. He appointed Roberto Farinacci, known as "Farinacci the Sadist," to head the

Cheka, and permitted him to give full vent to his psychopathic personality by wiping out, maiming, or beating 224 enemies of Benito.

As the message became clear that the *Duce* was really to be reckoned with, vocal opposition dwindled. Some of the more prominent loudmouths—Rossi included—were quietly shipped out of the country. By the time the real culprits, the five hired gangsters, were brought to trial, Mussolini once again had control over the populace. The murderers testified, in spite of visible evidence of repeated stabbing, that Matteotti had had a sudden attack of tuberculosis in the car and hemorrhaged to death on the spot. Farinacci, the defense counsel, maintained that Matteotti should have been "executed," not assassinated, for his traitorous activities. The "executioners" were given five-year sentences, but Mussolini pardoned them after five weeks of imprisonment. After the Matteotti affair, Mussolini was careful to keep himself abreast of all activities.

Many Italians were quite happy with the state of the country—especially the rich. Business and industry flourished. New construction was everywhere. Buildings sprang up. Swamps were cleared. Rivers were widened and deepened. Harbors were dredged, and dams constructed. Export business soared.

But the poor got poorer.

Mussolini saw himself as the savior of Italy. Pictures and statues of the short, stocky *Duce* abounded. Adored by his people, like an ancient god, he allowed no one to address him by name, but only as *Il Duce*. And all had to greet him with the fascist salute. "For one thing," he said, "it's more sanitary than shaking hands."

As for cleanliness, Mussolini still lived like an ordinary bum. He had to be reminded to shave, change his clothes, and wear underwear. He did not have the faintest understanding of protocol, and continually embarrassed himself and others by the things he did or did not do or say.

Benito Mussolini expected adulation from everyone. School children stood erect and saluted his picture in the classroom; crowds chorused their approval at him at mass meetings; soldiers strutted in a goose step that almost split their pants. Even his wife timidly referred to Benito as *Il Duce*. At all of this Mussolini smiled broadly—revealing his stained teeth, which, like his clothes, he often failed to wash for weeks on end.

Despite the adulation heaped upon him, there were many who thought Mussolini's proper place was not at the head of a government, but in some lowly position. Several assassination attempts were nipped in the bud. One "vulgar socialist," as *Il Duce* later referred to him, actually shot Mussolini. But the bullet-proof vest that he had been wearing spared him his life. "Everybody loves me," he bragged, "but some people are just plain crazy."

One who loved him from afar, and whose sanity has often been called into serious question, was none other than Adolf Hitler. When, in 1925, Hitler requested of Mussolini an autographed photograph, and received instead a rebuff, he vowed that one day he would eclipse that conceited Italian. Years later, Mussolini tripped along behind *der Führer*, sycophantically proclaiming: *"Ja, der Führer hat immer recht."* ("The *Führer* is always right.")

When Hitler came to full power in Germany, Mussolini was not pleased. Not only was he frightened at the prospect of an arms and troop build-up in a country that had a history of getting involved in warfare, but he was annoyed that a second dictator had emerged in Europe, and that this man had reached a position of power by employing exactly the same tactics as he. "He had no originality," Mussolini thundered.

It was true; much was the same. But it was a winning combination. Brown shirts—Black shirts; Gestapo—Cheka; persecution of Jews—persecution of Christians. National Socialism was hardly different from fascism, despite Mussolini's insistence that there was "a world of difference between the two."

The major difference, however, lay in the people themselves. Mussolini wondered whether he could ever whip the Italian people into proper military shape to equal the Germans. Hitler, for his part, was convinced that the Italian army would be nothing but a hindrance to his plans. They were both right, but this led to little rejoicing by either dictator.

The two men met for the first time in June 1934. Mussolini was, at the time, still the dominant European personality, and he chose Venice as the meeting place, which held for him an obvious psychological advantage. He also wore his fascist uniform—while Hitler was in mufti—hoping to express in another way his superiority. Benito led off the discussions by reprimanding Hitler for harassing his old friend, Engelbert Dollfuss, Chancellor of Austria, and suggesting that Hitler curb his anti-Jewish activities because of the poor international impression they were creating.

Hitler thought it a bit odd that Mussolini should be opposed to persecution in view of his own treatment of Christians and

Freemasons. He expressed his point of view directly to Mussolini, adding that there was a distinct difference in the case of Germans persecuting Jews, for here one was dealing with one of "the inferior dark-skinned races." When Mussolini asked Hitler if the Italians were to be counted among those "inferior" peoples, Hitler answered in the affirmative—along with the Arabs, Greeks, Turks, and others.

"They all have Negro blood in their veins," he explained. For once, Mussolini felt he was part of the Italian people, a nation he had all too often spoken of with the same disdain as Hitler. Mussolini lacked the courage to continue the argument.

The first encounter between Mussolini and Hitler was a complete fiasco. Subsequent meetings were much more successful, but only because Hitler took control over each situation, leaving Mussolini powerless. Both men fulminated against each other when they returned to their respective capitals.

Just as Hitler sought *Lebensraum*—or used *Lebensraum* (imperialism) as an excuse for conquest—so too did Mussolini. In fact, that was Benito's avowed reason for moving into Abyssinia in 1935. Actually, he had more grandiose plans than merely punishing "those Ethiopian barbarians." He hoped to conquer the world. In this respect, too, he was exactly like Hitler.

But Mussolini was no tactician. Instead of leaving his generals alone to work out their own battle plans, he was constantly sending messages—some contradictory of others that had been sent to the front just a short time earlier. What was to have been a speedy victory in Ethiopia turned into months of combat in which Italian troops were bogged down in mud and slime, fighting against untrained Ethiopians armed with weapons that were no more than relics. Until General Pietro Badoglio took command and pushed his way into Addis Ababa, the capital city, the rest of the world was almost amused at the plight of the Italians.

When Hitler hammered his way into Poland on September 1, 1939, Mussolini proclaimed Italy's neutrality. He had decided to make no commitment and hoped to ally himself with the winning side at the proper time. He followed this course although, inwardly, he admired the Germans. "The Italians are a weak and stupid people; they don't know what is good for them," he said more than once. "What they need is a shot of Nordic blood." He went so far as to order thousands of trees planted in a section of central Italy to make the region cooler. "Maybe the people will take on some Nordic traits and become energized," he theorized.

Despite his misgivings about Italian military effectiveness,

Mussolini continued to assert himself, only to suffer humiliation and defeat. When he decided to publicly support Germany, Hitler accepted, but treated him shabbily. He undertook military campaigns without consulting Mussolini, and when Mussolini took the initiative, more often than not he had to call upon Hitler to bail him out of a difficult situation.

Such "rescues" were more painful than defeat would have been. In Greece, the Italians were soundly thrashed until Hitler marched in. Throughout North Africa, the Italians lost campaign after campaign until the Germans came to their aid and completed the operation swiftly. Mussolini was humiliated; he was in a state of constant depression.

At the front, Mussolini was reduced to a non-entity. Tripping along behind Hitler like a puppy dog, his opinion counted for little. The German generals had no respect for him, his commanders, or the Italian troops. Bad enough that Rommel did not even deign to pay him a visit in Africa, but what pained Mussolini the most was that he shared Rommel's contempt for the Italian people—"A bunch of sheep" he called them, and "a people gone flabby by art."

Mussolini dreaded every meeting with Hitler. The conversations were totally one-sided, Mussolini being the audience for Hitler's three-hour marathon harangues on politics, religion, race, war, and a score of other subjects. "The man is mad," he confided to his son-in-law, Count Galeazzo Ciano. In Germany, Hitler described Mussolini as a "fool."

As time went on, Mussolini became increasingly anti-German. Privately, he would lash out at Hitler and other members of the General Staff. But then, never knowing his own mind, he would castigate the Italian people for their cowardice, using the Germans as an example of a people with purpose, and a will to fight.

Mussolini once wrote: "At the first bombing that might destroy a famous campanile or a painting by Giotto, the Italians would go into a fit of artistic sentimentality and would raise their hands in surrender." When the Allies were pounding the city of Naples to pieces, Mussolini expressed his joy. "The breed will harden," he said. "The war will make of the Neapolitans a Nordic race."

By 1942, Mussolini was a thoroughly sick man—mentally and physically. The strain of prosecuting a war so hopeless, the humiliation of dealing with Hitler, the frustration of attempting to perform tasks for which he was not educationally equipped—all of these problems overwhelmed him. Added to this, Mussolini's physical condition was declining: his syphilis had started to bother him again, and he was now suffering from amoebic dysentery and an acute ulcer.

In view of all this, it is not surprising that Mussolini frequently made gross errors in judgment, and went off in flights of fantasy. In one such fantasy, he saw Italy fighting on the side of the United States one day, and on the next, he dismissed the United States as an effete nation not to be reckoned with. He had even become anti-Semitic and tried to abolish Christmas, because it was "founded by a Jew." This same Jew, he went on to explain, is to be blamed for the existence of the Christian Church which had "debilitated the world" and who persecuted him through its popes and priests. These latter he described as "jackals." The megalomaniac had become paranoid.

Italian leaders and the people themselves were aware of his condition. They decided to remove him from office. In a resolution presented to the Fascist Grand Council on July 24, 1943, Count Dino Grandi called for the *Duce's* resignation and the appointment of the king as Commander-in-Chief of the Armed Forces. The vote was 19 to nine in favor.

Grandi and his co-conspirators fully expected to be executed for their insubordination. Grandi had been to confession that morning, had written his will, bid his family good-bye, and pocketed a pistol and two hand grenades—but the ill Mussolini took no punitive action. Quietly, Mussolini left the council chamber, and the next day answered King Victor Emmanuel's summons. He accepted the fact that it was all over. In Mussolini's place the king appointed Marshal Badoglio as Chief Secretary of State. Fascism was dead.

Mussolini was first imprisoned on the island of Ponza in the Gulf of Gaeta situated off the western coast opposite Naples. He was confined to a poorly furnished, tiny room. He grew increasingly depressed.

After 10 days he was moved, for security reasons, to the small and uncomfortably hot island of La Maddalena, off the coast of Sardinia. He had lost all hope of being rescued from his miserable plight. He did nothing but sit and stare vacantly into space.

In his third and final week on La Maddalena, a 24-volume edition of Nietzsche's collected works arrived as a gift from Hitler. Mussolini tried to read, but his mind balked at swallowing anything Germanic.

Mussolini was next incarcerated in a hotel, named the Albergo Rifugio, located on the Gran Sasso, high up in the Abruzzi.

It was a pleasant enough place, and although Mussolini looked tired and drawn, he complained little. Most of his time was spent gazing out a window overlooking the gorgeous mountains. The peace of the open countryside contrasted sharply with the radio news of crushing Italian defeats, and the king's and Badoglio's flight to Brindisi. Mussolini gave surprisingly little thought to Italy's problems. He began to compare himself to Caesar, Napoleon, and Jesus Christ.

When Mussolini heard a radio report that a major condition for Italy's surrender was that he be turned over to Allied hands, his thoughts turned to suicide. He contemplated slashing his wrists with a safety razor that was in his possession—but never did so.

During Mussolini's entire imprisonment, the Germans had tried to determine his whereabouts. They feared that if captured by the British, he might reveal secret military information. But by the time they had learned that Mussolini was on Ponza, he had been moved to La Maddalena. By the time they had made plans to capture him there, he had been moved once again. At best, the rescue attempt can be construed to reflect Hitler's personal loyalty to Mussolini, and the assumption—roundly discounted by Rommel and Goebbels—that if fascism were to be resurrected, Mussolini was the essential figure for the Italian people to rally around. Further, if fascism was, indeed, at an end in Italy, its fall presaged a similar fate for National Socialism.

The kidnap operation was directed by Captain Otto Skorzeny of the Friedenthal Waffen SS, a covert unit assigned particularly difficult tasks. The help of an Italian general was finally solicited, and Skorzeny, the general and several German commandos located Mussolini and whisked him off in a light plane to a nearby airfield. There they transferred him to a larger aircraft, and flew him to Vienna. On September 14th, 1943, he was taken to Hitler's Wolf's Lair in East Prussia.

Mussolini was grateful, but not in the way Hitler had calculated. Assuming that they were of the same stripe, Hitler had surmised that Mussolini would be anxious to butcher his enemies and attempt to regain power. But the *Duce* was a tired, sick, old man; he only wanted the war to end so that he might find some peace.

It was not to be. Under Hitler's browbeating, on September 18th, 1943, Mussolini was forced to announce to the Italians over Munich radio that he was returning to establish a new fascist socialist republic, the *Repubblica Sociale Italiana*. He called on his people to support him, but most Italians were weary of war and their alliance with the Germans, and listened with indifference or disdain. In northern and central Italy, guerilla groups were lashing out at troops commanded by Marshall Albert Kesselring who, since September 11th, had put Italy under German military control. In the south, paisanos were welcoming the advancing Allies with women and food. The Italians had switched sides for good.

Mussolini installed himself at Saló near Lake Garda. He had no illusions that this was entirely his headquarters and viewed the Germans around him more as jailers than fellow soldiers. He was well aware that his power was backed by Hitler alone. His wife was still urging him, as she had been for some months, to give it all up, but Mussolini spurned her advice.

"What is there for me to do but cooperate?" he moaned. "Hitler will kill me if I give up."

The first positive step taken by Mussolini was to bring to trial in January 1944, all those "traitorous" members of the Fascist Grand Council whom he could find. In this action he was firmly backed by Hitler and by members of the new government.

The most important of these "traitors" was his son-in-law, Count Galeazzo Ciano. Ciano's wife, Edda, came to her father and pleaded with him to save her husband. But Mussolini was adamant. Ciano was executed along with four other ministers. "A true patriot never hesitates to sacrifice even his own children," he announced testily.

The northern part of Italy was in a state of near civil war from June through November 1944. Partisans and Germans and die-hard fascists were fighting each other bitterly at every turn. Mussolini became more despondent as the Germans moved his headquarters from one location to another. He likened his plight to being aboard a rudderless raft in the middle of a stormy sea.

On April 27, 1945, heading a detachment of German troops assigned to guard him, Mussolini departed from Milan, and stopped for the night at Grandola on Lake Como. He could clearly see that his end was near, and he penned a long farewell letter to his wife who, with the children, was staying a short distance away until such time as she could safely escape into Switzerland. His only remaining hope was the promise made by Alessandro Pavolini, his new party secretary and former Minister of Popular Culture, that 3000 loyal troops were ready to join his convoy. With the help of the troops, Mussolini hoped to breach the partisan lines and make his escape into Switzerland.

Mussolini was excited when a solitary armored car drew up at the hotel early the next morning. Pavolini stepped down and announced the arrival of the long-awaited troops. "But where are the men?" inquired Mussolini. "Right here, Excellency," said Pavolini,"—all 12 of them!" Mussolini was crushed when he learned how the Italian people had turned against him.

Through his final ordeal Mussolini had the support of his mistress of nine years, Claretta Petacci. Of all the women in his life—aside from his wife—Claretta occupied the position of greatest notoriety. Benito met her in 1933, when she was a young woman engaged to be married and he a man of 50. Within three years he had made her his mistress and, until the beginning of the war, was discreet in his relations with her. Thereafter, his affair became a public scandal.

Surprisingly, Rachele knew nothing about the liaison until 1943. When she did discover it, relations between her and Benito became strained. Yet, she soon forgave him. Benito, for his part, never behaved differently toward his wife—but he refused to give up his mistress.

At the town of Menággio, the convoy was halted by Italian partisans who were searching for fascists. They arrested all Italians in the group, including Claretta. Mussolini was disguised in a German uniform and dark glasses, and was allowed to pass through, unrecognized, with the Germans.

At Dongo, on the northwestern shore of Lake Como, the convoy was again stopped by partisans for inspection. Here, Mussolini was recognized and taken prisoner. When he was deposited at a nearby partisan camp, he cast off his German disguise and donned other clothes. "I never want to see another German uniform," he blurted out.

After several hours' sleep, Mussolini was taken by car to a village a few miles north of Como. There he was joined by Claretta, who had persuaded her captors that she be permitted to die with her lover. Mussolini was grateful, but was silent. An embrace said it all.

After a night in a farmhouse near Bonzanigo, the couple was transported—on April 28th—to the Villa Belmonte on Lake Como. They were marched in through the gate and ordered to stand up against a rock wall. In tears, Claretta pleaded with the partisans not to shoot the *Duce*.

Walter Audisio, commander of the group, slowly read Mussolini's death sentence and ordered the execution. Claretta was shot first as she flung herself in front of the *Duce* to protect him. Four bullets were then fired into Mussolini's chest. He collapsed backward with a thud.

Tossed on a truck, the bodies were sped away. The next day

they were brought to the Piazzale Loreto in Milan and dumped atop 17 other fascist corpses for the populace to view.

The Italian mob went wild, and began to mutilate the bodies. Some people in the rear of the crowd claimed they could not see, so Mussolini, Petacci, Pavolini, and Gelormini were strung up by their heels on the girder of a half-built filling station facing the square.

A prophecy Mussolini once made had been fulfilled: "It's my destiny to end my days only when I'm once more raised to the heights I've always occupied—high above the mob!"

5. Hitler

In 1945 a sizeable portion of the world lay in ruins. Its condition was not the result of natural disaster, but the inevitable outcome of the ambitions of a madman.

Adolf Hitler, would-be Austrian artist of mediocre talent, who rose to become Chancellor of the Third Reich, was born on April 20, 1889. His birthplace was the small town of Braunau on the Inn, a river separating Austria and Germany—two countries he was destined to join.

Adolf's father's work as a customs official had taken him to Braunau, but the family—on both sides—had come originally from an area northwest of Vienna. The fact that Adolf was of peasant stock became a source of pride and propaganda for him. That a man of such modest background could rise so high has been a source of wonderment to the world, and has been explained, in part, as being due to a combination of luck and the needs of the German people at that point in history. But an even more poignant factor may be found in the mad genius of the man himself.

Adolf's parents, Alois Hitler and Klara Poelzl, were second cousins. Klara was 23 years younger than her husband; she was his third wife. Adolf was their fourth child. Of the six children born to Alois and Klara, only Adolf and his younger sister, Paula, lived to adulthood. Adolf's half-brother, Alois, married and spent part of his life in Ireland and England. His half-sister, Angela, became his housekeeper after he became Chancellor. Adolf's love affair with her daughter, Geli Raubal, is a strange and violent story.

When Adolf was three, the family moved to Passau in Germany. His father had been promoted to a higher rank in the customs service, and was assigned to regional headquarters. By a special agreement worked out with the German government, the Austrian officials lived in Passau. Even at this tender age, little Adolf favored Germany over his native Austria.

The family spent two years in Passau, although the father departed for Linz after one year, because he had been appointed to an even better post. At the time of Alois's promotion, Klara had just given birth to their fifth child.

But Linz was not to be their home for long. Shortly after his 58th birthday, in the year 1895, Alois decided to take early retirement, and the family moved to Hafeld, a village approximately 30 miles from Linz. Adolf began his schooling there, but two years later the family was uprooted again.

Alois sold his property in Hafeld and took an apartment in Lambach, a medium-sized community between the cities of Linz and Salzburg. In Lambach, Adolf attended a Benedictine monastery for one year. It was here that Adolf saw a swastika for the first time, for there were a number of decorative swastikas throughout the buildings and grounds. A previous abbot by the name of Theodorich von Hagen had them put up as a sort of pun on his name, which closely resembles the first part of the German word for swastika.

In November of 1898, Alois moved for the last time. Longing for a house and some land where he could tend his bees and raise vegetables, he bought a place outside Linz in a village called Leonding. There he lived for five years until his death in 1903 at the age of 65.

The family remained in Leonding until 1905 when Adolf, now the head of the family, left school. He had been commuting to school in Linz—and later in Steyr, near Linz. His mother sold the house and took an apartment in Linz proper. Adolf lived at home, but could not find a productive job. Instead, he spent his time drawing, taking walks, and attending the opera. This "lazy streak" was to remain with him all his life.

Other characteristics marked Adolf's childhood.

First of all, he was a mama's boy. He lived in dread and awe of his father who, with his curling mustache, large frame, advanced age—he was over 50 when Adolf was born—and splendid uniform of the customs service, presented a most imposing figure. Adolf was as stubborn as his father, and the two of them were engaged in constant arguments—particularly about Adolf's desire to become an artist. This early clash with authority was a factor that later drove Adolf to seek power over others, but as a youngster he sought refuge behind his mother's skirts. The very mention of his father invariably conjured up hostile feeling, but his love for his mother was fathomless. He never found a woman who could quite measure up to his mother.

On the whole, Adolf was a poor student. Even in drawing—his favorite subject—he never consistently earned the highest grades. Much of his time in school was spend in mischief-making. He liked nothing better than to tease and torture his teachers, employing tricks and asking questions calculated to embarrass them. He saw them all as authority figures—molded in the image of his father—and they had to be put down. Throughout life he harbored a particular dislike for academic types.

While in the Linz *Realschule*—a non-classical secondary school—Adolf continued to perform inadequately, and was on the verge of expulsion when his mother removed him and enrolled him in a similar institution in Steyr. Upon completing his final examination there, he celebrated by getting roaring drunk.

After sobering up, the next day, he was distressed at not being able to find his school-leaving certificate. Fearful of an upbraiding from his mother, he went back to the school to ask for a duplicate. After a long wait, the director ushered Adolf into his office and held up his original certificate. It had been torn into four pieces, and had arrived in the mail that morning.

From the appearance of the mutilated and stained paper, it was obvious that Adolf had wiped himself with it. The director was beside himself with rage, and gave the boy a scolding that he never forgot. Years later, Hitler recalled his humiliation with rancor. The incident increased his hatred for teachers and learning, but it also taught him a lesson. He swore that he would never again get drunk—and he didn't.

Young Adolf was a child of moods. Although given to playful pranks and to bursts of occasional enthusiasm, he was usually a somber and withdrawn boy. He was not well liked by his peers, and, until the family moved to Linz, he had no close friends. There he linked up with August Kubizek, an aspiring musician of about the same age. Together they would take long walks, visit museums, discuss art, and go to the opera. Adolf was fond of August. He was able to assume the role of leader in their relationship.

In the spring of 1906, Adolf traveled to Vienna where, inspired by the magnificent buildings and world of culture, he was determined to return the following year as a student enrolled in the Academy of Fine Arts. It never occurred to him that he did not have sufficient preparation or talent. As one biographer noted: "Hitler had the artist's temperament without either talent, training, or creative energy."

In October 1907, Adolf took the qualifying examination for entry to the Academy and failed. He applied one more time, in 1908, but this time was even refused permission to sit for the examination. He then applied to the School of Architecture, but wouldn't even be considered because he could not show his school-leaving certificate. Devastated, Adolf abandoned virtually all contact with his family. He had only one friend—Kubizek—who had joined him in Vienna some months previous. They shared a room which quickly was overcrowded when August's piano and Adolf's drawing board were installed.

August and Adolf walked together and talked together often, until, in the summer of 1908, they returned to Linz for the summer. Then, Adolf went his own way, and when August returned to Vienna in the fall, he looked for his friend but was unable to locate him. For the next five years, Hitler disappeared among the down-and-out of Vienna.

During the first two of those years, he led a hand-to-mouth existence, often sleeping in doorways during the warmer weather. During the winter months he spent his nights in a flophouse in back of the Meidling railroad station. Toward the end of 1909, he changed his lodgings and moved into a men's hostel down near the Danube River. He remained there until the spring of 1913.

The Vienna years are important in explaining Hitler's drive for power. Sleeping in a cubicle beside drunks, dope addicts, and ne'er-do-wells of every description, and eking out a bare subsistence through the sale of his hand-painted picture postcards, he appeared to be a person totally devoid of ambition. It was only when one engaged him in conversation that his inner turmoil became evident. Hitler viewed every democratic institution with suspicion, every intellectual with distrust, every capitalist with disdain. He fulminated against Jews in particular, ascribing to them every ill in the world for which the Communists were not already responsible. He ranted against the ethnic mixture of Vienna—primarily against the Slavs, for whom he had the direst contempt. He once described them as "sub-human." Hitler's idea of earthly paradise was a nation of nothing but Germans.

He espoused these same views during the year and a half he lived in Munich. Years later, his landlady commented that Hitler was a strange duck. He spent long periods in his room preparing a poster or advertisement or reading books he had borrowed from the library. When she met him, he was often muttering to himself.

Part of each day, Hitler spent in a café or restaurant, engaging in heated political discussions. She also remembered that Hitler seldom had any money, and was habitually late in paying his rent. To her, he was a total failure, a common bum.

But when Germany declared war on August 1, 1914, Hitler was to begin a new phase of his life which would intensify his spirit of nationalism and increase his hatred of bolshevism.

On August 3rd, Hitler applied to the Bavarian king for permission to enlist in the army. He was allowed to volunteer immediately, and was assigned to a training camp until October. Toward the end of the month, his regiment was sent to the front. His job was to run messages from one headquarters or unit to another. He carried out his orders efficiently, conscientiously, and bravely, and was cited many times. Except for a brief period in 1916 when he received a leg wound, and another one month before the end of the war when he was temporarily blinded in a gas attack, Hitler spent almost the entire war at or near the front lines.

He gave all his energies to fighting for Germany and could not understand the griping of soldiers that he heard on all sides. He took no pleasure in drink or women, but was content to spend what little free time he had talking, reading, or brooding. The army gave Hitler a sense of accomplishment, status, and a measure of excitement that he had never before known. He was not anxious to return to civilian life. Neither were millions of others, and it was from this pool of discontented veterans that many extremist groups, among them the Nazis, were able to recruit so successfully.

At the time of Hitler's return to Munich in the fall of 1918, the city was a hotbed of confused and chaotic political activity. For a time, Bavaria was controlled by the Social Democrats, a party led by a Jewish intellectual named Kurt Eisner. Less than three months after taking office, however, Eisner was shot by a fanatical right-winger. From then until the spring of 1920, Munich was the stage for the creation and demise of numerous parties and factions intent on overthrowing the Weimar Republic and avenging the so-called "stab-in-the-back."

After a period of guard duty in Traunstein, Hitler was back in Munich once more, doing a job for the Press and News Bureau of the Political Department of the Army. His task was to smoke out parties inimical to the army and to lecture to soldiers on the dangers of democracy and left-wing ideologies—the latter a curious assignment, to be sure, in view of the army's oath to support the democratic Weimar Republic. Hitler took to his duties like a duck to water. One of the suspicious parties he was to investigate was the German Workers' Party, the forerunner of the Nazi party.

Hitler was not enthusiastic about attending a meeting of this group, for it seemed to be completely innocuous. Unlike most other worker parties, it was neither communist nor socialist, but rather a sort of ineffectual right-wing group. He attended because he was so ordered.

The meeting took place in the dimly-lit, smoke-filled back room of a tavern. Hitler listened to the proceedings and was bored. However, when an unknown professor began to criticize the economic theories of Gottfried Feder, a half-baked economist whom Hitler had heard lecture the previous month, he rose and delivered a verbal drubbing such that the professor slunk out the back way. A wan-looking man, wearing thick glasses, then ran up to Hitler and pressed a pamphlet into his hand. The man's name was Anton Drexler, a locksmith by trade, and the founder of National Socialism.

Hitler did not read the booklet until early the next morning. He was astonished—and pleased—to discover that Drexler's ideas coincided with his own. The basic premise was that no nationalistic party could be effective without the wholehearted support of the lower classes. Later the same day, Hitler received an invitation to attend the next meeting of the German Workers' Party. After much thought, he decided to go. He was annoyed that he should be attending meetings of somebody else's party and not founding his own, but his curiosity had been whetted by the booklet.

The meeting was dreary and poorly attended. The treasury was practically empty; there were no interesting ideas discussed, and no political action contemplated. Hitler was both repelled and fascinated. Two days later, after considerable reflection, he decided to join. His reason was simple: He saw in this scruffy, scraggly bunch a chance to lead.

The party leadership consisted of the founder, Anton Drexler; a promoter, the drunken poet Dietrich Eckart; the ideologist, a homosexual army captain named Ernst Roehm; and the screw ball economist, Gottfried Feder. But it took a tramp named Hitler to unite them all, and produce a movement that was to scar the world forever.

The first major meeting took place in February of 1920. Hitler was in charge of all preparations. He rented the huge festival hall of the famous Hofbräuhaus in Munich, and prepared all the publicity. He arranged to have a main speaker, but he also saw to it that he himself had a place on the program. And it was he who held forth the longest and received the most applause. During his speech, he set down the program of the party. The points included the bringing together of all Germans into a union, the abrogation of the treaties of Versailles and St. Germain, and "the creation of a strong central power of the

State." (This last point indicates the line of Hitler's thinking even in his earlier years.)

During the spring of 1920, Hitler changed the name of the party to the National Socialist German Workers' (Nazi) Party. For dramatic effect, he devised an appropriate emblem, combining a black swastika on a white disc, superimposed on a red background. The emblem was introduced immediately on armbands for his rough-and-ready bodyguards and ushers at meetings. By midsummer, the Nazis were flying a flag of the same design. The white symbolized nationalism, the red the socialist aspect of the program, and the black swastika the strength and creativity of the pure Aryan. It was an unbeatable combination of colors, shapes, and ideas.

Hitler personally handled all party propaganda. Every poster and announcement showed his touch. Each placard was of a particular size and shape, and was posted in a very carefully selected place in Munich. Various sizes of type were employed to highlight particular ideas. Spacings, underlinings, and quotation marks were employed to gain the fullest effect and to capture the reader's attention. The admission price was "played down"; so was the fact that Jews were not to be admitted—at least initially. If a Jew or two did manage to attend a meeting and start a ruckus, Hitler liked nothing better than to watch his bullies toss them out. The same applied for communists, who appeared more often. He was convinced that brawls added to the excitement of meetings and engendered public awe of him.

Hitler was already tasting power of a more potent sort. He had left the army, and now usually wore a simple suit to meetings. However, his bodyguards stood in a relation to him much as subordinates do to their general—and Hitler relished this relationship. Night after night, month after month, Hitler was the featured party speaker. He packed the people in, and held them spellbound for hours on end.

On the night of July 29, 1921, before a full house at the Zirkus Krone meeting hall, he was introduced for the first time as *Unser F*ührer, Our Leader. In a short while he was to become simply *Der Führer, The* Leader—as if he were not merely the leader of the Nazi party, but of the German nation and, perhaps, the world. He compelled the party leadership to grant him dictatorial powers, and these powers he never relinquished.

From this time forward, the party continued to flourish. It won over converts and was able to succeed because of its appeal to the uneducated masses who lacked insight and were unable to discriminate among viable political possibilities.

Public dissatisfaction with the various governments in Berlin, and the search for a scapegoat to explain Germany's defeat in World War I, also played a part. But it was mostly Hitler's effective propaganda program under the triple guise of order, reason, and logic—punctuated by fear and violence—that attracted and held the German people.

The incisive comments in the diary of Captain Truman Smith, assistant American military attaché in Berlin, are a clue to Hitler's growing strength and madness. Smith wrote in November 1922, after an interview with Hitler: "A marvelous demagogue! Have rarely listened to such a logical and fanatical man." Smith recognized that logical fanaticism will produce marvelous demagoguery. Hitler was as consistent and logical in his arguments as any intelligent person might be; it was only his premises that were totally unfounded.

Hitler's reliance on violence and men of violence became part of his ruthless plan to gain and hold power. By the end of the spring of 1922, he had several hundred storm troopers under his command. They frequently paraded up and down the streets of Munich, usually to the accompaniment of a band, with flags flying and armbands flashing. After beer hall meetings, they cracked every communist head they could find, and at huge outdoor rallies they "maintained order" by dispersing themselves among the crowd, pretending to be policemen.

After the immensely successful rally on Königsplatz in Munich on August 16, 1922, at which time Hitler railed endlessly against the government in Berlin and called for its overthrow, he began to export his politics to outlying towns and cities. It did not matter whether there was a law prohibiting mass assemblies; he continued to speak and use his storm troopers to write and enforce his own laws. Once, when a train crew refused to transport the storm troopers back to Munich from a rally, Hitler threatened to arrest and shoot the crew on the spot, if they did not obey his orders. He had no compunctions about assuming authority, and taking the law into his own hands even to the point of executing anyone who did not obey his command.

Hitler was now beginning to see himself as dictator of Germany. Except for his insufficient military forces, he felt reasonably well prepared to carry out a coup d'état. But two events that took place at this time gave him an extra measure of courage and confidence to move ahead with his plans.

On September 25, 1923, Hitler met with the heads of the various rightist private armies, and convinced them to declare him commander of the entire group. He knew that he would need a sizeable force when he marched on Berlin, although he did not take sufficiently into account the importance of being in a state of military readiness equal, at least, to the forces he might encounter when he met his enemy.

Also, during September, he decided to pay a visit to Richard Wagner's widow and the rest of the family in Bayreuth. Hitler admired Wagner greatly. His music reflected Hitler's idea of pure Germanic culture. He was amazed, and tremendously gratified, at the reception tendered him. The accolades heaped upon him by the Wagner clan, and the display of loyalty expressed by the local storm troopers increased his ego to the bursting point. There was no doubt in his mind that he was, indeed, the appointed savior of Germany. He could go forward with his plans, protected by God and supported by the people.

Upon returning to Munich, Hitler could hardly wait to put his plan into operation. It was a simple one—in fact, in retrospect, too simple to have worked at all. If it had not been for an element of luck he enjoyed throughout his life, the story of Hitler's reach for power would have ended in ridicule, or a burst of gunfire.

Bavaria was essentially under the control of three persons: Generalkommissar Gustav von Kahr and the heads of the army and the state police, General Otto von Lossow and Colonel Hans Ritter von Seisser. As Hitler saw it, all he needed to do was to arrest these three men. He did have the help of General Erich Ludendorff, who he expected would support him all the way.

Plans went forward to arrest the ruling triumvirate on November 4th, during a ceremony for the war dead, but at the last minute it was decided to bring off the "putsch" at a meeting in the Bürgerbräukeller four days later. Hitler felt that the plan was more apt to succeed in the presence of less military opposition.

There then followed one of the weirdest events in modern political history.

Hitler arrived at the meeting at 8:00 p.m. In contrast to the well-dressed Kahr and his associates, Hitler was garbed in a trench coat.

After 30 minutes of listening to Kahr's speech, Hitler became restless. He cocked his ears upon hearing the sound of nearby trucks. He looked at his watch: It was 8:30. At that moment, a wave of helmeted storm troopers burst into the hall and took up positions along the walls, machine guns pointed at the assembled crowd of 3,000. Hitler leaped from his seat, and joined Hermann Goering in the aisle. Together they rammed their way up to the speaker's platform.

Hitler raised his revolver over his head, sent two shots flying toward the ceiling, and punctuated the sudden silence with
his screams for attention. Like an obstreperous class caught
misbehaving, the crowd stopped their excited chatter and fixed
their gaze alternately on the wildly gesticulating madman on
the platform, and the gun snouts that ringed the room.

His voice rising higher and higher, and at times breaking,
Hitler declared that the revolution was now underway. "The
Bavarian government is deposed! The Reich government is deposed!" he screamed. Always adept at the big lie, he declared
that 600 men were in and around the building, and that others
had taken over the police and the army barracks. In truth, probably no more than 60 or 70 storm troopers were present; neither
the police nor the army had been taken; and the government
had not been deposed.

Arresting all the other dignitaries on the stage, he escorted
Kahr, Lossow, and Seisser into a back room for a consultation.
When they hesitated to accept the proffered deal of a place in a
government headed by him, Hitler brandished his gun and proclaimed: "I have three bullets for you and one for me!" To make
his point even more dramatically, he lifted the pistol to his temple, as if to shoot.

If Ludendorff had not walked in at that moment, we might
have found out whether Hitler was bluffing. Seeing and talking
with the famous general, however, convinced the three to swear
allegiance to Hitler.

Hitler spent the rest of the night making speeches all over
Munich. When he awoke the next morning, he was not aware
that Kahr, Lossow, and Seisser had spent their night having
misgivings about the promise they had made to Hitler.

Marching at the head of 3000 men, Hitler and Ludendorff
struck out for the center of Munich in late morning. Blocks
away, on the edge of Odeonsplatz, armed police waited under
orders from Seisser.

At first, the encounter between the two forces was more
show than action. But then a shot was fired—no one knows to
this day from which side—and at that, the police commenced
firing at the pavement directly in front of the advancing National Socialists. When ricocheting bullets began wounding and
killing persons, panic set in. Storm troopers—noticing for the
first time that their rifles lacked firing pins—headed for doorways or hid behind monuments, pillars, and corners of buildings.
Even Hitler was about to beat a rapid retreat when his compan-

ion, Max Erwin von Scheubner-Richter, was struck in the heart by a bullet. Ludendorff's valet lost half his head when he rushed in front of the general to protect him. Hitler's bodyguard, Ulrich Graf, was hit by six bullets as he tried to cover Hitler. Only Ludendorff, apparently not in the least worried about the flying lead, continued straight across Odeonsplatz and into the Feldherrnhalle.

When Scheubner-Richter was hit, he and Hitler were walking arm in arm. The force of the falling dead body dragged Hitler down so hard onto the cobblestones that he injured his left shoulder. Thinking he had been shot, he began crawling immediately in the direction of Max-Josephplatz where, according to a prior arrangement, he was to be picked up in case of emergency and driven away to a place of hiding.

His destination was the home of a musician, Ernst Hanfstaengl, in an outlying village. Stuffed in the attic, Hitler passed a bad night in pain and fear of capture. Mrs. Hanfstaengl reported later that Hitler was beside himself, and that when she went to check on him the next morning, he greeted her with ravings about never letting "those swine take him," and swearing to kill himself first. At one point he produced a pistol and threatened to shoot himself. But Mrs. Hanfstaengl, a hefty woman with steady nerves, wrested it from him and flung it across the attic. Always uncourageous with women, Hitler let the gun lie where it had landed—in a flour barrel.

Hitler hid at the Hanfstaengl home for three nights. On the third night, three policemen arrived and arrested him. Like a small child refusing to take a trip with his parents, Hitler was pulled down from the attic, screaming and yelling about Germany's ruined destiny, and led away to prison at Landsberg on the Lech.

By all rights, Hitler should have been hanged for treason. Instead, he was given the minimum sentence of five years, but his actual imprisonment lasted a mere 13 months. During the time of his incarceration he enjoyed privileges not easily obtainable in a first-class hotel. His co-conspirators also received light sentences, and Ludendorff was released unpunished.

Why were Hitler and his crooks treated so kindly? Partly because of a few friends in high places, partly because of the lack of a threat from either the right or left in Germany at the time, partly because of undeserved mercy, but probably most because of an innate fear of this madman. His rhetoric, his eyes which could penetrate one to the core, his persistent frown, unnerved virtually everyone with whom he came in contact. Hitler possessed a mystic power which radiated from his being and, like wild fiery flames, incinerated both conscience and soul of those who fell prey to his personality.

When he was first arrested, Hitler was in a state of deep depression and exhibited definite suicidal tendencies. Within a very short time, however, he realized the tremendous impact his abortive putsch had had on the nation. His actions and statements at his trial were reported in detail in the press throughout Germany and the world, and when he was released on December 20, 1924, he had become a world figure. He began immediately to take advantage of this fact and set out to complete a book that he had started writing in 1922. It was a long discursive combination autobiography and political treatise which he completed in 1924 while in Landsberg prison. It was published on July 18, 1925 and was finally named *Mein Kampf*.

His book was read by millions of the wrong people: the Germans. Had it been read carefully by others, it would have been recognized for what it really was: a dangerous master-plan of a madman for world conquest. Had it been read merely by a committee of psychologists, it would have been considered sufficient evidence for Hitler's committal to a lunatic asylum. Replete with historical inaccuracies, mythology, and half-baked truths, insultingly repetitious, filled with obfuscations and blatant lies, its mystical pull was nevertheless so powerful and appealing to the masses that it was read and believed and accepted as a kind of truth that could only be characterized as emanating from one endowed with divine truth. Although the book held only disdain for every class—and practically every nation—it is strange that the reader did not see himself as the subject of attack. But the German people of the 1920s and 1930s found themselves, despite themselves, part of Hitler's "struggle," and they discovered, on every page of *Mein Kampf*, not themselves, but some other person, group, race, or nation as the cause of their problems and the object of their hate on whom they could unleash their suspicion and avenge themselves.

Hitler's favorite target was the Jews. His fear and dislike of them knew no bounds. Of all the themes in *Mein Kampf*, of all the functional psychoses afflicting him, his hatred of the Jews stands out and typifies all his thinking and actions. Hitler always insisted that the masses were stupid and could comprehend only very few and very simple ideas at one time. These ideas had to be clear-cut—black or white, right or wrong—and they had to be hammered into the people relentlessly. From the start of his career, Hitler drummed into the German people the idea that the Jews were a depraved race, grossly inferior to "pure Aryans."

For Hitler, an Aryan was a Caucasian of non-Jewish descent. In fostering this concept, he mistakenly connected Aryanism with race because he assumed that a common language—namely, Indo-European—meant a common racial origin of those who spoke it. It did not occur to him that the Slavs, a people he detested almost as much as the Jews, were also Indo-European.

Never one to permit himself to allow the truth to interfere with his preconceived notions, Hitler promoted the idea of a satanic people—the Jews—a people who believed in liberalism, democracy, freedom of speech, and the like. Jews, he declared, were a threat to the noble qualities embodied in the Aryan. Hitler was convinced—to the point of madness—that the Jews were intent on destroying the "pure Aryan race" by controlling them economically, politically, and even physically—by means of miscegenation. So convinced was Hitler that his mad theory was truth that he set out, systematically, to eliminate this people—the object of his hate. And, indeed, he did manage in large measure to achieve his objective. Ruthlessly, he caused the death of more than 60 per cent of European Jewry before he was stopped.

Between the time of his release from Landsberg, in 1924, and his accession to full power in 1933, Hitler continued to work with, and for, the party. By court order not permitted until 1927 to make political speeches, he used his party newspaper, the *Völkischer Beobachter,* as the vehicle for his inflammatory anti-government ideas. This was not to say that he refrained from all speaking engagements. Quite the contrary. In fact, almost immediately after his release, he assembled 2,000 people in the very same Bürgerbräukeller where he had launched the unsuccessful putsch. Fearful of loss of his parole status, however, he went off to address less publicized gatherings, often traveling far from Munich to express his revolutionary ideas.

The people who surrounded Hitler in those days are important figures, for their opinions and work often shaped the party and gave it direction and tone; their personalities affected Hitler's approach and decisions.

Since Hitler's henchmen were all extensions of his own personality, it is unnecessary to list them by order of their appearance, or to attempt to evaluate which of the group was the wisest or the most vicious. It was their collective effect and influence that is the important element and that figured the most in the rise and fall of Hitler—and in Germany's collapse.

Paul Joseph Goebbels first became attracted to Hitler when he heard him speak at a rally in 1922, but it was three years before he became closely associated with the workings of the party. Goebbels was eight years younger than Hitler, but revered him like a father. His admiration for the *Führer* is all the more strange because of the tremendous educational gap between them. Goebbels held a Ph.D. from Heidelberg University; Hitler had a haphazard and modest grammar school education.

But they had at least three things in common. Both were powerful orators, effective writers (although Goebbels failed in his literary attempt), and criminals. Only five feet tall, thin, crippled, dark, and with a mouselike face, Goebbels in his devotion to Hitler gave the impression of a black, female bat buzzing around her human lover.

Hermann Goering, a much-decorated flyer in the First World War, was the exact opposite of Goebbels in physical appearance. Obese, but still in possession of that charm and basic good looks that made him a dashing war hero, Goering admired Hitler. However, he was unafraid to speak his mind and did so on many occasions. No sychophant, he demanded and got his own areas of control. Basically a brute, he unhesitatingly pushed people around, especially when his mind was unclear because of the drugs to which he was addicted.

In the earliest days of the party, Gregor Strasser was second only to Hitler in popularity and effectiveness. More jovial in nature than the rest of the gang, Strasser seemed the typical Bavarian. He was not unintelligent, and he served the party well when he succeeded in winning over to the cause two of his former secretaries: Goebbels and Heinrich Himmler. Strasser's brother, Otto, was expelled from the party because of his overly socialistic views.

Ernst Roehm had joined the party before Hitler, but he recognized very early Hitler's peculiar talents and status within the party. He despised the Weimar Republic as much as Hitler, and worked doggedly for its destruction. Hoglike in appearance, with beady eyes behind draped folds of fat, and a nose half shot away in the war, he was not attractive to women. But he did not care—he preferred men.

Julius Streicher taught school in Nuremberg. From the adulatory poster poems written to him by the girls of the seventh and eighth grades, one would think he was a saint. In point of fact, he was anything but a saint. Like Hitler, he was often seen carrying a whip—which he used on anybody who displeased him. But his greatest pleasure was found in taking time-released photographs of himself, in a mirrored room of his house, having intercourse with obliging young schoolgirls. Streicher also edited a newspaper called *Die Stürmer* (The Stormers), in which his favorite target was Jews, a people he described as "perverted, subhuman monsters."

Wilhelm Frick was perhaps the least odd of the core group. An efficient bureaucrat not unlike Hitler's father, he gave the party a measure of respectability so useful in the early days. He never failed to do Hitler's bidding and was especially pleased to arrest an annoying bunch of clergymen who complained to Hitler that the regime had taken on a definite anti-Christian attitude.

Criminality and ruthlessness were common factors present in Hitler and his gang. Where Hitler had a weakness, one of his associates made up for it. Where he had strengths, others fortified them. Even physically, Hitler's unimpressive body, his wan complexion, and his unsmiling face were complemented by the build and physiognomy of his cronies.

It seemed that the people surrounding Hitler were all members of his biological family with many of whom he had had incestuous relations.

Actually, incest was not anathema to Hitler. In the summer of 1928 he rented a villa in the mountains near Berchtesgaden, and set up housekeeping with his half-sister, Angela Raubal, in charge. Angela was widowed, and she brought along her two young daughters, Geli and Friedl. Geli, a lovely girl of only 20, caught Hitler's eye immediately. Everywhere he went, he took Geli along. In September of 1929, he moved out of his spartan quarters on Thierschstrasse in Munich, and rented an elegant apartment on Prinzregentenstrasse. He set aside a room for Geli.

For three years, he courted her and would have probably married her, had she consented. But, apparently, although she undoubtedly dispensed her favors to him, she did not love him the way he loved her. Also, Geli was still just a young girl who wanted to continue her career in music. Adolf could not bear the thought of her leaving him to take singing lessons in Vienna. He made this absolutely clear to her one morning in 1931, as he was about to leave for Hamburg. The next day, she was discovered dead in her room. She had shot herself in the heart.

Hitler was grief-stricken, and threatened to take his own life. He swore that he could never love another woman. He did, of course, have a long and close relationship with Eva Braun, but he never did love her as deeply and as completely as Geli. He waited until the day before his death to marry Eva.

Hitler now carried two pictures with him at all times: a photograph of his mother and one of Geli. A huge painting of Geli adorned the reception hall at Obersalzberg, his mountain retreat. Below it stood flowers which were changed daily. Hitler abhorred and feared death. Keeping freshly cut flowers near her picture was his way of denying the reality of Geli's suicide and assuaging the guilt he carried in connection with her death.

Life in Germany in the mid-20s was much too stable for Hitler's taste. He longed for a crisis to catapult him back into the public eye. He did not have long to wait. By the late 1920s inflation and growing unemployment were rampant. The country was in a depression. On October 3, 1929, Gustav Stresemann, the statesmanlike foreign minister and co-signer of the Kellog-Briand Pact, died, taking the new relationship of peace and harmony established with the Allies along with him to the grave. Added to his, before the month was out, the New York Stock Exchange had crashed.

Despair grew, and the situation was made to order for Adolf Hitler. He knew how to take advantage of moments of crisis and despair: find a scapegoat—in this case, convince the masses that the cause of their misery was the Jews and the communists. And then convince them that their savior was Adolf Hitler.

The elections in September 1930 reflected the magnitude of Hitler's success. Eight times as many votes were cast for the Nazis as in the elections two years earlier!

Hitler decided to wait for the proper moment. For a while he had thought another putsch would be necessary. But remembering his earlier fiasco, he resolved to make his bid for power through legal means. He set up party offices in the former Barlow Palace facing Königsplatz in Munich, and created a decor that gave the impression of wealth and efficiency.

The party had, in fact, been taking in a good deal of money. However, now with the purchase of the Brown House, as it became known, the treasury was considerably strained. Hitler thought the purchase was necessary—for the sake of the party's image. Spit-and-polish Nazi officers came in and out all day. Busy, busy, busy. The people were watching. It looked like a party that was on the move—upwards.

By July 1932, Hitler received 37.4 per cent of the total popular vote. But it took more than votes to gain the chancellorship. Hitler enlisted the support of wealthy and influential industrialists. These associations brought him in contact with the intrigues swirling around the aged president of Germany, Paul von Hindenburg. It was a situation custom-made for Hitler's purposes.

Von Hindenburg had appointed a general by the name of Kurt von Schleicher as his chancellor. Despite his name—which means "intriguer"—and many of his actions, von Schleicher was not able to put together an effective government, and von Hindenburg dismissed him 57 days after he took office. Hindenburg recommended a government shared by himself, a powerful politician and nobleman named Franz von Papen, and Hitler.

Hitler refused to accede to this arrangement, and insisted on the chancellorship. The infirm Hindenburg gave in to his demands. On the morning of January 30, 1933, Hitler took the oath of office as chancellor. By evening, as he took the salute from tens of thousands of storm troopers streaming through the Brandenburg Gate, he was already working out a way to become dictator.

The first step was to eliminate or reduce the political opposition of the communists. Working from membership lists stolen from headquarters, SA (*Sturmabteilung,* storm troops) men rounded up communists and threw them into prison. Of necessity, this was done rather quietly. But Hitler sought a means of dramatizing his action and of presenting the communists to the public in a bad light.

The Reichstag fire was the answer.

On the night of February 27, 1933, the Parliament building, known as the Reichstag, burned to the ground. Goering, who was one of the first on the scene, began raving that the communists were responsible. He proved this by wresting a confession from a half-blind, dim-witted Dutchman who was found stumbling around the burning building and who was in possession of communist papers. Hitler, who was eating dinner with Goebbels at the time of the fire, hardly interrupted his meal—and with good reason. Later evidence showed that he had ordered Goering to set the fire. Goering admitted it himself nine years later.

Hitler now stepped up his terror campaign. He dispatched his troops into the field to check up on the leadership of local governments. When they discovered other than simon-pure Nazis in control, immediate arrests were made. Soon the swastika flag was seen on every public building in the country.

But Hitler still did not have absolute control over the nation. He needed more than his army of Brown Shirts; he wanted the full support of the regular army. He had not been able to accomplish this because the regular officers suspected that he was preparing to use his Brown Shirts to overthrow them.

Hitler's plan was simple. He would murder the leaders of the SA, in an action that has been called "The Night of the Long Knives."

Ernst Roehm, the chief of the SA, had proposed that his organization be made the core of the new army, thus assuring him vast personal control. In view of Hindenburg's and the regular army's obvious objections to such a scheme, Hitler considered the plan politically unwise from a personal point of view. He succeeded in winning from the army a promise of support as the successor to Hindenburg upon the latter's death. All he needed now was to show his good faith by decimating the officer ranks of the SA.

Goering, chief of the SS (an arm of the SA), and Himmler, the newly-appointed head of the Prussian Gestapo, were more than willing to help. Goering, who had recently been appointed an infantry general in the regular army, was particularly anxious to demonstrate his loyalty.

Hitler permitted rumors of plots by Roehm to fly about for three months before he took action. After a speech by Papen on June 17th criticizing the Nazi movement and calling for immediate reforms, Hitler could see that he had once again lost the confidence of the army and President Hindenburg. It was time to set things right.

At two o'clock in the morning, on June 30, 1934, Hitler and Goebbels took off from the airport at Bonn for Munich. They intended to settle the score with Roehm. Hitler had also given orders to wreak revenge on various other enemies in the process. With the dictatorship within grasp, he had no intention of permitting it to slip through his fingers—regardless of the cost.

Arriving in Munich two hours later, Hitler found that some groundwork had been laid. A number of SA men had already been arrested, among them August Scheidhuber, who was also the Munich chief of police. When Hitler came face to face with Scheidhuber, he was violently angry. Raving like a maniac and spitting out the word "treason" three or four times in quick succession, Hitler shoved Scheidhuber backwards with one hand, and, with the other, tore off the chief's Nazi badge. This was not just for show; Hitler was actually in a frenzy. True to his character, he treated the object of his fury as he did every enemy—real or imagined. His madness erupted like a volcano spewing forth hate and derision.

In 15 minutes, Hitler was on his way again—this time to a hotel on Tegern Lake outside Munich. There, still sleeping, were Ernst Roehm and numerous SA men. One homosexual pair was yanked out of bed and was gunned down as they raced out to the street. Then, Hitler entered Roehm's room alone, and, in one of his towering rages, upbraided him for his "treachery." Forgotten were the years of friendship and cooperation. Roehm, more than anyone else over an extended period of time, had raised Hitler to his present position of prominence. As he left the room, Hitler deposited a pistol on the nightstand. But when Roehm did not oblige him by killing himself, Hitler sent in two SA officers who blew Roehm apart at point-blank range.

It is not certain how many persons were killed on this date. While Hitler was at work in the Munich area, Goering eliminated 150 SA officers in Berlin. Gregor Strasser was one of those. Papen escaped. An old enemy of Hitler's, former Bavarian monarchist leader Gustav von Kahr, was found axed to death in a quagmire outside Dachau.

Upon his return to Berlin, Hitler received the accolades of the army and the president for his swift action against those responsible for acts of treachery. When the cabinet agreed to legalize the recent butchery in the name of expendiency, Hitler knew he was now in full possession of a license to slaughter.

Hindenburg died on August 2, 1934. Hours before his demise, a law had been passed, under pressure from Hitler, that the offices of president, chancellor, and commander-in-chief were to be abolished. In their place, a single office—that of *Führer* and *Reichskanzler*—would exist. *He* would fill that office even though he had not called for an election to determine Hindenburg's successor, as he was bound to do by the Constitution. Instead, he demanded that all members of the armed services swear allegiance to him personally—not to their country.

The Third Reich had now begun in earnest.

The Nazi murder of Austrian Chancellor Engelbert Dolfuss in 1934, the annexation of Austria in 1938, the seizure of Czechoslovakia in 1939, the attack on Poland, followed by a declaration of war from France and England—all these are well-known facts. Hitler's sweep through Scandinavia, Holland, Belgium, and France and his mad attempt to conquer Russia are equally familiar episodes. The Rome-Berlin-Tokyo Axis and the Allied Powers became huge symbols for evil and good—or good and evil, depending upon one's nationality.

By the time Hitler had become absolute ruler of Germany, he had demonstrated every aspect of his particular madness. Now, with full power in his hands, the madness was intensified; conquest and murder multiplied. The nations that watched as he ranted and raved at foreign ministers, gassed and incinerated millions of Jews, and swallowed up whole countries were too naive to believe that the blueprint had been before them since 1925 when it was committed to print in *Mein Kampf*.

By the summer of 1944, it had become evident to many German military leaders that the war was lost, and that Hitler was leading the country to total destruction. A number of senior officers, fully aware of Hitler's mental state, conspired to kill him by placing a bomb in a briefcase during a planning session at the Wolf's Lair—his wartime hideout in East Prussia. At the last moment, however, somebody moved the briefcase a few feet away, and Hitler survived.

Slightly injured, and thoroughly shaken by the event, Hitler took immediate action and had the culprits strung up on meathooks. But, despite his anger, he regarded the event as prophetic, a sign from Providence that he was indeed the savior—else why should he have been spared?

It was precisely this attitude that led him then to insist on all-out war—regardless of the consequences for Germany. In the face of all good military advice, he meant to fight to the last man. Still living in a world of dreams and fantasies, the megalomaniac could not admit that the end had come until the Russians and Americans were within two blocks of the chancellery.

On April 30, 1945, as Germany lay in shambles, Hitler's life ended in his Berlin bunker where he spent the last days of his life raving like a maniac.

6. Trujillo

Trujillo was a man of many contradictions. He was both ruthless and cruel but had a deep and enduring love for his family, especially for his son, Ramfis.

Although Trujillo was virile and strong, he loved to bathe himself in perfume. He was five feet seven inches tall—rather tall for a Dominican. Nevertheless, he felt impelled to increase his height even more, and so, with the help of elevator shoes, he added two inches, and his five-foot nine-inch stature earned him the nickname, "Big One."

He lacked eloquence. His voice was high-pitched and unpleasant. And because he was unable to sway people with words, he decided to use guns instead.

"Big One" was as superstitious as any Haitian peasant, and prone to imaginative excursions. One of his greatest illusions was that he was an expert in the field of medicine. He liked nothing better than to summon prominent physicians to the presidential mansion and to suggest to them exotic cures for every conceivable illness.

His knowledge of commerce and industry was minimal, yet he accumulated more personal wealth than entire governments have been able to. Such power and wealth as he had could have been used for the good of his people—but he was corrupt and selfish from the very start.

He often acted as though he were more powerful than God himself, yet he filled his homes with the symbols of Christianity. But when he finally defied the clergy, it was they who toppled him from power.

Trujillo—one of the most vicious dictators known to the Western world—once had the audacity to declare, "Above all, I am against dictators!" He used these words of accusation against President Horacio Vásquez in his fight for the presidential nomination of the Dominican Republic in 1930. When victory came to him, it was the beginning of the harshest, most iron-fisted dictatorship in Latin American history.

Trujillo recognized no higher earthly authority than himself. In fact, he saw himself equal to God. Not long after promoting himself to Generalissimo, he erected a huge neon sign in Ciudad Trujillo (the capital he renamed in *his* own honor) on which was inscribed: GOD AND TRUJILLO. A fearful press often quoted the motto as TRUJILLO AND GOD—for, after all, who was more important?

A story current during the 1950s characterizes the audacity and superego of Trujillo:

Stalin, Hitler, and Trujillo appeared before the Judgment Seat of the Almighty. The first two confessed that they had been cruel men, but explained that they had acted in the best interests of humanity.

The Lord rose, shook their hands, and said: "Go! There is a place here *even* for the likes of you two."

When Trujillo's turn came, God dispatched him merely with a wave of His hand.

St. Peter, observing the proceedings, asked why the Lord did not rise from his throne to shake Trujillo's hand as he had done with Stalin and Hitler.

God replied: "If I had left my seat for an instant, that scoundrel would have taken it from me!"

Rafael Leonidas Trujillo Molina was born in 1891 in a small town called San Cristóbal, located on the west bank of the Nigua River. It was slightly inland—about 18 miles from Santo Domingo, the capital of the Dominican Republic. There, amid dirty streets shaded by luxuriant fruit trees, he spent his youth.

Rafael was different from his playmates, largely in his fastidiousness. He was constantly bathing, combing his hair, brushing his clothes. This unorthodox and unusual behavior for a young boy was a pattern that was to remain with him throughout his life. By the time he became an adult, his excessive self-grooming had reached obsessive proportions.

Trujillo was particularly fond of sweet-smelling fragrances, and he loved to spray himself with mother's perfume. This practice did not cause Rafael's brothers or friends to exclude him from the group, nor did they consider him a sissy. Instead, the distinctive perfume odor that pervaded the area in which he was present served him well at different points in his life. It made him different. It made him stand out. In a sense, it was a subconscious repudiation of his humble origins.

As a young man, Trujillo displayed a fondness for flashy clothes. Neighbors grew accustomed to seeing Rafael, dressed in his finest, astride his father's horse, riding around town and through nearby fields on a Sunday afternoon.

Much later, as President, he maintained an unbelievably expensive and extensive wardrobe of ornate uniforms. One uniform is reputed to have cost $10,000. A complete wardrobe was kept in each of his 12 homes. Each wardrobe consisted of hundreds of custom-made shirts, cuff links of gold or platinum, and all the accoutrements of the well-dressed man. Rafael Trujillo cut a figure like a prince.

The article of clothing he most dearly cherished was the necktie. Neckties attracted attention even more than his braided, custom-made uniforms. He possessed thousands of them. Many were handpainted, costing upwards of $100.

Rafael was the third of 11 children. His older sister, Flérida, was no threat to him, but Virgilio, also older, had always been considered by their teachers the most studious of the children. This angered Rafael.

Rafael and Virgilio squabbled constantly as each jockeyed for the position of leader among the children. Younger brother José, nicknamed Petán, was also anxious to assume the leadership role, but he was quickly put down by Virgilio or Rafael. Fortunately for Rafael, both Virgilio and Petán left home as young teenagers.

Socially and economically, the Trujillo family was within the top third of those of San Cristóbal, but even at that they were not much above the rest of the poor community. The Trujillos owned a house, and had food enough to eat, but they could never hope to be accepted in Santo Domingo "society." This rejection was to be a cause of the self-doubt experienced by Rafael throughout his life, and it led him to abhor aristocrats and highly educated people.

Rafael's formal education was equivalent to little more than grammar school training. It was acquired largely in the homes of local teachers; his small home town could not even boast of a school building. His maternal grandmother, who was known to be a woman of great charm and culture, ran one of these "schools" where Rafael was taught to read and write.

What affected Rafael most of all was the negroid strain on his mother's side. Although he himself was athletic, well-built, and healthy, he showed his embarrassment over being copper-skinned by using blonde face powder. On his hair, he used straightener! When he had achieved power years later, he spoke on one occasion of the need for "white blood to improve our line." How strange then that he loved his dark-complexioned mother, and preferred her love to that of his white father!

Trujillo's father was a nondescript, small businessman who,

with difficulty, eked out a bare living. His one claim to status was that he held the rank of colonel (although he never used the title). He had never served in the armed forces, so the title was as worthless as the army which had bestowed it upon him. It indicated merely that José had been a supporter of Ulises Heureaux, the tyrant who ruled the Dominican Republic from 1882 to 1899. Heureaux was second only to Rafael in viciousness.

The Trujillo children did not admire or respect their father, but they adored their mother, looking upon her as a saint. Even after becoming President, Rafael would pay his mother a visit practically every night, and, as First Lady, she was accorded innumerable honors.

In 1907, when Rafael was 16 years old, he obtained employment as a telegraph operator and part-time ranchhand. After three years he gave up this kind of regimented employment, and attached himself to a gang of miscreants devoted to petty and sometimes serious criminal activity.

The years 1910 to 1916 were probably the most significant of Rafael's early life, for it was then that he became expert at robbing, blackmailing and killing. The details of his activities during these six years are speculative and unproven, but they range from check forgery to stealing money from the Santo Domingo post office, to rustling cattle.

As President, Trujillo did his best to suppress or destroy all records of his past. He wanted to ensure an esteemed place for himself in history, and went to any lengths to cover up past activity that might be questionable.

Since the turn of the century, life in the Dominican Republic had been marked by political intrigue, insurrection, and financial disarray. France, Germany and the United States had had great difficulty in protecting their citizens residing in the Dominican Republic. Finally, in 1916, when the Republic was bankrupt, the United States dispatched Marines to protect American lives and American interests.

Some elements of the U.S. Forces, however, were so inept and ruthless in carrying out their mission that it became necessary, by 1918, in the interest of maintaining harmonious relations, to establish a Dominican National Guard. This was done by the Military Government under Executive Order No. 27, issued April 7, 1917. Rafael Trujillo was among the first to apply for a commission. He became a second lieutenant on January 11, 1919.

The U.S. government recognized Trujillo's organizational talents at an early stage and welcomed him as a loyal ally in their effort to bring order out of chaos. Using him as an informer and as an expert at extorting confessions from anti-occupation elements, the United States was actually responsible for encouraging (and training) Trujillo in the skills which he later used against the people of the Republic. Trujillo rose rapidly in the ranks of the National Guard, and later in the new army. He had found his calling.

By 1922, the country had regained a measure of stability, and negotiations for the removal of U.S. troops began. With the departure of the last U.S. Marines in September of 1924, and with the election of Horacio Vásquez as President of the Dominican Republic a bit earlier—in March of 1923—the country seemed headed in the right direction. But there was a price that had to be paid for the new peace that settled over the country. As head of the National Police, Trujillo stifled all dissent! While doing this, he was wise enough to keep a low profile, never giving a hint of his political aspirations.

However, when President Vásquez' health suddenly deteriorated in the fall of 1929, and he had to travel to the United States for a kidney operation, Trujillo knew that Vásquez could no longer be successful as candidate for re-election the following year. It was then that he began to plan his first major political maneuver.

Vásquez had managed for nearly four years to maintain a balance between two major warring political factions. Now that he was ill, the two leaders, José Alfonseca and Martín de Moya, saw their chance to capture the presidency. Trujillo, also, saw his opportunity at hand.

With two political convicts incarcerated in the Ozama prison, Trujillo conspired to take over the government by duping de Moya and Rafael Estrella Ureña (a brilliant young lawyer and spokesman for a small, splinter political group) into thinking they would each fall heir to the government. They, in turn, thought they were using Trujillo to further their own ends. They did not appreciate the cleverness of the man with whom they were dealing.

In February 1930, shortly after Vásquez' return from hospitalization in the United States, Trujillo, as Chief of the Army, engineered a "popular" revolt by arming a small group of civilians and having them "take" the army fortress in Santiago. The troops in the fortress had been issued old, and virtually useless, weaponry. Their officers, bribed by Trujillo, put up a short, weak fight. The two groups then joined together in a march toward

Santo Domingo.

This incident brought about the collapse of the Vásquez government, and Estrella Ureña was inaugurated as Acting President on March 3, 1930. Trujillo lacked the title, but he possessed the real power. He convinced Estrella that to preserve order he should collect all weapons in the hands of rebel units.

Elections were scheduled for May. It was becoming increasingly clear to many that, if legal means were denied him, Trujillo would gain the presidency by force. In protest, Estrella resigned and was succeeded by Jacinto Peynado, a strong supporter of Trujillo.

The Central Electoral Board followed by resigning *en masse*. Not wanting to be associated with a rigged election, Peynado appointed Roberto Despradel—one of the original two convict-conspirators—to be Chairman of the Board. Despradel saw to it that only Trujillastas sat with him.

With the army guarding the ballot boxes, the "election" was predictably a farce. Less than 30 per cent of the people turned out to "approve" what everybody knew was a *fait accompli*. Trujillo was certified "elected" on May 30, 1930, and inaugurated on August 16th of the same year.

Acting in the manner of dictators everywhere, Trujillo began liquidating his personal and political enemies as soon as he took control. Sudden disappearances and mysterious murders of a great many of Trujillo's enemies, including cabinet ministers, politicians of all sorts, journalists, businessmen, students, labor leaders and the like, make it obvious to all that a Trujillo plot to eliminate all opposition was in progress.

The manifestations of Trujillo's streaks of madness now began to emerge in earnest. Strong-arm squads, working from a blacklist, dragged people from their homes and shot or hanged them. One of these squads, *La 42*, was reminiscent of *La 44*, a band of young toughs of which Trujillo had been a member back in 1916. Nightly, four or five of the "42" group would pay visits to selected enemies of the regime and murder them in cold blood. And just as often, *La 42* members would cruise about Santo Domingo in a red Packard, suddenly draw up at a bus stop where a crowd of people was waiting, poke the noses of their machine guns through the car windows, and indiscriminately mow down 10 or 12 innocent, unsuspecting people. There was no way to link Trujillo to any of these acts, but they could not possibly have been carried out without his foreknowledge and approval.

On September 3, 1930, only 18 days after Trujillo's inauguration, a hurricane ripped through Santo Domingo. Within hours, thousands of buildings were blown down and thousands of Dominicans were killed. Just prior to the storm, Trujillo's henchmen had been assiduously at work systematically eliminating people on the enemies list. The bodies had been piling up faster than they could be disposed of. Trujillo ordered his thugs to cart the victims of both the hurricane and the massacre to the central plaza, and to burn them. He publicly announced that he was protecting the public against a plague.

Trujillo started to establish permanent control over Dominicans. He lost no time in regulating the economy so as to achieve his own ends. He acquired extensive cattle lands—and then controlled the market by selling meat, dairy products, tobacco, edible oils, rice, and even cement at "fixed" government prices. He became a master at connivance and extortion.

Trujillo found ingenious ways of applying pressure to private business. In one instance, he closed a series of privately owned dairies by requesting his health department to decree that any milk not dispensed under the auspices, and with the approval, of the government was unfit for human consumption. Naturally, his own dairies had no trouble obtaining health department approval. As a result, Trujillo's wealth grew quickly and steadily. It was estimated that Trujillo's private fortune amounted, at one point, to more than eight hundred million dollars.

In all these unsavory actions, the only acts of generosity displayed by Trujillo were to members of his own family. He helped many of them amass small fortunes. Whenever he himself could not personally control a monopoly, he put relatives in such positions of power: a bread trust for brother Virgilio; real estate and prostitution for two sisters; a hardware business for his wife. Of course, other favors, in addition to money and business control, were also bestowed upon family members.

Trujillo's brothers and sisters ran him a close second when it came to selfishness and viciousness. Virgilio was nasty, mean, conniving, lazy, arrogant, and only slightly less lecherous than Rafael. Petán, perhaps the biggest brute and bully of them all did, at least, possess some business sense. Had he been honestly motivated, he might have amassed an *honest* fortune. Aníbal had a certain charm about him, but his deviousness, dishonesty, bloodletting, and sexual excesses put him on a level with the rest. The remaining three brothers were similarly tainted; the only difference was that they were less colorful.

The four sisters were no better. If they seemed less corrupt than their brothers, their husbands made up for it by their crooked dealings in high government places.

All in all, the Trujillos were a morally bankrupt family. Its sheer size and the powerful personality of its corrupt head, Rafael, gave the government of the Dominican Republic the reputation of being one of the most depraved and ridden with nepotism in all of history.

Trujillo was married three times. Aminta Ledesma, a colorless, but kind woman from San Cristóbal was his first spouse. She bore him two daughters, only one of whom lived. By 1928, he had achieved the position and rank of Army Chief of Staff and Brigadier General, and cast his eyes upon Bienvenida Ricardo, a lady of some social standing, but no money. Aminta obliged him with a divorce. She was scarcely heard of again.

But even Doña Bienvenida was not able to satisfy his appetite. He met María Martínez, was charmed by her, and divorced Bienvenida. However, his new marriage did not prevent him from paying conjugal visits to Bienvenida in the sumptuous home he had given her. In fact, she bore him a child shortly after María had presented him with Ramfis, the son who was to become his favorite.

Rafael was anxious for a large family, and he achieved his objective, although some of his children did not have the benefit of legitimacy. The fact is that Trujillo had a never-ending thirst for women that no one chicken-plump, wide-faced wife could satisfy. Like father, like son: José Trujillo Valdéz and Rafael stopped at nothing to prove their masculine vigor. It is even said that the old man died of an excess of women and testosterone injections!

Rafael's daughter by Aminta, Flor de Oro, returned to the Dominican Republic in 1932 after two years of higher education in Paris. A young lieutenant, serving as aide to Trujillo, caught her eye. Only a few years before, he had been a nobody, managing amateur boxing matches in a seedy part of town. However, he had had the good sense to join the army upon his return from school in Paris. He was not unintelligent, and he displayed a certain loyalty to the Generalissimo. Seeing a way to cement his relationship with Trujillo and advance his fortune simultaneously, he married Flor de Oro.

The young man's name was Porfirio Rubirosa. Although the marriage with Flor de Oro was short-lived, it catapulted Rubirosa upward and onward to undersecretary of state for the presidency, president of Trujillo's insurance company, and, finally, to undersecretary of state for foreign affairs. Rubirosa never forgot to employ the technique of furthering his own career by conning wealthy females and enticing them into marriage.

In any discussion of the Trujillo family, the power wielded by Rafael within the group must be underlined. Though in his appointments and distribution of favors Rafael preferred his family to outsiders, he nevertheless felt distrustful even of them. Removal of appointments, dispossession, mysterious banishments were not uncommon.

When elder brother Virgilio began wooing political bosses and army leaders in an effort to win allegiance to himself, Rafael promptly assigned him to a diplomatic mission abroad.

Petán also cherished dreams of unseating Rafael, but before the plot could take effect, Rafael learned of it through his secret police. He took swift action and eliminated every single conspirator except his brother. Fortunately for Petán, the secret police commander thought it advisable to warn him. Petán was found hiding, quite literally, under his mother's bed!

Aníbal also incurred "Big Brother's" wrath—not for trying to overthrow the government, but for something rather amusing. He was dismissed from the army for trying to outdo Rafael in snappy uniforms!

Only one relative—his son Ramfis—had his undying devotion. By the time the child was four, Rafael had made him a colonel with equivalent pay and privileges. By age nine, when still unable to lift a sword, he was made a brigadier. Rafael's attention to Ramfis was rewarded in later years with doglike affection as they waded together through the muck and mire of crime and passion.

But Rafael and his father did not feel mutually about each other. Once, upon entering old Don José's house and finding his father seated comfortably in a chair, Rafael bellowed forth, when his father merely nodded his way: "Father, rise to your feet when the President of the Republic arrives!"

Rafael's superabundance of ego is further reflected in the many slogans devised by him. On private as well as public buildings, on churches as well as on military bases, in cities and villages alike, appeared such catch-phrases as: "Trujillo is My Protector," "Trujillo Forever," "We Thank Trujillo for Our Water." Even pushcarts and shoeshine boxes sported many of these sayings.

Probably the most cruel and ironical display of ego was reported by Dr. Jesús de Galíndez—the celebrated exile who was kidnaped and murdered by Trujillo thugs in a New York subway in 1956. He described how over the main door to the insane asylum in Nigua there appeared the declaration, "We Owe Everything to Trujillo!"

It was, of course, not abhorrent to Trujillo to make a profit even from the adulation that was bestowed upon him by himself. A plaque that he ordered to be made read on one side: "In this Place Trujillo is the Chief." On the other: "National Symbols: Rectitude, Liberty, Work, and Morality." These plaques were exclusives with the first lady's hardware company and were sold for $30 each. They were displayed and were sold in virtually every place of business in the country. Also found displayed in most business establishments was a picture of "El Jefe"—and perhaps one of Ramfis, as well. Such displays were considered sensible and protective moves by the wiser of commercial entrepreneurs.

Trujillo also had prudish and ludicrous aspects to his personality. Once, he became enraged when several guests appeared in frock coats minus vests. By official directive, men had to wear a jacket and tie at all times while on the street in Ciudad Trujillo. No bare feet were permitted in town. If you did not own a pair of shoes, you could rent one just outside the city!

Smoking while riding in a car was punishable by a substantial fine. All homes, even rickety huts, had to be equipped with toilets (bought, of course, from Mrs. Trujillo's hardware monopoly). One could be arrested for carrying one's coat over one's arm. (This law was not as foolish as it might seem; a gun might be hidden underneath.)

The letters-to-the-editor section of the newspaper, *El Caribe*, often carried communications written by the Chief himself, or by his most trusted lieutenants. They would harangue people—ordinary citizens and cabinet members alike—for laziness, sexual deviations, alcoholism, and other vices. The accused individuals felt obliged to offer lengthy apologies, although the charges were often untrue or greatly exaggerated. It was a sign of Trujillo's rule that a newspaper would print such libelous trash.

Trujillo did not trust anyone, particularly if that person happened to be more intelligent or popular than he. The fates that befell such persons were not to be envied: maiming, being dumped into shark-infested waters, bullets in the brain. . .

In committing his crimes, Trujillo was on his guard not to create antagonism in the United States. He was well aware that widespread distrust of him by the administration in Washington could bring about his downfall. Often, he employed blatant lies to keep the American press from becoming aroused. Once, when a Puerto Rican youth was shot for speaking "disrespectfully" of Trujillo, the latter explained the incident to Washington as the action of an overly zealous officer—whom he had promptly executed.

But Rafael Trujillo never felt obligated to concern himself with individual or isolated murders. He was also an early master of genocide, as proven by the Haitian massacre of 1937.

The Dominican Republic is a small land, perhaps no larger than Vermont and New Hampshire combined. But an even smaller country is the other half of the island of Hispaniola—Haiti. But, in 1937, it contained about twice the number of people as the Dominican Republic.

The border area separating the two countries was often unmarked and was easily passable, and many Haitians crossed over onto Dominican soil in search of a livelihood. Quite often, unsuspecting Haitians on the move in search of employment would cross the border, and find themselves unwittingly living in the Dominican Republic.

An agreement between Haiti and the Dominican Republic had been signed in February 1935, but the encroachment of Haitians continued. Trujillo's patience was at an end. In October, he ordered a number of Haitians living on the Dominican side of the frontier gunned down. Upon the heels of this incident, Trujillo learned of the arrest of his secret agents in Haiti. They had been sent there to undermine the government. Throwing all reason to the wind, Trujillo ruthlessly ordered the massacre of between 15,000 and 20,000 Haitians living in border areas.

Bodies were strewn everywhere. Blood streaked the roads as bullet-ridden bodies were hauled by the truckload to dumping spots in rivers, valleys, and meadows. For 36 continuous hours the massacre continued, and the evidence was carried off to be buried.

Trujillo remained cool and unconcerned. His frigid comment at the time was oft-repeated: "While I was negotiating, out there they were going sha-sha-sha." The "sha-sha-sha" was the sound of the machete as it whizzed through the air lopping off heads of Haitian after Haitian.

News of the massacre was long in reaching the outside world. Trujillo was able to control the news that left the country, and the world was slow in discovering the monstrous, inhuman actions transpiring in the tiny, obscure country. But, eventually, the news was out, and Trujillo was compelled to pay $550,000 in reparations to Haiti.

The repulsive reaction of the United States government to

the massacre compelled Trujillo to begin to act more prudently. When "elections" came up in 1938, he announced that he would not run. Instead, he installed a puppet—who served for two years—and then another, who served for an additional two years.

Thus, it was not until 1942, four years later, that Trujillo deemed it safe to reassume the presidency. He wined and dined important Americans by the dozens, and sold himself as an archenemy of communism. To show his good faith, he allowed the United States to set up a guided missile tracking station in the Dominican Republic. "What a good guy; we need more like him," was the attitude of many people in Washington.

Even as late as the mid-1950s, some Americans were still being fooled. In 1955, Vice-President Richard Nixon was photographed hugging Trujillo. Both had big smiles on their faces.

But all was not well in the Dominican Republic. For some time prior to 1960, rumblings of discontent at home and abroad were growing louder and louder. When Trujillo accused the Church of Rome of plotting to overthrow him, the die was cast. In Washington, Eisenhower had finally seen the light and growled: "This kind of attack is usually the last desperate resort of a dictator."

During three decades of the Era of Trujillo, the Church had not challenged the dictator. With the coming of a new papal nuncio, Archbishop Lino Zanini, things began to change.

Zanini was an honest, energetic, and forthright man, and he immediately launched a cautious campaign to discredit and expose Trujillo. His famous pastoral letter, read in all churches on Sunday morning, January 31, 1960, spelled the beginning of the end of the tyrant's reign. It spoke of the grave offense against God, of the suppression of human rights—and mentioned the bereavement of many families because of recent arrests and tortures.

Since 1952, when Héctor became puppet President, prayers had characteristically ended with the formula: "You are requested to pray for the health of Trujillo, the Benefactor of the Country, and for his brother, the President." Now the clergy went so far as to add the words: ". . . and for all those who are suffering in the prisons of the country, and their afflicted families."

Trujillo was beside himself with rage. He tried every stratagem in the book to thwart the hierarchy. Perhaps the most bizarre attempt to halt Church interference was his dispatching of a well-known spell-caster to Rome with instructions to stare at the pope in such a way as to kill him. In his desperation, Trujillo had fallen back upon the "evil eye."

By this time, the Organization of American States, under the leadership of President Romulo Betancourt of Venezuela, had indicted Trujillo for "flagrant and widespread violation of human rights." Trujillo struck back by attempting to bring about the downfall of Betancourt's governmemt. Not succeeding in this, he enlisted the support of the very governments whose system he claimed to despise—Cuba and Russia.

But it was too late. The restlessness and dissatisfaction at home swelled to even greater proportions. The army was particularly disgruntled, and a group of officers finally decided that the time had come to remove Trujillo. Assassination seemed the surest course to follow. After many months of careful planning, the plot was set in motion.

It was learned that on the evening of May 30, 1961, Trujillo would be driving out to his palatial ranch, Estancia Fundación. Shadowed by one car from one point along the Avenue, and met by another along a fairly desolate stretch near the water away from businesses and nightclubs, Trujillo and his chauffeur were cornered. What led them to venture forth without bodyguards is unclear, but they did have the foresight to equip themselves with machine guns and sidearms.

When the first bullets ripped through the rear of the car in which Trujillo was riding, he spurned his driver's suggestion to turn around and flee.

"We must stop and fight," he yelled.

But it was useless. Others had joined the assailants, and together they cut him down just as he stepped from the automobile—his own gun drawn and set to fire. He fell to the pavement. The Era of Trujillo had come to an end.

Members of the family who were abroad were hastily summoned home. All but Virgilio appeared. He was apparently too busy, and not at all moved by the event. Others were, likewise, not terribly affected, including the beloved Ramfis. However, in an attempt to placate his violently vengeful mother, Doña María, Ramfis had his father's conspirators removed from prison, shot in his sight, and dumped into the sea, where sharks fed on their corpses.

One of the captured conspirators caught was General José René Román Fernández, Secretary of State for the Armed Forces, and Trujillo's nephew by marriage. It is reported that he received very special treatment: His eyelids were sewn to his eyebrows. Days later, sulphuric acid was poured over him while he was beaten with a club. His tormentors then castrated him, set hordes of ants loose on his body, and shocked him repeatedly in an electric chair. They finally ended his life with a machine gun.

For a short time, it seemed as if Trujillo were still alive, so persistent was his tradition of cruelty. But he was, indeed, dead. In fact, the body was checked and certified twice.

After a lengthy temporary interment, Trujillo's body was placed in a mausoleum in the Père Lachaise Cemetery in Paris —on August 4, 1964. There it lies to this day behind a door with three panels depicting Christ, the Virgin, and St. Rafael. Inscribed on the front of the mausoleum are the usual words *Requiescat in Pace* and underneath, the Greek letters *theta*—presumably for Trujillo—and *omega*—for the end.

PART II: Assassins

7.Booth

Ask any schoolchild who killed Abe Lincoln, and the answer will be swift and correct: John Wilkes Booth. Whereas the names of the other presidential assassins—with the possible exception of John F. Kennedy's assassin—have faded into obscurity, the name of Booth, as the first assassin of an American president, continues to be remembered.

Had it not been for John Wilkes' monstrous deed, he and his brothers would be clearly remembered for their superb acting talents. But the assassination has so overshadowed the family's accomplishments, that their madness remains most prominent in our minds.

The madness, though of a benign sort, began with John's grandfather, Richard Booth. He passed it on to his son, Junius Brutus. In turn, it became the legacy of Junius's sons—of whom John received the most virulent dose.

The Booth family had its origins in London, although Richard's forebears had been forced out of Portugal for their overly liberal political views. By 1796, when Junius was born, Richard had acquired solid respectability as a barrister.

As a young boy, Richard nursed a strong desire for adventure. He longed to travel to the New World, but his father, a more practical sort, tried to convince him to take up law. Richard had decided to travel, however, and he was actually on his way to America via France, when his father had him arrested and returned to England.

Richard settled down in England, but never forgot America. Years later he was to reach his destination, but during the greater part of his life he contented himself with reading about the new, fascinating country that lay on the other side of the Atlantic. An immense portrait of George Washington hung in his house, and, it is said, he required his visitors to bow low before it.

95

Richard became a widower at the birth of his third child, Jane. Upon him, then, devolved the care of his children. He was, on the whole, a good father, but not very strict or watchful of their activities.

Junius—the father of John Wilkes Booth—had a definite affinity for getting into trouble with girls. Two of his teenage romances led to pregnancies. One of these resulted in a court action against Junius and, at the last minute, it prevented him from sailing to America. Like his father, Junius harbored an enormous wanderlust.

Richard now considered the future of his offspring more closely, and he decided to lead Junius in the same direction his father had led him. But a law book in the hands of Junius had an unexpected effect. He detested the law, and it drove him further into a life of idleness, purposelessness, and fantasy. Most of Junius's time was spent reading and attending plays.

In precisely such activity did Junius discover himself. He found that he possessed an unusual ability to predict the outcome of a play which he had never seen, and a precocious appreciation of the dynamics of dramatics. He, therefore, decided to become an actor, and he joined a traveling troupe. In 1814, against his father's wishes, he left for Holland. It was on this trip that his penchant for women and his love of the stage became fatefully entwined.

Finding it necessary to seek lodgings in private homes because of wartime crowding of hotels, Junius had the good fortune to come upon a nice home in Brussels inhabited by a widow and her three daughters. They welcomed Junius.

And Junius liked the Delannoys—especially the youngest daughter, Adelaide. She was four years older than Junius, and not very pretty, but reasonably bright. Junius was lonely, and when the troupe continued on its travels, he took Adelaide with him—without asking the permission of her mother. Four months later, Junius and Adelaide informed Madame Delannoy of their whereabouts, and expressed their desire to get married. The mother was not particularly unhappy over this prospect, but she did stipulate that Junius would have to find more gainful employment than acting. Junius and Adelaide then left for England.

Being out of funds, they moved in with Junius's father. He was not exactly pleased with this newest of his son's exploits, and demanded that the two young people pay for their keep and submit to holy wedlock. On May 8, 1815 they were married by an Anglican priest.

For five years Junius and Adelaide lived happily together. A daughter was born to them during the first two years of marriage, and she died in infancy. In 1819 a son, Richard, was born. He was to figure prominently in his father's later life.

Junius had become a success overnight. Playing some of the most important theaters in the country—among them Drury Lane and Covent Garden—he was competing, at 24, with England's most famous actors. His finances and social stature improved greatly. Adelaide was especially fond of her role as the well-dressed wife of a budding tragedian.

One day, while playing Covent Garden, Junius strolled through the flower market, next to the theater, and stopped somewhat absent-mindedly before a stall. When he looked up, his eyes met those of a girl he had never seen before. She had dark, widely-spaced eyes, long black curls, and soft rounded features. He thought she was a beautiful girl—and he told her so.

The flower girl had recognized Booth, and was immensely flattered by his compliment. When he took her hand, asked her name, and begged to see her the next day, Mary Ann Holmes could not believe her eyes or ears. She consented immediately.

From that day forward, Junius Brutus Booth never loved another woman. He seized every opportunity to be with Mary Ann, never letting on to Adelaide what had happened. Using the pretext that he had to be off on an acting assignment, he spent days and weeks with Mary Ann in distant parts of England and France. The thought of ever having to part with her distressed him.

Once, while with her on a voyage to Madeira, a ship bound for America docked at Funchal. Junius proposed that they not return to England, but instead go to see the glorious land of which his father had so often dreamed and talked. When they sailed, still unmarried, Mary Ann was pregnant with the first of their ten children. John Wilkes was the ninth of their offspring and—of all of them—the most potent mixture of his mother's beauty, his father's talent, and the family's madness.

During the first year of his residence in the United States, Junius played various cities from Boston to Charleston. He concentrated on making appearances in smaller towns whenever possible in order to avoid encountering members of the profession he had known in England, and who would, undoubtedly, ask questions about his family life. He had written Adelaide that he would send money for her support and little Richard's, but he was not anxious that she learn about Mary Ann—particularly now that he had another son, born just before Christmas in 1821. He also decided to set up housekeeping far away from the highly populated cities and towns.

He chose a spot in the country about 25 miles north of Baltimore. He was happy with his choice, because it was located roughly halfway between the important cities of the North and South. The house was a comfortable log cabin on the farm of Elijah Rogers. It was to remain—with considerable enlargement and improvement—the main home of the Booth family for all of Junius's lifetime.

In the summer of 1822, old Richard suddenly appeared at the Rogers farm. Disgusted with his daughter for having married a lazy bum by the name of Jimmy Mitchell, he had gathered together his belongings and, in secret, boarded a ship for the land of his dreams. The old man was surprised to discover that Junius had a second family, but he was quick to forgive in return for a room on the farm. There he read during the day and caroused in nearby taverns at night. Richard and Junius continually castigated each other for their drinking habits. To hide their addiction from each other, they never drank together.

While at home on his farm, Junius was a considerate and loving husband, and a kind and good father. Away on tour, he waged a constant and unsuccessful battle with liquor and moodiness. Usually, the latter was an outgrowth of the former.

An article in a Boston newspaper of 1829 reported a performance in which Booth, apparently after a drinking bout, so completely muffed his lines that he turned to the audience and admitted the same by saying: "Ladies and gentlemen: I really don't know this part. I studied it only once before, much against my inclination. I will read the part, and the play shall go on. By your leave, the play shall go on, and Mr. Wilson shall read the part for me."

At this juncture, the stage manager began to drag Booth off the stage while Booth, with a foolish look on his face, yelled through cupped hands at the astonished audience: "I can't read —I am a charity boy. Take me to the lunatic asylum!"

That is exactly what the management intended to do, but when they tried to find Booth the next day, he had left for Providence, Rhode Island on foot—with no overcoat—in the middle of November.

By the end of 1833, Mary Ann had given birth to seven children, of whom three died. Junius was away when two of the children became seriously ill, and returned home only as they were breathing their last. He was performing in a play when the third child died. He rushed home upon receiving word, dug up the body from the back yard, and attempted to resuscitate the child.

In 1836, the family—minus Old Richard—made the second of two voyages back to England for a visit. Each time they managed to excape Adelaide's scrutiny, although on one occasion Booth actually spent a brief time with her. It was on this trip that Junius extended an invitation to his sister to move to America with her eight children, provided she would leave her no-good husband, Jimmy Mitchell, behind. The Booths returned to Maryland, and it was not long before Jane and her brood appeared—but together with Jimmy. Mary Ann—neat, orderly, and serene—was aghast at the crudeness of her sister-in-law's brood. Father Richard was so repulsed that he moved out of the house.

For nearly four years the Mitchell clan sponged off the Booths. The worry and bedlam caused by these people drove Junius increasingly to drink until, in 1840, he finally summoned enough courage and common sense to oust them from his property.

Into this confusion were born the last of Junius's two children: John Wilkes on May 10, 1838; and Joseph on February 8, 1840. Still living were, in order of their birth: Junius Jr., Rosalie, Edwin, and Asia.

Richard, Adelaide's boy, journeyed to America in 1842 to seek his fortune. Junius paid his passage. When Richard learned of his father's infidelity, he advised his mother. Adelaide, furious, departed for the States, and took legal action against her husband. She acquired a divorce in 1851 and, after 31 years, Junius became the legal husband of Mary Ann.

In view of all these vicissitudes it is perhaps not surprising that Junius achieved the reputation of being a thoroughgoing madman! Tales of his drunkenness and weird doings were legion. He would sometimes appear on stage in such a stupor that he would fall forward into the pit without uttering a line. On one occasion he climbed up onto the catwalk above the stage and refused to come down to play Hamlet. While the stagehands worked to get him down, he crowed like a rooster.

Once, while taking a boat trip through Charleston Harbor, he leaped into the water at the spot where a well-known actor had committed suicide. Ten crew members were needed to haul Junius out of the water. On still another occasion, after much heavy drinking, he attacked a friend and fellow actor with an andiron. His sons, Junius and Edwin, were witness to much of this sort of behavior when each, in turn, accompanied him on tour as his dresser.

Junius never wanted his children to become actors, but three of the boys succumbed to the fever. After a brief acting career, Junius Jr. became a theater manager on the West Coast, and Edwin rivalled his father as a tragedian. John had to compete against the combined reputation of his father and brothers. He sought quick recognition, not wanting to do the work required to achieve the goal.

None of the boys ever achieved the international fame of their father, but all three were certainly possessed of superior talent. Unfortunately, they fell heir to their father's less desirable traits.

John, or Johnnie as he was often called, was his parents' favorite. He was praised frequently and always allowed to do as he wished. Very early in life he became a spoiled brat. He adored his mother not only because she indulged him in his every whim, but because she was very beautiful and affectionate. When he died, his last wish was that his mother would understand why he had killed the President.

Like his father and brothers, John was slender and rather small of stature, but nevertheless, he was strong and vigorous. He was an expert horseman and a marksman of repute. He always strove to be the best—or the most noticed—in a group. He was eager to be the center of attraction on all occasions.

Unlike his father and brothers, John did not immediately achieve recognition as an actor. He had accompanied his brothers on tour from time to time, but had never been apprenticed to his father. He lacked the determination and ability to *study* acting, but he did inherit his father's flair for the dramatic.

By 1859 John had acquired a place for himself on the stage. However, it was marred somewhat by his vociferous defense of the southern attitude on slavery, an issue which was beginning to divide the nation. Theater managers were especially unhappy over his outspoken views. One incident in particular stands out.

In October 1859, John Brown, celebrated in the folk ballad, "John Brown's Body Lies Mould'ring in the Grave," carried out the now famous raid on the government arsenal at Harper's Ferry, near Charlestown, for the purpose of establishing a haven for runaway slaves. Booth read of this incident in the Richmond papers with more than a little interest. During the summer, he had been on the verge of joining a militia group, but had been dissuaded from doing so by his mother. Now, a second opportunity presented itself. But, again he did not join—perhaps out of respect for his mother's wishes, perhaps out of fear. Instead, he went about criticizing the North, going so far as to threaten to kill every Abolitionist he met. This bitterness and hatred grew with each passing year.

The rebellion at Harper's Ferry was quickly quelled, and Brown was taken into custody. He was tried in November, and sentenced to be hanged on December 2, 1859. Because the authorities were afraid that Brown's friends would attempt to rescue him before the execution, the militia in Richmond was ordered, during the middle of November, to head for Charlestown to prevent potential uprisings.

John watched as the soldiers marched past the Capitol on their way to the train station. He was on his way to the Richmond Theatre where he was to act in a play that afternoon. Suddenly, he changed his direction. In half an hour he was back —dressed in a borrowed uniform—and striding toward the depot.

The soldiers aboard the train did not welcome Booth; in fact, they tried repeatedly to throw him off, convinced that he was nothing but a crackpot. But John found a hiding place on the train and arrived in Charlestown with the rest of the men.

When the trap was sprung on Old Brown, Booth was 20 feet away, obviously relishing his part in the whole affair. He was later to claim that he had assisted in capturing Brown. Actually, Booth was a braggart and quite a coward. He had been willing to come to Harper's Ferry only when the danger had past.

In the winter of 1860, following Lincoln's election, there was much talk of war. As always, John Wilkes Booth spoke openly in support of the Southland that had been so kind to him. It did not matter where he was when he expressed his opinions—in the South, in the North, on a street corner, in a fine restaurant, or even on the stage.

John Wilkes Booth was making his Albany, N. Y. debut at the same time that Lincoln, on his way from Springfield to Washington to assume his presidential duties, stopped off to make an extemporaneous speech. Booth was in the crowd waiting to catch sight of the President as he stepped down from the train. This was the very first time Booth had seen Lincoln, but the President had already long before become a symbol of John's hatred of the North. What a gaunt, sick-looking man—what a vapid speaker, thought Booth, as he studied Lincoln.

He began to speak out openly—and violently. His fellow actors soon began to fear that he would be arrested for his treasonous statements. Booth was even heard to say, shortly after seeing Lincoln in Albany, that he was a great admirer of Brutus and Charlotte Corday. On another occasion, he spoke of "the glorious opportunity for a man to immortalize himself by killing Lincoln."

The war issues divided many families of the North and South—and the Booth family was no exception. Junius Jr. and Edwin could not understand their brother's reasoning. When the three of them discussed the war, only hard feelings were aroused; no insights were gained. The two older boys found it impossible to understand John's ever-growing fanaticism, and what they even considered madness.

Once, shortly after the war began, John was riding on a train with his brother-in-law, John S. Clarke. Clarke mentioned some news from the front and ended his remarks with criticism of Jefferson Davis. Enraged, Booth rose from his seat and, acting like a maniac, clutched his brother-in-law by the throat. He would have choked him to death, had not several passengers intervened. They tried to pull Booth away from Clarke, but he held on doggedly, forcing Clarke against the coat rack and window. By the time Booth came to his senses, Clarke was nearly unconscious.

Despite his vicious remarks against the North and references to assassination, John's first thoughts were to *abduct* the President—not kill him. His reasoning was not as harebrained as some maintained.

It was January 1865. It appeared that the war was winding down, but it was not going the way of the South. Booth calculated that by capturing members of the administration, including the President, he could assist the South in striking a deal, whereby the North could be forced into a prisoner exchange that would be advantageous to the South. Large numbers of Confederate soldiers were imprisoned in the North, and many Yankees were being held in the South. The South needed the men more than the North, and, with the President as hostage, the South could have regained a substantial number of troops. Further, Booth reasoned, the North would be demoralized by the loss of their President, and might agree to halt the war and agree to the establishment of a Southern nation.

The plan failed, not so much because of any inherent weakness—even the escape route was reasonably well-conceived —but because of a faculty and incomplete plan of action, and also because of the spineless types Booth chose as his accomplices. Aside from persons situated along the escape route, the group of conspirators consisted of seven men—excluding Booth—and one woman. They were a scary, gossipy, careless, marginally intelligent bunch—with perhaps the exception of Lewis Paine. He was rough and tough—well suited for this kind of endeavor.

Booth had learned that Lincoln would be attending a performance at Ford's Theatre in January and made plans to abduct him at that time. One of the conspirators, Edward Spangler, worked in the theater stable, and made arrangements to store Booth's horse and buggy there for use in the getaway. But Lincoln failed to appear on the appointed night. The conspirators became suspicious. They feared that their plans had been discovered.

The group disagreed as to the next step to be taken. Once agreement was reached, delays arose in implementation of a new scheme. Booth became thoroughly discouraged, and turned to drinking even more heavily than usual. His mental condition deteriorated to such a point that he ranted and raved at his fellow conspirators. The strain pushed him inexorably closer to the edge of insanity.

Within a month, a prisoner exchange program was arranged. Everyone, except Booth, considered the abduction project unworkable and pointless. Samuel Arnold, one of the conspirators, stated that Booth's insistence on carrying out the abduction was a "heartless ambition on his part . . . He was a madman," Arnold asserted some months later.

Booth's attitude began to change. Murder of the President was now on his mind. Sensing that the plan was taking a different turn, Booth's fellow conspirators backed off, maintaining that they would have no part in murder.

Booth became more and more agitated. He started dressing in riding garb, and kept himself armed with a pistol and dagger. On one occasion, when suddenly startled by a fellow actor, he pulled a knife. He seemed to be in a trance, the actor reported.

On another occasion, when attending a ceremony conducted by the President, a bystander noticed that Booth had a wild look on his face as he studied Lincoln. His hatred for the man and his frustration over the abduction plans had reached a peak.

Booth was determined to accomplish his mission. He dispatched Lewis Paine and John Surratt to check out the presidential box at the theatre. Later that same evening, the entire group assembled to discuss the role that each individual would assume in the abduction. When Booth explained that they were to lower Lincoln onto the stage from his box, Arnold declared this a stupid idea. Booth became enraged, and threatened to kill Arnold on the spot.

The group did eventually reach a concensus on how to proceed, but the next day they learned that the President would be attending a play at the nearby Soldiers' Home. A plan to intercept the coach was immediately put into action. However, when the coach was spotted, it was seen to contain someone other than the President. This turn of events convinced the conspirators that the White House knew of their plans. They disbanded forthwith.

In the spring of 1865, the Confederacy was collapsing. Just before the arrival of Union troops in Richmond, President Jefferson Davis, together with his family and several cabinet members, boarded a train (on April 2, 1865) and headed south to Greensboro, North Carolina. On April 9th, Lee surrendered to Grant at Appomattox. Booth was distraught: the war was over, and the South had lost.

"The darned thing didn't even flicker; it just went right out," someone remarked. Europe was amazed that the South accepted defeat so readily and gentlemanly. There was not even a government in exile. But Booth refused to admit that the struggle was over. In his diary, he wrote:"Our cause being *almost* lost, something decisive and great must be done." There was no doubt that he intended to assassinate Lincoln.

Of the original conspirators, all of whom had been in favor of *abducting* the President, only Booth, Paine, and David Herold were willing to *murder*. Booth was to kill both Lincoln and Grant; Paine was assigned the task of doing away with Secretary Seward; and George Atzerodt was to eliminate Vice-President Johnson. At the last minute, Atzerodt lost his nerve and refused to carry out his part. Herold assisted Paine.

On Thursday night, April 13th, there were impromptu parades in Washington to celebrate the northern victory. Booth was among the crowds of milling people, but he was not laughing and joking. Grim-faced, he returned to his room at the National Hotel, and for a long time sat with his hands over his ears, trying to shut out the sounds of merriment below. In his mind, he reviewed the plan again.

That same night Lincoln had a dream: He was on a ship drifting inexorably toward some very indistinct shore. He could not comprehend its significance. He had had this dream before some of the decisive battles of the war were fought. But now the war was over. He mentioned his dream to Grant at a late-morning cabinet meeting, but Grant could offer no explanation. This was hardly surprising, for Grant did not have a mystical fiber in him.

Good Friday, April 14th, was gray and drizzly, but the decorations from the previous day still adorned the streets of Washington. Parades were passing by, and the mood of the people was bright in spite of the dull weather. Lincoln had forgotten his dream and was looking forward to this evening's production of *Our American Cousin* at Ford's Theatre. He and Mrs. Lincoln had invited the Grants to accompany them, but the Grants had declined, so a Major Rathbone and his fiancée, Miss Clara Harris, completed the group.

Booth arrived at the theater a little early, and dropped in at the bar next door for a few quick drinks. He was tense, but not sufficiently to arouse suspicion. He talked and joked with people around him. But when somebody suggested that John would never be the actor his father had been, all joviality drained from his face, as he said, "When I leave the stage, I'll be more famous than any man in this country!"

With that, Booth strode out of the bar toward the theater. He looked at the clock in the theater foyer. It was after 9:00. Cracking the main door, he looked up at the presidential box. Lincoln was not there! Perplexed and angry, he stepped back, went into the street and cursed under his breath. What had gone wrong? He walked half a block down 10th Street, trying to figure out what to do, when he saw the White House coach draw up, and the Lincolns and their guests step down.

Booth was surprised not to see Grant in the party, but that did not alter his plan to kill Lincoln. He hurried to the theater stable, got his horse, and led it around to the stage door. Handing the reins to stage carpenter Ned Spangler, who apparently knew nothing about the assassination despite his original involvement as one of the conspirators, he disappeared around the corner of the building. Spangler then passed the reins over to a flunky named "Peanut John," explaining that Mr. Booth would come back for his mare in a few minutes, but that he was to hold, not tie, her because she was very skittish.

The second act was in progress when Lincoln arrived. A little later, at about 9:30 p.m., an intermission was called, and the Lincolns and their guests remained seated in their box. Booth was in the vestibule downstairs anxiously awaiting the start of the third act. Shaking, he dashed next door for a shot of brandy to calm his nerves. Now, he had less than half an hour in which to kill the President and start out for the Anacostia

Bridge across the Potomac where he was to meet Paine and Herold. He hoped that by now they had gained entry to Seward's house.

The second scene of the third act was underway when Booth entered the passageway leading to the presidential box and bolted the door behind him with the wooden bolt he had rigged up the day before. Looking through a small hole he had previously bored in the door of the box, he saw the President seated with his back to the door.

Flinging the door open, Booth pointed his derringer at the back of Lincoln's head and fired a bullet through his brain. At the sound of gunfire, Major Rathbone turned quickly and grappled with Booth, who screamed, *sic semper tyrannis!* ("Thus always to tryants"—the motto of Virginia). Booth then dropped his pistol, and began chopping at Rathbone violently with a long dagger. Rathbone suffered a deep cut on his left arm, and momentarily released Booth. Booth leaped up onto the railing of the box.

For a brief moment, everyone in the theater froze. Mrs. Lincoln stared transfixed at her husband. Lincoln had slumped forward. Rathbone tried to utter a scream, but no sound came forth. The audience below, with their stunned, upturned gaze, gave one huge gasp.

Then Rathbone finally screamed: "Stop that man!"

Like a movie projector started up again after being stopped to view a scene, frantic action began. Booth jumped from the railing to the stage, 14 feet below. Mrs. Lincoln leaned forward, looked over the edge, and then shrieked, "The President has been shot!"

In his leap, Booth had caught his left spur in the folds of a flag draped beside the presidential box. Thrown off balance, he landed with his left leg under him such a way as to break it just above the ankle. Unmindful of the pain, he sprang to his feet and dashed backstage, past stunned performers and stagehands, and out the back door. In a moment, he mounted his horse and galloped toward the river.

Paine had not been as successful as Booth. Gaining entry to Seward's residence by pretending that Herold, who was a drug clerk, had some medicine for the ailing secretary, Paine dashed upstairs in search of his victim. Met at the top of the steps by one of the secretary's sons, Paine cracked the boy over the head so hard with his pistol that he damaged the gun. After manhandling another son and a guard, he lunged into the bedroom and hacked away at Seward's face, head and throat with a knife half as long as a bayonet. Seward would never have survived had he not been wearing a steel collar to protect a recently broken jawbone.

Also riding toward the river, but still some distance away, was Herold. He was alone, having deserted Paine when the screams of Seward's family and servants frightened him. Paine was, at this moment, wandering aimlessly about, totally lost without Herold. After three days he showed up at Mrs. Surratt's and was immediately arrested.

Lincoln was shot at 10:13 p.m., and lapsed into unconsciousness instantly. He was carried across the street to a boarding house, and cared for until he died at 7:22 the following morning.

Booth, actor that he was, persuaded the Anacostia Bridge guard to let him pass. Herold, appearing ten minutes later, was detained a short while, but eventually was given permission to cross. The two men met just north of Surrattsville, exchanged horses, and rode on together to a tavern in Surrattsville itself, where they picked up some weapons they had hidden with a fellow conspirator. They then continued on to Dr. Samuel Mudd's house. Dr. Mudd had been in on the discussion of the original plot, and treated Booth's leg.

For the next nine days Booth and Herold made their way southward along a route parallel to the original abduction escape route. At one point, they were befriended by two young Confederate soldiers who helped them cross the Rappahannock River at Port Conway, leading them to the Garrett farm just southwest of Port Royal, Virginia. Booth was in constant pain because of his hurt leg. Feeling more and more discouraged about their chances of reaching Richmond, he remarked several times that he would kill himself before he would be captured.

In the early afternoon of April 24th, the four men rode up the little road leading to the farm of Richard Garrett, a southern sympathizer. Unknown to all concerned, the War Department in Washington had learned of the general whereabouts of Booth, and dispatched a detachment of men to capture him. It is not clear to this day who furnished the information.

For the rest of that day and night, and for the next day as well, Booth remained at the farm. The other men came and went. The Garretts apparently did not suspect the identity of Booth, but accepted the story that he was a wounded Confederate soldier. They did think, though, that he and Herold might steal their horses, so the Garrett boys surreptitiously locked the men in the barn the second night.

By this time, the military detachment had discovered Booth's hiding place. At two o'clock in the morning the detachment surrounded the farmhouse, rousted old man Garrett out of bed, and tied him to a tree. They asked the whereabouts of Booth, and Garrett claimed ignorance. When the soldiers threatened to hang Garrett if he did not divulge where Booth and Herold were hiding, Garrett's sons came to the rescue, and pointed to the locked barn. Colonel Conger, who was in charge of the soldiers, ordered young John Garrett to open the door and persuade the fugitives to surrender. When Garrett entered the barn, Booth forced him out at gun-point.

Conger then delivered an ultimatum: He would set the barn afire if they didn't emerge in ten minutes. Five minutes later Herold surrendered. Booth wanted to make a deal: He would come out and fight the entire detachment if they would step back 20 yards. "No," said Conger, and the barn was set afire.

The fire cast a bright light on Booth through the slatted walls. He was standing up leaning on the crutch Dr. Mudd had made for him. He held a carbine under his right arm. At that moment, one of the soldiers pointed a gun barrel between the slats. Booth saw it, dropped his rifle, pulled his pistol out of his belt, and shot himself through the upper neck, severing his spinal cord.

He was carried from the barn and laid on a mattress on Garrett's front porch. There he lay paralyzed, uttering an occasional word or phrase—"Tell mother—I did—what I thought—was best for my country." He died at 7:15 the next morning, April 26, 1865.

Booth's body was transported to Washington and properly identified. In order to thwart any plans fanatic Southerners might have to steal the corpse, authorities pretended to sink it in the Potomac. Later, they buried it secretly under a slab in a cell in the old penitentiary. Years later, the Booth family succeeded in claiming it for reburial.

Of the conspirators, only John Surratt was acquitted—because of a legal fluke. Surratt's mother, Atzerodt, Herold, and Paine were hanged; the rest received prison sentences.

The story of John Wilkes Booth should—and properly does—end here, for it has been authoritatively proven that he died under the circumstances just related. However, rumors persisted for many years that he actually escaped and lived until 1903, first under the name of John St. Helen, and later as David E. George. A Tennessee lawyer named Finis L. Bates wrote a book "documenting" these last 38 years of Booth's life.

A mummified "John Wilkes Booth" was actually put on display. Even into the 1920s myths abounded about his life. Some are still believed.

8.Guiteau

Charles Guiteau's favorite word was "high-toned." It signified dignity, intellectualism, lofty morals, superior social rank, and good manners. His life was a reflection of his attempt to achieve this status through education, religion, and politics.

In many respects, Guiteau was not different from many other Americans with the same high principles and goals. But his education was extremely limited and casual, his religious expression too fervent. They combined to focus on politics, and brought about the death of the 20th President of the United States, James Abram Garfield.

The prosecution at Guiteau's trial argued for his sanity, explaining his actions as arising from moral debauchery. The defense insisted that Guiteau was hereditarily insane and, thus, not accountable for his deeds. Guiteau himself raged when the idea of his madness was suggested as a defense, conceding only that the words: "not guilty by reason of insanity" (at the time of the assassination) be used and understood only in their legal and technical sense. He asserted that God had taken from him his free will by "inspiring" him to kill Garfield. It was therefore the Deity Himself who was guilty. The jury convicted Guiteau of the crime.

The events leading up to Garfield's assassination comprise, in a sense, the entire lifetime of Charles Julius Guiteau, for so much of his life was abnormal and unbalanced.

Born September 8, 1841, in Freeport, Illinois, Charles was the fourth child of Luther and Jane Howe Guiteau. Two children. were born after him, but neither one survived infancy, so Charles grew up as the youngest of four offspring.

When Charles was seven, his mother died. There had been some question as to her sanity, although her self-imposed, ten-week isolation after Charles's birth might today be interpreted as severe depression following childbirth. An older sister, Frances, took over the job of looking after Charles. She continued in this role throughout Charles's life, up to the time of his execution.

Charles's father, Luther Wilson Guiteau, came from a fairly

prominent, rural New York family. He himself was a successful businessman. The family was imbued with a heavy dose of religious piety, and attributed their good fortune in life to heavenly rewards for right thinking and Christian actions. The necessity of doing God's will was inculcated in Charles from an early age. When "the Devil got hold of Charles," his father was quick to beat it out of him.

Although Luther Guiteau exhibited many of the characteristics of typical 19th century evangelical Christianity, his church alliance was far from conventional. During his years in New York, Luther had been attracted to the teachings of John Noyes, founder of the strange, perfectionist Oneida Community. The main tenets of this faith were that Christ had already come for the second time when the Temple was destroyed in 70 A.D., and that man could become perfect in this life by overcoming sin. Sin took many forms, but its most obvious and virulent manifestations were smoking, drinking, and swearing. Charles eschewed these vices all his life. Neither did he associate with "lewd characters." He associated only, as he put it, "with high-toned people." He saw no religious or moral inconsistency in his wifebeating, petty thievery, or the murder of another human being.

Charles was a lonely, withdrawn child with virtually no friends. Until he was 12, he gave the impression of being retarded. He had a speech impediment and encountered great difficulty in learning to read and spell. When his father remarried, Charles started to emerge from his shell and made considerable progress in his school work. In fact, within a year he had become an avid and proficient reader. Horace Greeley was his model, and he devoured every issue of the New York *Tribune*. No doubt, it was in this publication that he first discovered Republicanism.

At age 18, Charles announced to his father that he wanted to go to college in order to better himself. His father, a nononsense type of self-made man, viewed higher education as a frivolity, and stated that he had no intention of paying for his son's education. But Charles got lucky. His maternal grandfather died about this time and willed him $1000. Charles quickly calculated that he now had enough money for his entire education—with some left over. Exuberant, he registered at the University of Michigan in Ann Arbor.

Charles was not cut out to be a college student. Firstly, his previous training was so poor that he had great difficulty coping with the academic demands. Secondly, Charles was unstable, and could not address himself to a rigorous course of study. Unhappy, he soon began to look elsewhere for personal gratification. As always, he turned inward. His introspection led him to seek solace in religion. He decided to join the Oneida Community of which his father was so fond. Disliking his father as he did, this was indeed a strange move.

In June 1860, Charles took up residence at the Community. He signed over what remained of his inheritance—the tidy sum of $900—and gave every evidence of spending the rest of his days serving God and His representative, John Noyes. For once, Luther Guiteau was proud of his son.

Charles stayed with the community for five years. During the last of those two years he was restless and dissatisfied, partly because he felt himself rejected by most of the members, and partly because he suspected that his future lay elsewhere.

He chose journalism as his field. Not one to start at the bottom, he aspired to an editorship. He fully expected, in a short time, to outshine Horace Greeley, and it was this unmitigated egotism that caused his associates to despise him and avoid him.

Charles hoped to establish a daily religious newspaper that would change the hearts of Americans. He imagined that truth-hungry people would snap up such a paper. For three months he walked the streets of New York City, pounding on doors to get subscribers, but he was not successful. Humbled, but not despairing, he returned to the Community and "re-donated" his inheritance.

Within 15 months, however, Charles departed from the Community once again—and this time for good. He asked for, and received, the remainder of his inheritance. Within nine months, he had squandered all of it.

Badly in need of money and suddenly resentful of the Community for having robbed him of six years of his life, thereby "thwarting him in his life-long objective of becoming a lawyer," Guiteau threatened to sue Noyes in order to recover $9,000 in wages he would have earned had he been paid by the Community. He also drew up a set of particulars, accusing the Community of corrupting influences. Among other things, he stated that the Community practiced free love and sexual deviation. This accusation was later to backfire when he admitted having taken part in several sexual acts.

Not one to be toyed with, Noyes responded to Charles's threats by initiating his own suit against Guiteau. This frightened Guiteau, and he left New York quietly in February of 1868, and surfaced in Illinois where he stayed, for a short time, with his father, and with his sister, Frances, and her husband, George Scoville. He found a job in a Chicago law office doing clerical work. He pursued his law studies at the same time. Frances gave him a little money now and then, and after several months Charles felt prepared to take the bar exam. To the amazement of all, he passed—even if by the skin of his teeth.

Charles was in high spirits. He now had a profession, and looked forward to a great future. But first he needed a wife; and he found one at the YMCA.

Charles was a voracious reader. He met Annie Bunn, the YWCA's librarian, during one of his frequent visits to the library. From then on, they met often and had many discussions. One night, only two months after their first meeting, Charles proposed. Annie was flattered. Charles had given her the impression that he was an important lawyer, and a fine, Christian gentleman. Several months later they were married.

Annie expected great fulfillment from her marriage, but was to receive nothing but disappointment. As a lawyer, Charles was a dismal failure. His entire practice consisted of collecting past-due bills, at which he was amazingly adept. His tenacious manner coupled with his weird, fearless approach produced results. However, he did not have a sufficient number of clients to earn an adequate livelihood. The debtors he dunned owed such small amounts that he began to scrape off considerably more than his allotted commission—a practice that hardly endeared him to collection agencies.

Personal relations between Annie and Charles were strained from the start. Charles considered his wife a smart aleck—a know-it-all. When she dared to criticize him for his laziness and swindling, or when she expressed her views on religion or politics, Charles flew into a towering rage. He would, unhesitatingly, slam her in the mouth or yank her around the house by her feet or by her hair. "I am your master," he would scream, "and don't you ever forget it!" If beating did not produce submission, he often resorted to stuffing her into a closet for hours on end. On two occasions, she nearly suffocated.

The Guiteaus stayed married until 1874. Annie had wanted to file for a divorce for a long time, but in New York, where they had been living since 1871, the law permitted divorce only on grounds of adultery. Annie had had a pre-marital affair, but adultery was a different matter. Very likely, she feared for her life, for Charles would certainly have looked askance at such an action. "High-toned people don't behave that way," he often said. But, high-toned or not, Charles himself committed adultery in a whorehouse for the express purpose of allowing his wife to sue for divorce.

During the better part of the next year, Charles busied himself with the job of securing backers for his anticipated purchase of the Chicago *Inter-Ocean,* a newspaper of considerable reputation. He had decided that it was more sensible to buy an existing newspaper than to found one. His goal became to convert the *Inter-Ocean* into the greatest publication of the Midwest, but he was singularly unsuccessful in convincing people to invest their money in such a scheme despite the promise of great profits. To one prominent Chicago businessman, he promised the presidency of the United States.

By June of 1876, Charles was destitute. His fantastic schemes died even before seeing the light of day, and he sought out his sister, Frances, as he had done so often in the past. She and her husband were spending the summer in their cottage in Wisconsin. They were both surprised and alarmed when Charles turned up suddenly one morning, quite unannounced. He had a strange look about him and had taken to muttering under his breath.

But the Scovilles took him in. Frances washed his clothes, fed him well, and talked to him encouragingly. In a few days Charles looked much better. His old optimism even returned as he spoke of undertaking a career in theology.

One day, unexpectedly, Charles acted in a bizarre way. Sent out into the back yard to chop some wood, Charles was busy cutting away when his sister, on her way to hang up some clothes, passed by. Suddenly, he stopped his work and fixed a steady gaze upon her, his tongue lolling out of his mouth. Raising the axe over his head, he stepped toward her. In a panic, Frances ran into the house, locked the doors, and sent for the local doctor.

The doctor arrived within minutes and had a long conversation with Charles. He spoke to Frances privately, and told her that he was certain her brother was deranged and should be committed to an asylum forthwith. But when they went to look for him, Charles had vanished.

Earlier, Charles had explained to his sister that he felt called to preach the Gospel. Inspired by the evangelists of the time, he set out to make his mark. Traveling from city to city over the next several years, Guiteau preached in shabby buildings and flapping tents. The pattern was the same everywhere. His earnings were a pittance.

He would con printers into making up elaborate flyers, promising payment after the service. He would then hold forth, for five or 10 minutes, to a scraggly audience of 20 or 30 curious souls, gather up his enormous sheaf of partially read notes, and scurry out a side door. People were so stunned by his odd behavior that before they could react, he had fled.

In 1880, the lives of Charles Julius Guiteau and James Abram Garfield began to converge. Charles had become inordinately interested in politics, and saw, in the midst of the free-for-all arising out of Rutherford B. Hayes's refusal to run for a second term, a chance for espousing his views as a supporter of the Stalwarts—the arch-conservative faction of the Republican party. This right-wing group hoped that Ulysses S. Grant would run for a third term. Thwarted in their attempt to capture the nomination for Grant, the Stalwarts joined forces with the other, more liberal faction, the Half-breeds, and consented to Garfield's candidacy. On the 36th ballot Garfield won the nomination by a landslide.

Garfield's politics were not clearly known, but it was assumed that he was far more conservative than the Half-breeds' candidate, James G. Blaine. As a sop to the Stalwarts, however, Chester A. Arthur was made Garfield's running mate.

Guiteau was generally pleased at the outcome. He felt confident that the Republicans could win against the bland Democratic candidate, General Winfield Scott Hancock. He set forth his opinions in a rambling, incoherent, printed campaign speech called, "Garfield vs. Hancock," which he foisted on people at campaign headquarters, on the street, and through the mail.

Of course, Garfield did win the election, but to the surprise and utter dismay of Guiteau, he chose Blaine as his Secretary of State. At first, when pressing Garfield by letter for appointment to a European consular post, Guiteau was polite, even obsequious. When his letters were ignored, however, he began to see Garfield as a party turncoat. He repeatedly warned the President that Blaine was a corrupting and liberalizing influence. He seemed distressed that the President did not look upon certain Stalwarts with the same admiration as he.

One warm May night, in 1881, Charles lay dozing in bed. He hoped he could get some sound sleep. Of late, his head had been so full of confusing thoughts that he found it difficult to get a good night's rest. Suddenly, his mind cleared; he had an "inspiration." He was to "remove" Garfield.

True, he had conceived the idea himself, but the inspiration for the idea and the pressure to carry it out originated in "another world." The only problem was to decide whether it was Satan's or the Lord's work he had been appointed to do. A month later, after much prayer, he had sorted out things. The inspiration had indeed come from God. He could, therefore, act with impunity. Guiteau immediately bought a pistol.

During those last two weeks of June, Charles practiced with his revolver and reviewed his plan to kill the President. Once, while out walking, he encountered Garfield by accident, but he was unable to shoot. He continued to read the daily papers for clues as to President Garfield's whereabouts. Another opportunity arose that found Guiteau in a position to attempt the assassination, but once again he could not bring himself to carry out the deed. Finally, on the last day of June, he noted in the *Washington Post* that Garfield would be boarding a train at 9:30 a.m., on Saturday, July 2nd, at the Baltimore and Potomac station. This time he would accomplish his mission!

Charles rose early on Saturday. This was to be the most important day of his life: as God's agent, he would achieve earthly fame and a divine reward. He ate a substantial breakfast and set out on foot for the depot.

On the way, he stopped for a while at the river bank and fired several shots at a stick to test his marksmanship. After several weeks of this kind of practice, Guiteau had become an expert marksman.

Arriving at the station a whole hour before the President's scheduled appearance, Guiteau made arrangements with a hackman to be driven to the vicinity of the District of Columbia jail at 9:30. He then stepped around the corner to have his shoes shined. On the way, he paused in front of a small newsstand and handed a letter and a packet of papers to the attendant. "Someone will pick these up shortly," he said without further explanation.

In the meantime, the President and Secretary Blaine had just left the White House and were heading for a waiting carriage. They were chatting animatedly. The president walked leisurely despite the fact that his train was due to depart in 20 minutes.

With five minutes to spare, Garfield's carriage drew up to the depot. Still conversing, he and Blaine stepped down and entered the station. At that moment, a small, unkempt, bewhiskered man strode up behind the two and fired one shot at the President, striking him in the right arm. Hurrying forward a few paces, he then fired again, hitting Garfield in the lower back and felling him.

Without a word, Guiteau turned and walked resolutely out the station door and onto Sixth Street. A policeman, having heard the shots, rushed in. Seeing the President lying on the floor, and taking note of the suspicious man in a shabby suit and black slouch hat, he detained Guiteau. Charles put up no struggle. In fact, he proclaimed proudly: "I did it. I will go to jail for it. Arthur is President, and I am a Stalwart."

President Garfield lingered, in much pain, throughout the hot summer. At times, he seemed to be recovering, and encouraging bulletins were issued. Then, for a time, his condition worsened, only to improve again. That he survived as long as he did was a miracle, considering the limited knowledge of X-rays, antibiotics, safe operating techniques and pain killers (except for morphine). The President's family and intimate friends, as well as the entire nation as a whole, were almost daily reminded of Guiteau's heinous act. Their appetite for vengeance never waned.

James Abram Garfield died on the night of September 19, 1881. When the body lay in state in the Rotunda of the Capitol, the mourners viewed a skelton of their former chief. More than 80 pounds under his normal weight, he looked tortured and shriveled. The anger of the nation was once again at fever pitch.

Between the time of the shooting and the beginning of the trial on November 14th, Guiteau occupied himself writing countless letters to newspapers and influential people. exhorting them to publicize his reasons for killing Garfield and requesting gifts of money for his defense. He was convinced that the Stalwarts and certain important attorneys would rally to his cause.

But no one came to his aid and Guiteau remained virtually penniless. Ironically, his brother-in-law, George Scoville, took up his legal defense. Scoville just happened to be in Washington shortly after the attempt on the President's life. He was amazed to learn that it was none other than his own, unbalanced brother-in-law who was responsible for the deed.

The trial of Charles Julius Guiteau lasted until the end of January 1882. During those two and a half months, the public was subjected to some of the most bizarre courtroom antics imaginable. Guiteau was ecstatic at having a stage on which to perform. Never before had he had such a large, interested and captive audience. He would take his seat each morning, and reach first for the newspapers and continue to read about himself while court was in session. Admonished by the judge to pay attention, Charles would angrily reply that he needed to garner world opinion through the papers.

When the papers no longer intrigued him, he would give rapt attention to the proceedings. When he disagreed with a statement, he would unhesitatingly leap up from his seat and start shouting. It was irrelevant to Guiteau whether judge, counsel, or witnesses were speaking; if he had an opinion, it would be heard over everyone else's. At first, the judge reacted severely by threatening contempt of court citations—even manacling—but after eight or ten such outbursts, he gave up. After all, he did not want it to appear that he had muzzled the defendant in any way; he wanted no excuse for a retrial.

The outcome of the trial was never much in doubt and so it was Guiteau himself who became the focus of attention. The public always wondered what he would do next. As often as not, it was not what he *did*, but how he *looked* and *sounded* that drew eyes and ears his way. His posture changed from relaxed to rigid from hour to hour. His eyes sparkled with fire or rolled with distraction. His voice was alternately low and well-modulated, or shrill and cackling.

Guiteau's defense revolved about his claim of legal insanity at the time of the shooting. Any suggestion that he was totally mad was rejected by him, but his counsel and witnesses—often over Charles's objections—presented the jury with copious evidence to that effect. The courtroom became a forum for the debate between differing medical factions as to what constituted "insanity," and between medical and legal minds as to the effect of insanity on a legal ruling.

Dr. Edward C. Spitzka, a young, but well-known, European-educated psychiatrist—a witness for the defense—insisted that Charles was a congenital madman. He spoke of Charles's "tendency to delusive or insane opinion, and to the creation of morbid or fantastical projects," adding that there was "a marked element of imbecility of judgment," leading him to consider the defendant "a moral imbecile, or rather a moral monstrosity." He stated that Charles' appearance was a considerable factor in leading him to this conclusion.

Spitzka referred to Guiteau's wandering gaze, his misshapen head and face, and a tongue that lolled to the left. All of these characteristics clearly denoted a "primary monomaniac," he insisted, and led him to believe that Guiteau was born with a brain of unequal sides.

Either because of an inability to comprehend the substance and import of Dr. Spitzka's analysis, or out of an awareness of the effect the doctor's words might have on the jury, Guiteau rose to Spitzka's defense when the latter was being berated by District Attorney George Corkhill: "Dr. Spitzka has studied all over Europe and knows all this entire business of insanity. He has studied in all the high-toned colleges of Europe, and then for him to come here and be insulted by this little bit of a scamp. Why, Corkhill, he wouldn't spit on you outside, among all his high-toned acquaintances; he wouldn't condescend to go to that extent."

It fell to Judge John K. Porter, a native New Yorker and a nationally known trial lawyer, to be the final speaker for the prosecution. His remarks attacked Guiteau's basic logic that God had chosen him, a bum, to be his agent for the important work of "removing" the President. How could Guiteau possibly be qualified for such a task, considering "his life of imposture and of swindling and of beggary and of breach of trust and of wrong and of adultery and of syphilis?" That Guiteau could conceivably represent the firm to which he claimed to belong, that of "Jesus Christ & Company," was utterly beyond belief. "Very soon the defendant will feel something he has never felt before— divine pressure in the form of a hangman's noose," Porter concluded.

Charles had asked repeatedly for a chance to testify in his own behalf. Again, not wishing to allow grounds for a mistrial, Judge Cox finally acquiesced.

Guiteau rose, manuscript in hand, and began to read in a voice that ascended and dipped in keeping with the pathos and accentual underlining he gave the words. He likened himself to a patriot who had done his nation a great service. It was a religious act of merit, he maintained. "High-toned people are saying, 'Well, if the Lord did it, let it go'."

Judge Porter responded by calling Guiteau "cunning, crafty, remorseless, low, and brutal—the most cold-blooded and selfish murderer of the last 60 centuries."

Every juror's eye was on Porter. There was no chance for acquittal.

The sentence was for hanging between 12 noon and 2:00 p.m. on Friday, June 30, 1882. "And may the Lord have mercy on your soul," proclaimed the judge.

"And may the Lord have mercy on your soul," answered Charles. "I am not afraid of dying . . . I know where I stand on this business. I am here as God's man and don't forget it!" Delivering a curse to all his and God's enemies, Charles was led away.

On the morning of the execution, Charles wrote a poem which he planned to read from the scaffold. He had also hoped to appear wearing a long, white, flowing, vestment-like garment which he would remove at the last minute. He wanted to be hanged in his underwear. But a minister had talked him out of that stunt, stating that people would then surely consider him insane. The poem would have to suffice.

It went like this:

"I am going to the Lordy, I am going to the Lordy ... Glory Hallelujah!" ... and so on for five verses.

As Charles dropped his paper and, with a tremendous shout let out the words "Glory, ready, go!" the trap opened.

Was he insane?

The autopsy revealed brain lesions and other defects very much in accord with Dr. Spitzka's predictions.

Ironically, in October of the same year his sister, Frances, was committed to a lunatic asylum.

9. Czolgosz

"All Kings, Emperors, and Presidents should die!" This firm declaration of Leon Czolgosz was made during a police interrogation shortly after he assassinated President William McKinley.

To Czolgosz, William McKinley was a stranger who had done him no personal wrong; yet, to Czolgosz, McKinley was a symbol of the evil inherent in government. And government was a force to be eliminated! To an anarchist like Czolgosz this was a matter of uncompromisable principle.

Leon Czolgosz was not an ordinary anarchist. He was a misguided activist who imagined himself to be the savior of the "nobodies" in the United States.

In his first public statement after the murder, he said, "I killed President McKinley because I done my duty. I don't believe one man should have so much service and another man should have none." By "service," Czolgosz presumably meant "respect" or "homage."

Twenty-eight years old at the time of the assassination in 1901, Czolgosz was born in Detroit of Russian-Polish parents who had first come to the United States in 1859. The fourth of eight children, he was unlike other presidential assassins, all of whom were either only children or among the youngest of their families.

In one respect, however, he was very much like other assassins: he was a lonely individual, unable to give or receive love. His was a constant search for recognition and approval—rewards which would certainly be his if he were to devote himself to a fanatical idea. His extreme needs led him to the performance of one monstrous deed that could not pass unnoticed.

The sparse facts of Czolgosz's dull and tortured life conform quite well to the conventional blueprint of the typical assassin: Leon was a quiet, shy boy who had great difficulty making friends. In fact, he experienced as much trouble relating to the members of his own family as to outsiders. Of all the Czolgosz children, only his older brother Waldeck met with his approval.

A large part of Leon's inability to form friendships was a result of the frequent moves the family made from one Michigan town to another while his father searched for work as a common laborer. Time and again, just as the family settled in a new neighborhood, the father lost his job and the family had to uproot itself.

Leon regarded his father as a failure, and learned to expect very little from him or from life. "I never had much luck at anything," he said, "and this preyed on me."

When Leon was 12, his mother died. There is no indication that his mother's death was an unusual trauma for him, but the fact that the other presidential assassins have come from broken homes leads one to believe that the effect on him was significant.

When his father remarried, not long after the death of his first wife, Leon developed a highly antagonistic attitude toward his stepmother. The family had just moved to Alpena, in far northern Michigan and Leon attended school more regularly than he ever had previously. For a while, it seemed that the Czolgoszes were going to establish roots in a community.

But, then, after a short stay, the lure of a better job took the family to Cleveland where they made a permanent home. Neighbors in Alpena and Cleveland remembered Leon as an extremely religious and moral boy. He spent hours—sometimes days—in fervent prayer. Even as a teenager, his father recalled, he did not date girls, but passed his evenings—mostly in his room—brooding or praying. He never did establish a normal relationship with a woman.

Leon was a very compassionate young man, so kind, in fact, that he literally would not kill an insect. He was obsessively neat and orderly about his person and his belongings—so much so that other young people poked fun at him.

At age 16, Leon quit school and went to work. Within two years, he and his brothers were able to contribute enough to the family to purchase a run-down store in Cleveland and a tiny farm just outside the city, in Warrensville. Leon was a reliable and steady worker until he began to read books on socialism and anarchy. He had always believed that the working class was being exploited, but now, through reading and occasional contacts with socialists, communists, and anarchists, he was convinced of it.

His disillusionment finally became so acute that he quit his job and went to Chicago. Chicago was the "big city" where he hoped to find a *really* good job, and where he might meet others interested in working for social change. But disillusioned, he returned after several months and took a job in a wire mill in

Newburgh, a suburb of Cleveland. His continued reading of pro-anarchy propaganda and his conversations with various political agitators made him increasingly bitter. He spoke constantly of his "bad luck" and how it had made him "morose and envious."

Czolgosz's mental strain became progressively more apparent. By the time he was 22, he began to talk and behave strangely. Once, while engaged with his brother in fervent prayer over a strike at the wire mill, he suddenly stopped praying and announced that since those things for which he had prayed were not forthcoming, it was obvious that the priests were "fooling" him. Ultimately, Leon left the Church, convinced that the clergy were "out to get him." But he clung to his religious faith and retained his loyalty to socialism or anarchy.

In 1898, Leon was 25 years old. He gave up his job at the mill, and went to live on the farm. There, according to his brother, Waldeck, he had a nervous breakdown. He "simply went to pieces," Waldeck said. Irritable and suspicious, Leon made life unpleasant for all those around him. He was particularly vitriolic toward his stepmother, who often repaid him in full measure for his rancor. When not quarreling with a member of his family, he mostly sat alone in his room. Before long, he started to prepare his own meals and to eat them in his room. He became obsessed with the thought that he would be poisoned.

During this period of self-imposed incarceration, Leon read about the assassination of the Italian King Humberto I by an anarchist. Fascinated by it, he delved further into anarchy, attending lectures in Cleveland whenever possible. For many weeks, he slept with the Humberto article under his pillow.

One of the lectures he attended, in July 1901, was given by Emma Goldman, a vociferous female anarchist. Leon testified that she aroused his "craze to kill." He elaborated on his feelings: "She set me on fire. Her doctrine that all rulers should be exterminated was what set me to thinking, so that my head nearly split with the pain. Miss Goldman's words went right through me, and when I left the lecture, I had made up my mind that I would have to do something heroic for the cause I loved." Although the text is no longer available, one early biographer of McKinley has asserted that the Goldman lecture was largely theoretical, and did not urge direct violence. It was obvious that mental deterioration had distorted the perceptions of Leon Czolgosz.

One morning in late July, Leon announced that he was leaving the farm, and demanded return of the money that he had

contributed toward its purchase. The same demand had been
made before, but Leon was never taken seriously. Receiving no
response from his family, he threatened violence. The family
was deeply concerned, and managed to scrape together a partial
payment, with the promise that the balance would be forwarded
to him.

Leon departed for Chicago.

The very next day, he applied for membership in several
anarchistic groups, but was rejected by all of them. That night,
he marched back to his boarding house in a blue rage.

For a week, Czolgosz read, slept, and moped in his room. He
would go out only briefly—for an occasional meal.

One morning, he picked up a newspaper and read of President McKinley's impending visit to the Pan American Exposition in Buffalo. He became immediately excited. A sudden determination grew within him to *do* something, but he did not know
what. The thought of shooting McKinley ran through his mind,
but he did not—or could not—formulate a plan of action. He only
knew that he *had* to "help the little people." Then, without fore-
thought, that very day, he purchased a railway ticket to Buffalo.

Upon his arrival in Buffalo, he took a streetcar to West
Seneca, a nearby suburb. There he spent several weeks in a
sleazy boarding house, sleeping and eating. As far as is known,
he did not once enter the fairgrounds. In late August, he informed his landlady that he was returning to Cleveland. His
stay in Cleveland lasted for three or four days; the nature of his
activities is unknown.

On August 31, 1901 he caught a train back to Buffalo, and
registered at 1078 Broadway, at a hotel with a saloon on the
ground floor. It was owned and operated by John Nowak, a fellow Pole who was a political leader in his district. Czolgosz told
Nowak that he had come to see the fair.

Leon went to the fairgrounds more than once a day for several consecutive days. At some point during these visits the
resolution to kill the President became firm.

Czolgosz later explained his meager motivation and the intensity of his determination:

> It was in my heart; there was no escape for me. I could
> not have conquered it had my life been at stake. There
> were thousands of people in town. All those people
> seemed to be bowing to the great ruler. I made up my
> mind to kill that ruler. I bought a 32-calibre revolver
> and loaded it.

It was a Tuesday night, the third of September, when Czolgosz took that pistol with him to the fairgrounds and stood near the railroad gate where the presidential party was expected to enter. As it approached, he tried to get near McKinley, but the police forced him back. He maneuvered himself into another position and found himself very close to the President as he entered the grounds. He glanced around quickly, from side to side, and refrained from attempting the assassination because of the presence of so many presidential bodyguards. His fear was not of them, nor was he concerned that he himself might be hurt or killed. His only fear was that he might fail; that he would lose, forever, his chance to shape history. Inwardly, he cursed his rotten luck.

Fortunately for Leon, the President was to make another appearance at the fair on Wednesday. On that day, Czolgosz went back to the Exposition grounds and positioned himself right under the stand from which the President was to speak. McKinley arrived and, as he delivered his talk Leon fingered his hidden gun half-a-dozen times. Fearing that his aim would be misdirected by the jostling crowd, he did not shoot. He muttered to himself all the way home.

Thursday was a repetition of Wednesday, The President was just about to get into his carriage to leave the fairgrounds after giving his major public address. Czolgosz managed to worm his way through the crowd to within a short distance of the chief executive. But as a cordon of guards formed, he was pushed back several feet and out of range. Discouraged, Leon went home. He would try once more on Friday, he thought, if he could come up with a plan that would allow him sufficient time to take accurate aim.

That night, an idea came to him: He would place the gun in his right hand, tie a handkerchief around both his hand and gun, and stuff them in his pocket. When he would withdraw his hand, those around him would think that his hand was bandaged or that he was about to mop his brow. All that was now required was that he position himself as close to McKinley as possible.

McKinley had had to defer his visit to Buffalo from spring to late summer, first because of a trip to California and then because of his wife's illness. He was very anxious to attend the Pan American Exposition, for, he felt, with its emphasis on progress, it provided a most fitting setting for him to deliver a major address on the preservation of a prosperous economy. The rapidity with which industries were multiplying in the United

States had made the search for overseas markets imperative, and the President was anxious to win popular support for the reciprocity arrangements he had negotiated and had presented to Congress for approval.

A second problem that he wished to bring to the attention of the American public concerned trusts. There had been a marked tendency by big business to buy out small competitors. McKinley felt that small businesses were being discriminated against; and he intented to protect them against encroachment by large corporations.

Historians have pointed out that Czolgosz's act greatly affected America's foreign policy by thrusting Theodore Roosevelt into the presidency. Roosevelt was an internationalist with the requisite skills to carry out McKinley's idealistic foreign policy.

On Friday, September 6, 1901, the President rose early and felt refreshed, despite the long and arduous previous day which had involved a great deal of handshaking and speechmaking. It was already hot, but he attired himself in the customary stiff collar and shirt, vest, and frock coat. He pocketed a penknife and some change, picked up his gloves, and, after examining the brightening skies, stuffed three handkerchiefs in his swallow-tailed coat.

Usually grave-faced, the President began to smile. With one hand he smoothed the front of his shirt over his slight paunch, while with the other he slicked back his straight hair from his receding hairline. He studied the street below his window. Some of the gay decorations from the previous day's celebration of "President's Day" were still in evidence on the residential street where he was staying—at the home of Mr. Milburn, president of the Pan American Exposition. Peeping out from under the vines just over the front door below him, he could see an edge of red, white, and blue bunting that his host had had hung in his honor. He was pleased at what he saw, and it relaxed him. This day, thought McKinley, will be a restful one.

The Exposition management had decided that the Temple of Music was the ideal place to hold the President's public reception. Not only was it very large and airy, but it was centrally located on the fairgrounds. Further, it was an architectural showpiece, inside and out. It looked like a replica of St. Mark's of Venice, even to the point of containing a huge pipe organ.

At the front of the building was a raised platform on which the President and his party would sit. Those wishing to greet the President would be allowed to enter through one of the four doors, and could be easily controlled. They would use any of the other three as exits.

It seems doubtful that the possibility of assassination had occurred to Major Louis Babcock, Grand Marshal of the Exposition, for thousands of persons were permitted to enter the building in advance of the President. Although McKinley's schedule called for him to spend the morning and part of the afternoon in Niagara Falls, people had started to gather in the Temple of Music early in the day.

Had Babcock thought that assassination was a possibility, he would also have been wary of the exposed position of the dais. At lunch that day, a fellow Buffalo attorney, James Quackenbush, casually remarked to Babcock that "it would just be Roosevelt's luck if McKinley got shot." Babcock was not amused. Czolgosz had arrived at the fairgrounds at approximately the time Quackenbush made his prophetic remark.

During the early afternoon, the crowd milled about the Temple of Music, hoping to catch a glimpse of the President upon his arrival, and perhaps have an opportunity to shake his hand. McKinley was enormously popular, having beaten out his Democratic opponent, William Jennings Bryan, by almost one million votes in the election of 1900. He was an extremely friendly man and much to the distress of his secretary, George Cortelyou, the President was given to grabbing hands right and left when in a crowd. The Secret Service agents were overworked, for the few that were on duty could not keep an eye on the huge crowd of well-wishers. Cortelyou did not want the President to tarry outside the building any longer than necessary, and hoped that the reception inside the Temple would last no more than ten minutes.

At precisely four o'clock, Major Babcock ushered the President into the Temple, and asked him to stand to one side of the dais in front of a decorative screen that was draped with the Stars and Stripes. It hung amid a profusion of potted plants and bay trees.

As the final strains of the organ faded away, Cortelyou gave the signal for Babcock to allow greeters to enter through the east doorway, two at a time. Once inside the Temple, they were instructed to form a single line. It was hoped that in this way the President would safely be able to greet many people in a short period of time. Nevertheless, Cortelyou was nervous. After about five or six minutes he pulled out his watch. Babcock interpreted Cortelyou's action as a signal for him to close off the line. He headed for the door.

In the meantime, completely unnoticed, a short, slender, somewhat effeminate young man, clad in a black suit, had entered the building. Patiently, he stood in line and awaited his turn to speak to the President. Babcock slammed the door shut.

As the door closed, it was Leon Czolgosz's turn to greet the President. He pulled his handkerchief-swathed hand from his pocket and aimed the concealed pistol at the President. Simultaneously, he pushed away McKinley's proferred hand of greeting. Two shots rang out.

Not a word had passed between the two men. A look of total bewilderment and shock spread over the President's face. The face of Czolgosz was expressionless.

For a bewildering instant all movement was suspended. Suddenly, a fist struck Czolgosz hard in the face. Four or five others then joined in the pummeling, and Czolgosz was pinned to the floor. Fists and feet kept pounding away at his limp body.

Men shouted; women screamed. As those nearest the exits scrambled to get out of the building, those outside pushed forward in an effort to get to see what had happened. Panic and curiosity, fear and hysteria collided.

The same confusion was reflected later in the accounts of those persons who claimed to have been close enough to witness the dramatic moment.

Sympathetic arms lifted the President and placed him in a chair. Gasping for air, he called for his secretary.

"Cortelyou," he whispered, "do be careful about my wife. Don't tell her."

He clutched at his vest. When he drew his hand away, it was covered with blood. McKinley caught sight of his assailant lying prostrate on the floor, policemen and Secret Service agents hovering over him. The president noticed the livid face, pulpy and blood-stained from the blows that it had sustained. Placing his bloodied right hand on Cortelyou's shoulder, the President, overcome by inexplicable compassion, said, "Don't let them hurt him."

Ten minutes later, Czolgosz was being interrogated by the police. He gave his name as Fred Nieman—so suggestive of the German word for "nobody." At the same time, the President, conscious, but in deep shock, was being undressed by hastily summoned, prominent Buffalo surgeons. The lives of Czolgosz, a nobody, and McKinley, the President of the United States, had touched for three brief minutes—and the encounter brought an end to the lives of both.

On Monday afternoon, September 16th, the grand jury indicted Czolgosz for murder in the first degree. The prisoner was shackled and moved, under heavy guard, from the penitentiary to the jail across the street from City Hall. From there he was led through the tunnel under Delaware Avenue to the basement of City Hall, up the stairs, and into the Erie County courtroom for arraignment.

Handcuffed to a detective, he stood before the judge and trembled. With a ten-day growth of beard, Czolgosz looked filthy and unkempt. The judge intoned: "You have the right to counsel. Who is your counsel?"

There was no answer. One of the police officers reminded Czolgosz that the judge was speaking, and that he had better reply.

Czolgosz still did not answer. Instead, his face began to twitch, and his eyes, although constantly downcast, darted right and left. Some later said that he was feigning insanity, but the psychiatrists engaged by the Erie County Bar Association determined that he was sane, thus destroying the only effective defense that the court-appointed attorneys could have used.

On Monday, September 23rd, Leon F. Czolgosz was placed on trial for the murder of William McKinley. He entered a plea of "guilty," but he was advised by the court to change this to "*not* guilty."

By noon on Tuesday, in just one day, the prosecution had presented its whole case. Defense counsel had very few questions to ask; their client had been highly uncooperative. Czolgosz preferred to make no statement in his own behalf. Supreme Court Justice Truman C. White thereupon ordered the jurors to begin their deliberations.

Czolgosz had been sitting rigidly in his chair all afternoon, his hands gripping the arms, his feet flat on the floor. Frequently, he pulled out his handkerchief and daubed nervously at his face. Then he would reassume his rigid position. His head was usually cocked to one side facing downward, his eyes staring at the floor. He seemed oblivious to the crowd around him.

Following the expected verdict of "guilty of murder in the first degree," Czolgosz was led out of the courtroom back to jail to await sentencing on Thursday. The trail had consumed only eight hours and twenty-six minutes.

Several members of Leon's family arrived just as the trial was ending. Among them was his brother, Waldeck. Waldeck had visited him twice in prison and had persuaded him to call a priest. But the visit was cut short when Leon refused to listen to the priest, who advised him to renounce anarchy. When the priest returned uninvited one more time, Leon lashed out at him with a fury that convinced the cleric to abandon his mission.

The following day, when Waldeck called on his brother, he was subjected to Leon's verbal attacks. "Damn those priests. Don't send them here again. I don't want them."

Waldeck was uneasy.

"And don't you have any praying over me when I'm dead. I don't want it," warned Leon. "I don't want any of their damned religion!"

In the late afternoon of October 28th, Czolgosz suffered a "nervous attack," as the prison doctors termed it. They explained that his eyes were dilated, and he was sweating profusely. Guards noticed that he spent hours pacing up and down in his cell. He seemed to fluctuate between periods of great calm and great agitation. But his appetite was never adversely affected. In fact, he gained several pounds during his confinement.

As he was being strapped into the electric chair the next day, he was asked if he would like to make a final statement. Leon replied: "I killed the President because he was the enemy of the good people—the good working people. I am not sorry for my crime."

In sharp contrast to Czolgosz's remorseless statement stands a famous phrase first used by President William McKinley to describe former President Rutherford B. Hayes. It was later employed by one biographer to refer to McKinley himself:

"Good in his greatness and great in his goodness."

These words of the President, more than anything else, describe the character and express the sentiment felt by millions of Americans when McKinley died. A great, compassionate man fell victim to bullets fired by a *nobody*.

Did the *nobody* achieve his intense wish to become a *somebody* when he took the life of a President? To some degree he did, for the names of William McKinley and Leon Czolgosz have become inextricably bound. In a sense they are but opposite sides of a single coin.

10. Oswald

At 12:30 p.m. on November 22, 1963, President John Fitzgerald Kennedy, while riding in an open car past Dealey Plaza in Dallas, Texas, slumped into the arms of his wife, mortally wounded by an assassin's bullets. After meticulous police work and an exhaustive report by the Warren Commission, it was determined that Lee Harvey Oswald, one of life's consummate failures, was responsible for the death of the young president.

When it was learned that Lee Harvey Oswald was an avowed Marxist who had spent time in the Soviet Union and was married to a Russian, many jumped to the conclusion that the President's death was the result of a Communist plot.

When, on November 24th, Jack Ruby, a Dallas honky-tonk operator, shot Oswald in the basement of the city jail, many more were now certain that there had been a conspiracy, and that Oswald had had to be silenced. However, as days and weeks turned into months, it became more and more clear that Oswald had acted alone.

In reviewing Oswald's life, a dangerous pattern emerged. The question as to why he would want to kill a popular president was no longer relevant. As a personality, Oswald seemed to demand instant power and recognition, and fate provided him with the circumstances to carry out his deed.

Born fatherless in New Orleans on October 18, 1939, Lee was the youngest of three children, one of whom was a half-brother. His mother had to earn a living and, unable to care for her children, she placed Lee, at the age of three, in an orphanage with his brothers.

When Lee was four, the family moved to Dallas where, in May 1945, Mrs. Oswald married for a third time. Lee was fond of his stepfather, Edwin A. Ekdahl, and was delighted to accompany him frequently on business trips. Lee was greatly saddened by his mother's separation from Ekdahl in 1946.

Lee started first grade in Benbrook, Texas, but his mother withdrew him after her separation and re-enrolled him in the first grade in Covington, Louisiana, in the fall of 1946. He was a student there for a little more than two months, because in

January 1947 his mother returned to Texas to attempt to effect a reconciliation with Ekdahl.

The reconciliation did not materialize. Instead, Ekdahl sued and obtained a divorce in the summer of 1948. The split made an indelible impression on nine-year-old Lee and was at least partially responsible for the steady decline in his academic performance.

With each passing year, Lee became increasingly withdrawn. When he and his mother went to New York City in 1952 to be with John Pic (Lee's half-brother who was stationed there with the Coast Guard), Lee resisted being with other children and refused to attend school. After being forced to enter a junior high school in the Bronx, he created so many problems for the authorities that he was remanded for a psychiatric examination to Youth House, an institution concerned with juvenile delinquents and habitual truants.

The report of his examination is very revealing. He was described as a "seriously detached" child who felt unloved by his mother.

It is true that Oswald's mother was never home during the day. Lee usually left for school from an empty house, and returned to one at noon and again at night. Practically the only time he saw his mother was when they were in bed. He shared the same bed with her until he was 11.

In his interview with a social worker, Lee stated that he often indulged in the fantasy of being "omnipotent" so that he would be able to hurt anyone he wished to punish. Once, he had threatened to stab his sister-in-law with his pocketknife. The chief psychiatrist diagnosed Lee's condition as "personality pattern disturbance with schizoid features and passive-aggressive tendencies," and recommended continuing treatment.

Lee returned to school and completed the semester reasonably successfully. But, when he returned to classes in the fall of 1953, he had reverted to a pattern of emotionally disturbed behavior. His mother refused to admit that he needed psychiatric care and, against medical and educational advice, removed him from school and returned to New Orleans in January of 1954.

The change seemed to do the boy some good, and his grades improved slightly, but his attendance was still erratic. Just prior to his sixteenth birthday, he brought a note to school one day The note stated that the family was moving to San Diego. Lee had composed it and forged his mother's signature.

For the next year Lee worked at this job and that, in and around New Orleans. He was still exceedingly shy and withdrawn and spent all his spare time watching TV or reading.

Having no friends with whom he might socialize, he devoted more and more time to reading—mostly about Communism. Completely unequipped, educationally, to handle the ideas that he was being exposed to, he became hopelessly confused. Nevertheless, he was fascinated by what he read. It gave him a sense of importance. After all, Communism was an unpopular ideology in America and he was among the few who were conversant with it. Once, he told a fellow-worker that Khrushchev was an ideal ruler and that he (Oswald) would like to kill Eisenhower because of his exploitation of the working people.

Lee and his mother moved to Fort Worth, Texas in 1956, and Lee attended high school for several weeks. When he turned 17, he dropped out and enlisted in the Marines. For one who all his life had been hungry for affection, individuality and status, this was a curious step. It can be argued that what he needed most, and was seeking at that time, was a stability and predictability which could only come from a rigorous military life. But when one considers his bitter resentment toward all authority, the argument breaks down.

Lee spent almost three years in military service. He attended technical schools in which he studied the principles of aviation and radar scanning, and spent 15 months in Japan. For the most part, he remained aloof from other servicemen and preferred to spend his off-duty time reading and watching television. On two occasions, he was court-martialed—once for possession of an unregistered weapon and once for challenging a non-commissioned officer to a fight.

Oswald was constantly baiting his superiors with his knowledge of foreign affairs. When he found that they knew less than he—or were simply not interested in what he considered important—he openly stated that they were unfit to lead. His greatest pleasure was in belittling those in leadership positions. If he was punished for so doing, he used the incident as proof of his being mistreated.

By the time he was discharged from the military, Oswald had saved perhaps as much as $1,500. Although he had requested, and obtained, an early release from service on the basis of his mother's financial hardship, he spent only a few days with her before departing for New Orleans, where, instead of finding work as he had promised his mother, he boarded a freighter bound for France. From there, he went by train to the Soviet Union, arriving in Moscow on October 16, 1959.

When his six-day visa was up, he attempted—or feigned—

suicide. In his so-called "Historic Diary," (which was filled with spelling errors), he wrote, on October 21, 1959:

> I am shocked!! My dreams!...I have waited for 2 year to be accepted. My fondes dreams are shattered because of a petty offial....I decide to end it. Soak rist in cold water to numb the pain, Than slash my left wrist. Than plaug wrist into bathtum of hot water....Somewhere, a violin plays, as I wacth my life whirl away. I think to myself "How easy to Die" and "A Sweet Death, (to violins)"...

He was discovered, taken to a hospital, and treated for a week. Upon his release, he appeared at the U.S. Embassy and stated that he was a Marxist; that he wished to give up his American citizenship and remain in the USSR. He never did complete the legal forms necessary for a renunciation of citizenship, but the Soviet Union gave him a visa in January 1960 to stay one year, subject to renewal each subsequent year.

Oswald went to work as an unskilled metal worker in a radio and television factory in Minsk. In addition to his salary, he received a matching amount from the Soviet government plus better housing than that of Soviet citizens of similar age and position. Oswald did not complain about this preferential treatment, as one might logically expect from an idealist who professed the Communist doctrine of equal treatment for all. Rather, in fact, he later felt resentful that his future wife's uncle, who was an MVD colonel, earned much more than the average person, and had a better apartment than he. He described the colonel as just another of those "fat, stinking politicians like we have in the U.S."

In January, 1961, Oswald applied for another year's residency, and his request was granted. But, suddenly, in February, he became dissatisfied, and applied at the American Embassy for permission to return to the United States. His diary entries (still filled with misspellings) for August-September 1960, and January 4 through 31, 1961, give clues to his disillusionment and discontent:

> As my Russian improves I become increasingly concious of just what sort of a sociaty I live in. Mass gymnastics, complusory afterwork meeting, usually political information meeting. Complusory attendance at lectures and the sending of the entire shop collective (except me) to pick potatoes on a Sunday, at a state collective farm: A "patroict duty" to bring in the harvest. The opions of the workers (unvoiced) are that its a great pain in the neck: they don't seem to be esspicialy enthusiastic about any

of the "collective" duties a natural feeling. I am increasingly aware of the presence, in all thing, of Lebizen, shop party secretary, fat, fortyish, and jovial on the outside. He is a no-nonsense party regular.

I am stating to reconsider my disire about staying the work is drab the money I get has nowhere to be spent. No night clubs or bowling allys no places of recreation acept the trade union dances I have have had enough.

He did not leave Russia as planned, for in March he met a pretty, dark-haired, 19-year-old girl named Marina Nikolaevna Prusakova. Marina's home was in Leningrad, but she was working as a pharmacist in Minsk, and living with her aunt and uncle. She was much better educated than Lee, but was enchanted by the attention paid her by an American. It was a whirlwind courtship, ending in marriage after six weeks—on April 30, 1961.

For the balance of 1961, Marina and Lee inveighed upon Soviet and U.S. authorities to permit them to move to the United States. Their application was tentatively approved in December, and they made plans to leave as soon as they were contacted by the immigration authorities. They knew they could not leave immediately, in any event, for Marina was seven months pregnant.

In February, Marina gave birth to a little girl and had to stop work. Lee continued to work in the factory, but his salary was not sufficient for them to save for the trip to the States. When they received final permission from the Immigration and Naturalization Service, they had to request a transportation loan of $435.71 from the State Department.

In the middle of June, 1962, the Oswalds arrived at Fort Worth. There, they moved in first with Lee's brother Robert for about three weeks. They then went to live with Lee's mother, and Lee took a job as a sheet metal worker in a Fort Worth factory. By the early part of August, the young couple had found an apartment of their own, and settled down to a domestic routine.

Their lives were not always harmonious. Oswald was a dictatorial husband. Occasionally, he beat his wife, prohibited her from smoking, drinking, and using cosmetics, and tried to prevent her from learning English. She, on the other hand, hounded her husband to make more money, poked fun at his political views, and told him he was not the man he imagined—politically or sexually.

By October, Lee had become restless and dissatisfied and quit his job. Almost immediately, though, he began working for a commercial photography company in Dallas. For a while, particularly during his training period, he showed promise, but after a longer period on the job, his work became unacceptable. He had extreme difficulty getting along with the other employees. At times he was morose or argumentative, and his fellow workers were critical of his reading Russian-language newspapers on the job.

He was fired on April 6, 1963, and it is not certain what effect his discharge had on his mental state. Four days later, however, he attempted to carry out a deed which in some respects resembled the assassination of President Kennedy.

Oswald had in his possession a 6.5 millimeter Mannlicher-Carcano rifle which he had recently ordered from a mail order house in Chicago. In a notebook, he sketched plans for an attack and listed bus schedules for his getaway.

Shortly after dinner on Wednesday, April 10th, he left his apartment. His wife did not know where he was going, but she became concerned when he did not return by 10:30. She went to the bedroom and discovered that he had left a note containing information about a post office box key, the rent, utility bills, the disposition of his clothes and personal papers, expense money, and the location of the Dallas police department in case he was taken prisoner.

When Oswald returned home that evening, he told Marina that he had taken a shot at Major General Edwin A. Walker, a controversial political leader who had resigned from the army in 1961. The shot was fired from outside the house when Walker was sitting at his desk. Oswald ran away immediately after firing the gun, and was unaware that the bullet had missed the general's head. The police recovered the slug, but in the absence of a weapon were unable to solve the crime until Oswald's note was made available to them—some 10 days after Kennedy's assassination.

Oswald told his wife that General Walker "was a very bad man, a facist, the leader of a facist organization." Marina replied that even if that were true, he had no right to take a life. Oswald's answer was, "If someone had killed Hitler in time, it would have saved many lives."

Oswald expressed great disappointment to Marina when the following day he heard on the radio that Walker was still alive. He was concerned about his place in history; and felt that by killing Walker he would have been assured recognition.

After the Walker incident, Marina advised her husband to seek work in New Orleans, and Oswald agreed. He left on April 24th, and Marina and their baby moved in with Ruth Paine and her two children in the latter's house in Irving, a suburb of Dallas.

The Oswalds had met Ruth Paine in February. Mrs. Paine, who was separated from her husband, had become fond of Marina and her daughter June, and, in exchange for help with the Russian language, invited them to stay with her while Oswald was looking for a job.

On May 10th, Oswald wrote Marina that he had obtained work as a commercial photographer. After he found an apartment, Mrs. Paine drove Marina and the baby to New Orleans. In reality, Oswald was working as a greaser and oiler of coffee processing machinery, a rather menial task, and one of which he was ashamed. Because he spent too much time reading and hanging around a garage next door, he was dismissed on July 19th.

During the period he spent in New Orleans, Oswald, using the fictitious name of A. J. Hidell—the same name he used to order weapons—founded a chapter of the Fair Play for Cuba Committee. The chapter had no form or substance, but on two occasions Oswald spoke on the radio on behalf of the Committee. He also distributed leaflets in support of Fidel Castro's position and was once arrested in connection with a fight arising over the leaflets.

On September 23rd, Ruth Paine came to New Orleans to pick up Marina and June and take them back to Irving. Lee was going to continue his search for a job—perhaps in Houston. Marina was pregnant again.

But Lee did not go to Houston—or any other American city, for that matter. Instead, he caught a bus for Mexico City, arriving there on September 27th. The purpose of his visit was to secure visas to Cuba and Russia. He had not told his wife anything about his plans to leave the country.

The Cuban authorities were unwilling to grant Oswald a visa unless he could first obtain a visa to Russia. The Soviet government would not issue the requested visa, so Oswald left Mexico for Dallas. He arrived there on October 3rd, and rented a room in the home of a Mrs. Bledsoe. The next day, he got in touch with Marina and told her that he was seeking employment in Dallas, and would visit her and June on weekends.

Sometime during the next few days, Mrs. Paine found a job for Oswald at the Texas School Book Depository in Dallas. At the end of that first week, Oswald moved out of Mrs. Bledsoe's house, and took lodgings under the name of O.H. Lee, in the home of A.C. Johnson—on North Beckley Avenue. He started work at the Depository on October 16th.

On October 20th, Oswald's second daughter was born, and Lee began a regular pattern of weekend visits to Irving. He would arrive late Friday afternoon, and then ride back early Monday morning with Buell Frazier, a fellow employee at the Depository who lived close to Mrs. Paine. One weekend, he remained in Dallas at Marina's suggestion because visitors were coming to the Paine house. Marina called Lee on the following Monday, November 18th, and was extremely annoyed to learn that he was living in Dallas under an assumed name.

On Thursday, November 21st, Oswald asked Frazier for a ride to Irving to pick up some curtain rods he had stored there. He explained that he needed them for his room in Dallas. Ruth Paine and Marina were surprised to see Lee a day early, but not unhappy to have him. Marina thought he had come to explain, and perhaps apologize for his use of a phony name, but Lee wouldn't discuss it.

After supper that evening, Oswald went into the garage where his belongings were stored, and wrapped up his rifle. Neither Mrs. Paine nor Marina were aware of this, but Mrs. Paine did notice later on that the light was burning in the garage, and she went to turn it off. She didn't give the matter much thought, and could not remember later whether she had actually gone *into* the garage.

The next morning Oswald left the house earlier than usual, without awakening anyone. He left his wedding ring on the dresser. His wallet, containing $170, was in a drawer. Marina discovered these items later that morning and thought it odd that he should have forgotten them. He had never done so before.

He and Frazier drove to the Depository with the "curtain rods" on the back seat. Oswald preceded Frazier across the parking lot, and Frazier remembered seeing Oswald walk into the building carrying the package. There was no suspicion that the package contained anything but curtain rods.

Like much of the nation, Ruth and Marina sat in front of the television Friday morning, November 22nd, and watched the presidential motorcade wend its way through Dallas. They had seen President Kennedy arrive at Love Field at 11:40, but no one saw Oswald ascending the stairs to the sixth floor of the Depository at about the same time.

Oswald knew that the route of the motorcade was down Elm

Street, past the front of the building. From a window in the southeast corner, he had a clear, unobstructed view of the motorcade as it swung around Dealey Plaza. Resting his arms on two boxes of books near the window, he took careful aim through his telescopic sight just as the presidential car approached the western end of the building.

President Kennedy was seated to the right of his wife Jacqueline—both in the rear seat of an open limousine. Directly in front of him, on a jump seat, was Governor John Connally. The governor's wife was on the other jump seat. Two Secret Service agents were up front. In the follow-up car were eight more agents. Behind that vehicle were the vice-presidential limousine, another follow-up car, and several additional cars, motorcycles, and buses. Agent Rufus Youngblood, riding in Vice-President Lyndon Johnson's car, noted that it was exactly 12:30 p.m. according to the clock atop the Depository as the motorcade passed the front of the building. This was the scheduled arrival time of the presidential party at the Trade Mart, where the President was to make a luncheon speech.

Oswald fired three times. The first bullet hit the President in the neck, the next caught the governor in the back, and the third struck the President in the head. The governor survived, but the President was pronounced dead at Parkland Hospital at 1:00 p.m.

In the first few moments after the shots were fired, there was surprising coordination of action. Agent Clinton Hill, who was riding on the left running board of the presidential follow-up car, leaped off and ran and mounted the rear of Kennedy's automobile. Agent Roy Kellerman, in the front seat, turned around to assist the President and Governor Connally. Agent Youngblood jumped into the rear seat and sat on Mr. Johnson to protect him. Kellerman yelled to the driver, Agent William Greer, to get moving. Greer radioed the lead car to take them to the nearest hospital and to accelerate sharply.

Marrion Baker, a Dallas motorcycle policeman, who was riding several cars behind, had come up within 200 feet of the intersection at the Depository when he heard the shots. He looked up to see pigeons flying in all directions. He was so convinced that someone had fired from the building that he continued north on Houston Street, crossing Elm. He stopped his motorcycle, dismounted, and dashed up to the entrance, encountering Roy Truly, the building superintendent. Together they ran toward the elevators in the rear of the building, but finding both of them stalled on upper floors, ran up the steps. Less than two minutes had elapsed from the time of the first shot.

When they reached the second-floor landing and were about to turn left and continue up to the next floor, Baker spied a man through the window in the door leading to the lunchroom vestibule. The officer dashed through the door, and saw through another door that the man was now moving away from him in the luncheon area.

With drawn pistol, the policeman ordered the man to come to him. The man did so immediately, not at all ruffled at the sight of a breathless policeman holding a gun on him. This should have seemed suspicious to Baker and Truly, but when the latter recognized Oswald as an employee and so identified him to Baker, they released him. Oswald stepped over to a vending machine, purchased a soft drink, and walked through the building entrance and down the front steps, holding the full Coke bottle in his hands. Baker and Truly continued their search of the building.

Oswald walked seven blocks east on Elm, and boarded a bus heading west on Elm. It was only 12:40—a mere 10 minutes since the shooting. He had apparently hoped to ride this bus to the Oak Cliff section of southwest Dallas where his rooming house was located.

But the bus quickly got bogged down in the traffic jam resulting from the assassination and could not proceed more than a couple of blocks. Since it was headed for the confusion in front of the Depository, Oswald decided after three or four minutes that he had better get off. He did so, and in a few minutes found an available cab, which took him several blocks beyond his rooming house on North Beckley Avenue.

Just before 1:00 p.m. he walked into the house and out again almost immediately. The housekeeper noticed that he seemed to be in a hurry. She was surprised to see Oswald, since he was never there in the middle of the day.

A quarter of an hour later, Oswald was walking east on East 10th Street just past the intersection of Patton Avenue, nine-tenths of a mile from his rooming house. There, he was spotted by Patrolman J.D. Tippit. Tippit was cruising slowly in the same direction on 10th Street, looking for a man of Oswald's general description. As was the custom during daylight hours, Officer Tippit was alone in his car.

He pulled up alongside Oswald and called to him. Oswald came over to the police car and, resting his arms on the right-hand window ledge, apparently exchanged a few remarks with Tippit. Tippit then got out of his vehicle and at some point drew his revolver, but when he reached the left front wheel, Oswald also drew a gun and fired it repeatedly, hitting the policeman in the chest four times and killing him instantly.

A man in a truck was just then approaching the scene from the west. He stopped to help Tippit, and saw Oswald head back to Patton Avenue, emptying his gun of spent cartridges on the way. The man broadcast an SOS over the police car radio.

Two persons witnessed the shooting, and four more saw Oswald leaving the scene. The fourth individual, a shoe store manager by the name of Johnny Brewer, had just heard the announcement of the killing over his radio. At the sound of a siren, he saw Oswald duck into the entranceway of his store and wait a few moments with his back to the street until the police car was out of sight. When Oswald left, Brewer followed him surreptitiously.

He saw the suspect enter the Texas Theater on West Jefferson Street, about 60 feet away from his shoe store. Brewer went up to the cashier and told her a man had gone into the theater without buying a ticket. Explaining that the man was a sought-after killer, he asked her to call the police.

At 1:45 the police surrounded the theater. The house lights were turned on, and a group of officers entered the building. Patrolman M.N. McDonald approached Oswald, who jumped up from his seat and said: "Well, it's all over now."

As he said that, he drew a gun from his belt with one hand and struck McDonald with the other. But McDonald simultaneously struck Oswald with one hand and with the other grabbed the pistol. It took several officers to pin him down and handcuff him. They loaded him into the back of a police car, and drove to central police headquarters. It was 2:00 p.m.

At the very moment Oswald was brought to headquarters, the police issued an APB on Lee Harvey Oswald, the only warehouseman missing from among the employees questioned by Roy Truly at the Depository. They were astonished to find him already in the interrogation room, accused of killing Patrolman Tippit. It was suddenly obvious that the murderer of Tippit was also the murderer of Kennedy.

When Ruth Paine and Marina Oswald heard on television that the President had been shot, they cried. When it became clear that the shots were fired from the Depository, Marina slipped out to the garage and checked to see if the rifle was in its accustomed place. She found the blanket in which it was usually wrapped and, seeing the outline of the weapon, thought it was still there. She returned to the house in relief. She had never forgotten the Walker episode.

When the police came to the house a few hours later, they searched, and discovered that the rifle *was* gone. Marina was distraught.

Oswald lived only two more days. On Sunday morning, November 24th, as he was being transferred from the city jail to the county jail, he was shot to death by Jack Ruby in sight of millions of TV viewers. Ruby claimed he was so filled with rage against Oswald, and overcome by sympathy for Mrs. Kennedy that he took upon himself the task of ridding the world of Oswald. Ruby was immediately arrested and jailed. He was indicted on November 26, 1963.

In March 1964, Ruby was convicted of murder in the first degree and sentenced to death. In October 1966, however, his sentence was reversed by a higher court on the grounds that the judge had allowed illegal testimony. As a new trial was being awaited, fate took a hand, and the new trial of Ruby was called off. Ruby died of cancer on January 3, 1967.

Lee Harvey Oswald had achieved the notoriety he wanted. No assassination in history was ever more publicized. The Warren Commission Report alone covers more than 700 pages. Countless other books, reports, and articles, both popular and scholarly, have been written on Oswald and his deed.

Although there are partisans who insist that Oswald was not alone in the plot to assassinate Kennedy, there is little reason to expect that this will be proven. The only questions begging for clear answers are those dealing with the true state of Oswald's mind. Surrounding his search for acclaim clusters a complex of forces found among other madmen: hostility toward one's environment, the inability to establish deep and lasting human relationships, a nagging sense of failure, and a fanatical attachment to some ideal.

How environment and heredity combined to produce such a madman as Lee Harvey Oswald is the biggest question of all.

11.Corday

The madness of Charlotte Corday was an enigma.

Difficult to trace and hard to justify, it revealed itself at its height in the hours before, and in the days immediately following, the assassination of the French revolutionary leader, Jean-Paul Marat.

Her madness was not a foamy-mouthed insanity; neither did it lack reason. In fact, it took reason too far—to the outer edge of fanaticism. Here, Corday's zeal collided with the equally fanatical but opposite outlook of Marat. In those few minutes when Corday and Marat met for the first and last time, the whole tapestry of the French Revolution was seen in microcosm: a clash between fanatical stances, resulting in terror and bloodshed for all.

Marie Anne Charlotte Corday d'Armont was born in Normandy, on July 27, 1768. There is disagreement as to her exact birthplace, but all suggestions place it somewhere between Caen, in Calvados, and Argentan, in Orne.

A middle daughter, Charlotte came from a poor, but noble family of two boys and three girls. She boasted that the 17th-century dramatist and poet Pierre Corneille was among her ancestors. These two unrelated facts—poverty and Corneille—were to play a part in the story of her life.

The Corday family had owned extensive property. But, over the years, from the time of their ascendance to the ranks of nobility in 1077, it had been divided again and again among descendants. Charlotte's father, Jacques-François, was a third son, and, consequently, received from his father only left-over parcels of land. Some few acres were located at Corday, near Falaise—whence the family name—plus other small tracts at Argentan and Mesnil-Imbert. All together, the property did not amount to much—in acreage or productivity.

François de Corday was vocal in calling for reform of the laws of primogeniture, which spelled out the rights of the eldest son in a family to inherit all of his father's estate. He openly criticized the social and political institutions of his time and region, and published pamphlets decrying tyranny in any form.

Even though François de Corday's attitude toward despotic government and arbitrary laws was shared by many in those pre-Revolution days, the intensity of his feeling especially affected his family. In particular, Charlotte—or Marie, as the family usually called her—inherited from her father an excessive degree of pride, which to some extent compensated for a lack of money.

The poverty-stricken family could afford no more than the bare essentials. The children presented a pathetic picture as they pranced about in their old and tattered clothing. Some of the poverty, however, could have been avoided or overcome if the parents had not been so prolific, and if that ingredient of nobility—pride—had not been present in such concentrated doses. For it was pride—and hope for a better future for the family—that made François and his wife scrimp and save. They denied the rest of the family a decent existence so that their two sons might be sent to a training school to become officers in the royal army.

By the time all five children had been born, it became necessary to turn to relatives for assistance. Charlotte, accordingly, was sent to live with her elderly uncle, the Abbé de Corday, curé of Vicques, a tiny village close to Argentan. Charlotte stayed with her uncle, off and on, for three years. The two formed a close attachment to each other which was founded on a mutual admiration for their famous ancestor, Corneille.

For hours on end, the old man and the young girl would isolate themselves in the Abbé's study, reading to each other and discussing passages in Corneille's tragedies. Against such a noble backdrop their own day seemed crude and mundane.

When Charlotte was somewhere between 10 and 13—there is uncertainty about her age when she went to live with her uncle—she returned home to help her mother look after the house. Trained to do domestic chores, she cooked, cleaned and sewed for the family. Although the distance between her home and her uncle's village was short, the distance she had traveled, intellectually, in those few years was far, indeed.

The tone of Corneille's dramas was exciting and elevating, and, as every student of French literature is taught, possesses a stateliness unequaled in the theater. The Renaissance theme of the self-assertion and heroism of man is everywhere in evidence.

Charlotte loved to immerse herself in these words and thoughts, and she devoured her great-grandfather's dramas. She absorbed quotations such as these from *Le Cid*: "To conquer without risk is to triumph without glory." And, "Brave men are brave from the very first." A quotation from the second act of *Horace* had special significance for her from the moment Marat came to power: "Do your duty, and leave the rest to heaven."

By the time Charlotte entered her teen years she had already absorbed and embodied many attitudes found among the characters of Corneille's tragedies. She was long-suffering, patient, respectful of duty, modest, and proper. When, shortly after the family moved to Caen, her older sister died, and then, some months later, her mother died, Charlotte was able, at the tender age of 15, to take over the management of the household from her distraught father.

For two years Charlotte faithfully performed her household tasks; but always, in her free hours, she read. From Corneille she moved back in time to the Romans of Plutarch's *Lives* and found in them, in even purer form, those same virtues of self-sacrifice, patriotism, and stoicism which she had long nurtured in her fantasy world.

That she then progressed to Rousseau must seem to most a wondrous contradiction, for Rousseau's novels were transparent and sensuous in style, self-centered and smaller-than-life, sentimental and full of feeling. Rousseau himself, although Charlotte may not have known it, was erratic and unbalanced. His life was a mass and a tangle of sex problems, money problems, and personality problems. He 'was a masochist, a mismanager of his domestic affairs, and an insufferable egotist. He could get along with no one and even put his own children up for adoption. The characters in his novels reflect most of these same problems and, like teenagers of every generation, wade through life with great, ponderous solemnity, spouting their wisdom and half-baked ideals in every direction.

Rousseau's characters stop every few pages and philosophize on every conceivable aspect of man's condition. But the favorite subject is politics, and it is undoubtedly in this area that Charlotte Corday, and the rest of France, found Rousseau's writings so fascinating.

Rousseau's *magnum opus*, the *Social Contract*, begins with an unmistakable call to revolution: "Man is born free, and everywhere he is in chains." The book had great appeal to the disinherited and disfranchised hordes of French humanity whose rights had, indeed, long been ignored. However, few reflected on the first part of the opening sentence. If they had, they would have had to admit that man is not born free, but is born—and remains to some degree—dependent on others.

The system of anarchy advocated by Rousseau was, rationally speaking, unworkable—as France was to learn all too soon. Rousseau had adopted John Locke's proposition of the sovereignty of the people and their right to revolution, but unlike Locke he did not admit to the necessity for law and its restraints. Rousseau saw civilization and its institutions as degrading to man, whom he pictured as a virtuous and noble savage. So much that was wicked, brutal, and truly savage in the French Revolution turned about such words as "virtue," "right," "liberty," and "equality."

In 1785, Charlotte and her sister Eléonore were sent to the convent of the Abbaye-aux-Dames at Caen to complete their education. There, the sisters remained for nearly six years—until the closing of the convents in 1790-91—at which time they returned to their father's home at Mesnil-Imbert.

During her years at the convent, Charlotte continued to study the works of the classicists and those of Rousseau, Voltaire, and Raynal. From the nuns she also received careful instruction in the Roman Catholic faith and in matters of decorum. By her nature, Charlotte was predisposed to all these influences, and, by the time she left the convent, she was a well-read, polished, and devout young woman.

After a number of months in the country, Charlotte felt intellectually inhibited. She departed for Caen where there was a measure of political ferment. Ever since the assembling, in May 1789, of the States-General—that legislative body comprising the three estates, or social classes, of the clergy, the nobility, and the bourgeosie—she had followed the course of political affairs and revolution with fervor. Encouraged by Mirabeau, a National Assembly had been formed, consisting of members of all three estates, many of whom held conflicting persuasions. When the king locked the Assembly out of their meeting hall on June 20th, the group met on the old tennis court and swore that they would write a constitution for France. The king called his troops together, and a Civic Guard was formed. The die was cast; the Revolution had begun in earnest. Incited by a young attorney named Camille Desmoulins, the French people rose up against King Louis XVI and stormed the Bastille and subdued it on July 14, 1789.

During the next two years, the Revolution proceeded with considerable order and a minimum of actual conflict outside the city of Paris. But, gradually conditions worsened; people became hungry, jobless, and hopeless; various factions conflicted with each other. Onto this chaotic stage strode three men—Marat, Danton, and Robespierre—each with his own solution, and each prepared to use murder as his weapon against the ideas of others. It is fitting that a violent death awaited each of them.

The Legislative Assembly, that new body formed after the National Assembly had presented the country with a constitution, consisted of three distinct groups: the Constitutionalists, who were generally conservative, and considered the Revolution to be over; the Jacobins, primarily under the leadership of Robespierre and Danton, and who later were given to great excesses; and, the Girondists, the most powerful and most revolutionary of the three.

The Girondists were supported by the vast majority of the people who wished the government to be simple, just, humanitarian, and republican, with freedom and security for all. With every passing month they became more and more moderate and reasonable, trying to steer a middle course between royalist interests and the ultra-republicanism of the Jacobins. But their moderation was met only by opposing forces who had become more and more violent and unreasonable.

When the Legislative Assembly was replaced by the National Convention, there remained only two political parties—the Girondists and the Jacobins. By now the Girondists were looked upon as the conservatives, and the Jacobins as the radicals. A fight to the finish was in the making.

The group most vehemently opposed to the Girondists was a ragtag section of the Jacobins called the Mountain, after its seating location high up on the left of the President's tribune. Jean-Paul Marat was the self-appointed head of the Mountain.

In his filthy rags, smelling like a garbage man, and covered with the scabs and pustules of a terrible skin disease, Marat looked every inch the representative of the wild, screaming, ignorant Paris rabble. "I am the rage of the people," he proclaimed.

Marat, often with the help of Robespierre, labored to destroy the Girondists through intrigue and murder. When the Girondists began to totter, they sought to regain their strength in Paris by importing a mob of some 500 volunteers from outside the country. This was a dire error, for Marat was able to make a pact with, and use these same people—for the most part, cutthroats of the worst sort—together with large numbers of the dregs of humanity imprisoned in the jails of Paris. When he loosed this mob on those suspected of being in opposition to him, 1,400 people were killed—many in the most savage ways. Some were arrested and killed before actually reaching prison. Others were slaughtered in prison. September 2-8, 1792 is a period infamous in history, and is recalled as the September Massacres.

The most renowned victim of the September Massacres was Princess Marie-Luise de Lamballe, superintendent of the queen's household. It was her great misfortune to be imprisoned at La Force, for it was at this place, on the third day of the massacres, that the drunken, raving mob exhibited its most crazed behavior. The princess had come from England to be with her friend Marie Antoinette in order to give her comfort in those troubled days, but ironically, the king and queen were spared until January 21, 1793.

Brought before the "tribunal," the princess swore an oath to uphold liberty and equality, but kept silent when asked to express her disloyalty to the king and queen. She was condemned on the spot, and handed over to the mob. Some accounts say that a spike was first thrust through her body, and then her head was cut off; others, that her head was severed and carried through the streets with curses for all to see and revile. Additional reports say that her heart was ripped out of her body while still beating and consumed by the people. One final account maintains that her arms and legs were chopped off, and were shot through a cannon into the air.

The September Massacres spelled the demise of the Girondists. When their end came on May 31, 1793, 18 members made their way to Caen and established new headquarters. There, they hoped to raise an army of volunteers that would return to Paris and overthrow Marat and the Jacobins.

Charlotte attended many of the meetings and agonized over the plight of the party. Her inner self in turmoil, seething with anger, she was determined to kill the tyrant, Marat, and save France.

For Charlotte Corday, Marat was the epitome of evil, and was responsible for the evils wrought by the Revolution. He was a hate-filled, murdering maniac—the embodiment, in one person, of the entire mob of bloodthirsty revolutionists. To Charlotte, Marat's opposition to the Girondists was now almost incidental, so thoroughly had she abstracted him as the archenemy of mankind. To her, even his physical appearance was detestable.

But was Marat really the kind of man Charlotte imagined him to be?

Born in Switzerland in 1743, Marat was the son of a Swiss mother and a Sardinian father. The latter, a chemist by profession, also had a knack for foreign languages. These proclivities he apparently passed on to his son, for Jean-Paul was educated in England as a physician, and later wrote books on topics ranging from optics and electricity to politics. He claimed fluency in French, English, Dutch, German, and Italian. This was the young Marat.

But the Marat of the Revolution was, physically and mentally, a sick man. He dressed like a present-day hippie—perhaps largely for reasons of effect—no matter where he went, or whom he was to meet. Before the Convention, standing near the carefully powdered, well-dressed Robespierre and Danton, he presented a disgusting contrast. His hair was matted and caked with dirt and grease; his clothes were not only odd and dirty, but ripped and rotting. He had a face like a frog—great, bulging eyes and greenish skin with running sores. The stench was such that even his own people slid away from him on the bench.

It is indeed a study in contrasts to link Charlotte Corday and Jean-Paul Marat. But fanaticism and hate are the same for all men. By 1793, they had almost destroyed Marat; by that same year they were eating at Corday's soul.

At about noon on Thursday, July 11th, Charlotte arrived in Paris. Knowing nothing about the city, she asked the stagecoach guard where she might find a decent room. He inquired in the ticket office and returned with the recommendation that she stay at the nearby Hôtel de la Providence. A porter then appeared to take her trunk and show her the way.

The room assigned to Charlotte did not please her. It was dirty and messy—the bed had not even been made—but she nevertheless decided to stay. Despite her meticulousness, she had more important things on her mind this day than the condition of a hotel room.

She asked the valet-de-chambre to straighten up a bit, and, while he was doing so, she put some questions to him. For one thing, she wanted directions to the Palais-Royal and to the rue Saint-Thomas-du-Louvre. Most of all, she wanted to know what the Parisians were thinking and saying about Marat.

The valet assured her that the patriots loved Marat, but that the aristocrats feared and hated him. He added that Marat was now very ill and seldom appeared in public or at the Convention.

This last piece of news was distressing to Charlotte. For weeks she had planned to make a public spectacle of Marat's murder. She pictured herself stabbing him before a great throng assembled in the Convention hall. It would certainly be difficult to gain entrance to his house, and kill him there.

But even before concentrating on the main purpose of her

visit to Paris, Charlotte had to take care of an item of business.

Before leaving Caen she had sought out the most prominent leader of the Girondists, Charles Barbaroux, and asked him to intercede in Paris for her old friend from convent days, Alexandrine de Forbin. Madame de Forbin had been having difficulty regaining her pension after having been incorrectly classified as an émigrée.

Barbaroux had not received an answer to a letter he wrote to the Ministry of the Interior, so Charlotte departed for Paris with a letter of introduction from Barbaroux to his friend in the Convention, Lauze Duperret.

Although she was tired by the trip from Caen, Charlotte left immediately for Duperret's house on the rue Saint-Thomas-du-Louvre. She did not find him in, and so, instead, left a packet of papers containing her letter of introduction, the explanation of Madame de Forbin's problem, and news and documents dealing with the Girondist deputies headquartered at Caen.

Anxious to talk to him about political matters and to learn something about Marat's habits, Charlotte returned to Duperret's house at dinnertime that same evening. He interrupted his meal to read Barbaroux's letter and to listen to Charlotte. He agreed to accompany her to the minister of the interior the next day.

Duperret kept his promise, but they were unable to see the minister on Friday morning. Although they had been able to secure an appointment for eight o'clock that evening, Duperret decided that his influence might be more harmful than helpful, and advised against returning to the Ministry. He asked, nevertheless, to see Charlotte on Saturday, but she answered in the negative and asked that he not contact her.

When Duperret asked Corday when she planned to return to Caen, she answered evasively. For his own safety, she urged him to leave immediately for Caen, where he had many friends among the Girondists. He thought this strange and took her for some kind of intriguer, but he did not in the least suspect that she planned to assassinate Marat. If he had been aware of her plan, he would surely have taken her advice and left Paris. Charlotte was trying to forewarn Duperret without actually divulging her scheme; she was certain that he would be found and killed when their association was established. She was right.

Upon returning to her room, Charlotte spent some hours composing a document of several pages, entitled "Address to the French People, Friends of the Law and Peace." In it, she condemned the wicked political ambitions of the Mountain, and appealed to France to think of the murder of Marat as symbolic of overthrowing the despicable yoke of cruelty. The paper, together with her birth certificate, was found pinned to her fichu after her arrest.

On Saturday, July 13, 1793, Charlotte awoke very early and left her hotel. For more than an hour she walked serenely in the Palais-Royal garden. The tranquility of the place contrasted sharply with the murderous thoughts that pounded in her brain.

Shortly after 7:30 a.m., the shops on an adjoining street began to open. Charlotte stepped into one and purchased a long kitchen knife with a green, cardboard sheath. She hid it in her bodice. On her way back to the hotel, she bought a newspaper and learned that nine enemies of Marat were to be guillotined that very day. The anger and hatred within her raged like an uncontrollable fire.

After breakfast, which she took in her room, she went downstairs, hailed a carriage, and asked the driver to take her to Marat's residence. She did not know the address, and neither did the driver, but after some inquiries they learned that Marat lived across the river, at 30, rue des Cordeliers, in the Faubourg Saint-Germain quarter.

In midmorning, Charlotte walked to the door of Marat's house and rang the bell. Her ring was answered by Catherine Evrard, the sister of Simonne Evrard, Marat's devoted mistress. Catherine explained that Marat could see no one, that he was a very sick man. Undaunted, Charlotte insisted that she brought news from Caen that would interest Marat. As Catherine was about to weaken and admit Charlotte, Simonne and Albertine, Marat's sister, appeared in the background of the antechamber. Simonne was very direct. "M. Marat can see no one," she barked, and slammed the door in Charlotte's face.

A lesser woman might have given up at this point, but Charlotte returned to her hotel and sat down and wrote Marat the following letter:

> I have just arrived from Caen. Your love of our country leads me to assume you will be anxious to hear about the unfortunate happenings in that part of the Republic. I shall therefore present myself at your house at about one o'clock. Be good enough to receive me and grant me a moment's interview. I will put you in the way of rendering a great service to France.
>
> Marie Corday

Only in the moment before his death did Marat comprehend the masterful subtlety of the last sentence.

When after six or seven hours she had received no answer to her letter, she wrote another. It read:

> I wrote you this morning, Marat. Did you receive my letter? May I hope to have a moment's interview with you if you did receive it? I hope you will not refuse me, for the matter is very interesting. My unhappiness gives me a claim on your protection.

This note she intended to take with her, to be handed over at the door if she should be denied admittance once more.

Although she never paid undue attention to her physical appearance, Charlotte was, in fact, a beautiful woman. Perhaps now for the first time, as she changed clothes before a mirror, she realized that her beauty might be put to good use. She disliked deviousness, but something prompted her to don a white, muslin dress, and to change the ribbons on her big hat from black to green. She then sent for a hairdresser, who arranged her long, chestnut hair in the latest style. She remembered Marat's earlier reputation for being a woman-chaser.

Charlotte appeared at Marat's at 7:30 p.m. The door was answered by the concierge, who repeated the same phrases that Charlotte had heard earlier that day. But this time, she was able to step across the threshold into the foyer, where she noticed two women folding copies of *L'Ami du Peuple*, Marat's inflammatory revolutionary sheet.

Charlotte was insisting that she have a word with Marat when, once again, Simonne came into the antechamber to take charge of the situation. She explained that Marat could not see her, or any other stranger, under any circumstances.

At that moment a deliveryman and Laurent Bas, a commissionaire stationed on the rue des Cordeliers, came through the front door. The deliveryman had a bill for Marat, and Bas had brought more newsprint. Charlotte noticed that the deliveryman took the bill through the dining room to the right and into a bathroom beyond.

Marat, who was reading Charlotte's earlier letter about the time of her arrival, heard voices through the bathroom door—left ajar by the departing deliveryman. Among the high-pitched, rasping voices of his domestics, he discerned the low, musical tones of an unfamiliar voice. Summoning Simonne, he learned that it was the author of the letter he was now holding who was standing in his hallway and requesting an interview. He gave immediate orders that she be admitted.

Reluctantly, Simonne obeyed. As Charlotte closed the bathroom door behind her, Simonne shuddered, though she could not decide why.

Despite her complete composure, Charlotte was not prepared for the sight that met her eyes. Marat was sitting in hip-high water in his bathtub. The bathtub was a weird contraption resembling a high-top shoe. A sheet was slung over his shoulders, and a filthy, vinegar-soaked rag was tied around his forehead. His naked, shriveled body was a mass of sores oozing with pus. Indeed, she thought, he is already in a state of putrefaction.

Marat motioned Charlotte to sit down on a box next to the tub. He stopped the writing he was doing on his curious aquatic desk—a board laid across the tub—and he plied her with questions about the situation in Caen. Charlotte, anxious to fire up his malice, told him that the deputies had been successful in raising an army to march on Paris. They planned to drive out the anarchists.

While Charlotte was speaking, Simonne entered and offered to pour more almond paste and clay into the tub, but Marat waved her away and said the bath was fine. Simonne darted a suspicious look at the attractive woman seated beside the tub and then reached over her to pick up a plate of odoriferous calf brains and sweetmeats on the window sill behind the tub. The whole house smells rancid, thought the fastidious Charlotte, as Simonne backed out of the door and closed it.

"Names!" Marat shouted. "Who are these traitors at Caen?"

As Charlotte listed them...Buzot, Gaudet, Pétion, Barbaroux...Marat wrote them down with haste and near glee.

"Excellent," he said as he laid his pen down, "we'll soon guillotine them all in Paris!"

This remark galvanized Charlotte into action. With her right hand, she drew forth the knife from her bodice, and, securing it tightly with her left hand, she plunged the blade into Marat's chest. The power of the plunge cut through to the lung, and sliced the aorta. When she withdrew the knife, blood spurted forth rhythmically with the final pumping action of Marat's failing heart.

"A moi, ma chère amie, à moi!" ("Help me, my dear friend, help me!") Simonne, in answer to Marat's entreaty, entered the room. The water in the tub was red with blood. Unmoved, Charlotte had laid the knife on the desk-board and strode resolutely out the door.

"Oh, my God, they've killed him!" sobbed Simonne as she clutched at the lifeless form in the tub.

From this moment on, confusion reigned. Laurent Bas struck Charlotte over the head with a chair, and then he and another man pinned her down. The women of the house dashed from room to room. A dentist from downstairs came running in. He and several other men carried Marat to his bedroom and laid him on the bed. All the screaming and wailing lent an atmosphere of total madness to the house.

When, within minutes, a doctor from the nearby school of medicine appeared, he could only confirm what everybody in the house already knew: Marat was dead. The crowd that had started to gather outside knew it too, and demanded that the assassin be handed over to them for punishment.

For the next five hours, Charlotte was interrogated at the house by the police. Throughout the entire ordeal, she remained in control of herself, admitting her guilt, but giving careful answers. She insisted that she alone had conceived the idea of murdering Marat, and that it was not an organized plot. At one point she was led to Marat's bedside and made to identify the body. "Yes, I am the one who killed him," she said.

At about two o'clock in the morning she was taken from the house to the prison of the Abbaye. After some sleep, she arose and wrote several letters: one to her father, one to Barbaroux, and one to the Security Committee, requesting that a painter be sent to the prison to do her portrait, explaining that "there is sometimes a curiosity about the likeness of great criminals." A national guardsman by the name of Jean Jacques Hauer, who had already begun a sketch of her at her arraignment, was dispatched to her cell. Charlotte was very concerned that history not forget her.

On July 16th, she was transferred to the Conciergerie, the penultimate step to the guillotine. During that same day she was moved back to the Abbaye and then back again to the Conciergerie, without explanation. Charlotte did not expect acquittal; indeed, she did not want it.

The trial took place on the morning of July 17th. To the Tribunal president's question, why she had killed Marat, Charlotte quickly replied: "To give peace to my country."

"Do you think that by killing him you have killed all the Marats?" persisted the president.

"This one dead, perhaps the others will be afraid," was the answer. She should have known that Danton and Robespierre were even then emerging from the shadows.

Charlotte heard her death sentence impassively, and was led back to her cell. She had expected execution by noon and was disappointed to learn that she would have to wait another five or six hours. She passed the time talking to Hauer as he painted her portrait, telling him how happy she was that peace would now descend upon France. She truly saw herself as the avenging angel and savior of her country.

At six o'clock, Samson the executioner arrived to cut off her long hair. Charlotte gave a lock to Hauer and another to the prison concierge. Enthusiastically, she donned the traditional red chemise and climbed into the tumbril. Samson remarked later that he had never seen a prisoner so genuinely indifferent to his or her execution.

For nearly two hours Samson pushed his prisoner through milling crowds to the Place de la Révolution. When he half apologized for the delay, Charlotte assured him that they would "get there eventually!"

Joyfully, she laid her head under the knife. The blade fell; the head rolled into the basket. Samson's assistant snatched it up and struck it across the cheek. Those in the front of the crowd said it blushed.

If so, it was not from shame.

12. Princip

Ever since 1900, tensions in Europe had been mounting. Colonial ambitions clashed with nationalistic fervor to set nation against nation, race against race, dynasties against a new social order. Only a tiny spark was needed to turn the continent into a conflagration.

A wildly fanatical teen-aged revolutionary, unknowingly, provided that spark on June 28, 1914 when he assassinated the Habsburg Archduke Franz Ferdinand and his wife, the Duchess of Hohenberg. He thought he was striking a blow for Slavic unity, but he started a war that was fought on three continents, took nine million lives and cost $350 billion.

Gavrilo Princip was born in the village of Oblej, Bosnia on July 13, 1894. The product of an Orthodox peasant family, he learned early in life to detest Austria. Austria had administered Bosnia and Herzegovina since 1877. When she arbitrarily annexed Bosnia in 1908, the land policy that was instituted hardly differed from that of the hated Turks who had oppressed the South Slavs for so many years. The people were, in fact, still largely dependent on rich landowners who were Turkish and Moslem. To the Bosnians it was doubly bad to be subservient to a people of different race and religion; but it was a quadruple threat to their Slavic pride to be controlled now by Austria—a ruling nation of Germans and Roman Catholics. Princip decided to do something about the situation.

Like the Archduke, Gavrilo had been a sickly child. His parents, taken up with the task of grubbing out a meager living from the land, largely ignored him. Gavrilo turned to books on history and politics for company, and he read voraciously. He wanted to learn and keep learning; his curiosity was endless.

However, while he thirsted for knowledge, he was not a good student. Not only was he frequently sick and absent from classes, but he lacked the necessary intelligence to meet the relatively high standards of the Austrian-directed school system. Therefore, in May of 1912, he went to Belgrade, the Serbian capital, to study where demands on the students were not as great. This move had a tremendous impact on Gavrilo's life, for in Belgrade he became friendly with a group of students committed to reuniting Bosnia and free Serbia.

The Serbs, unlike the South Slavic minorities surrounding them, had managed to throw the Turks out, and to assert their independence from Austria-Hungary. Serbia was engaged at that time in the first of two Balkan Wars. When they had been resolved in her favor in 1913, Serbia succeeded in permanently ridding the peninsula of Turks and in making significant territorial gains to the south.

More than ever, Bosnia and Herzegovina longed to be one with Serbia. There were two groups that wanted to bring about a reunion—no matter what the cost. One group was open and legitimate. It was called National Defense. The other was secret and vicious, ominously named, *Union or Death,* and popularly known as the *Black Hand.* These groups distributed reams of anti-Habsburg propaganda and fomented unrest throughout Bosnia.

Shortly after his arrival in Belgrade, Princip volunteered to serve as a member of an armed band of Serbian partisans (*comitaji*) participating in the Balkan Wars. Much to his disappointment, he was rejected because of ill health; a medical examination revealed that he had tuberculosis.

Princip continued his studies, but in the evening he could often be found sitting in cafés sipping *slivovitz* and conversing with revolutionary fellow students from Serbia and Bosnia. It was in one of these cafés that Gavrilo ran into Nedeljko Čabrinović, an old chum from Bosnia who had been driven out of his hometown of Sarajevo five years earlier because of his fiery socialist views.

One day, in the late spring of 1914, Čabrinović showed Princip a clipping from a newspaper announcing the visit of the archduke to Sarajevo. Each admitted to the other that he had entertained thoughts of murdering the archduke, and now together, they began making plans to carry out the deed. They also considered killing General Potiorek, the pro-Austrian governor to Bosnia, but decided that the assassination of Franz Ferdinand would wreak greater vengeance on Austria.

"I looked upon vengeance as a sacred duty of civilized man," said Čabrinović at his trial.

Princip had a somewhat more personal view of the matter. He said: "I am not a criminal, for I destroyed a bad man."

.Both statements were evidence of how ignorant these two young men were of the political situation and the role of the archduke in its creation. Actually, the archduke had long been a supporter of the Slavic quest for recognition within the Austro-Hungarian Empire. Without attributing to him particular concern for the welfare of the Slavs, it was, nevertheless, Franz Ferdinand alone among the royalty who urged that the restive South Slavs be given home rule, and that they be set up in a separate state of their own. To extreme nationalists, however, the archduke was no better than the tyrannical empire of which he was a part.

Shortly after Princip and Čabrinović began to conspire, they realized that it would be difficult to secretly assemble the necessary weapons. They, therefore, recruited a third student, Trifko Grabež, in the hope that he would be able to arrange for guns and bombs. Grabež contacted a former *comitaji* commander, Major Voja Tankosić, who was now a member of the terrorist pan-Serb Black Hand organization. Tankosić was second in command to Colonel Dragutin Dimitrievič (also known as Apis), who was the undisputed leader of the Black Hand, and head of Military Intelligence of the Serbian General Staff. Within a week they had their weapons.

Due to poor security and the presence of undercover government agents, many aspects of the terrorists' plans became known.

But despite overt efforts on the part of the Serbian government to quash the plot, Tankosić arranged for the young men to secretly reenter Bosnia.

Princip wrote a detailed letter to Danilo Ilić, a former teacher dedicated to revolution and reunion, explaining the entire operation and requesting that he recruit three more students in Sarajevo.

On Wednesday, June 24th, the three young conspirators departed from Belgrade on a train headed for the Bosnian border—approximately 65 miles away. They were traveling second-class, on reduced-fare tickets procured by agents of the Black Hand. To the casual observer, they appeared to be three schoolboys going on vacation.

Once they reached the frontier, their behavior changed drastically. They had been told to seek out a particular captain in the border patrol, give him a letter of introduction, and await his instructions. Princip located the captain and handed him the message. He was instructed to return after dark with Čabrinović and Grabež. They would then be able to cross the Morava River, which separated Bosnia from Serbia, and make their first contact with Bosnian nationalists at a nearby farmhouse.

Čabrinović went on his way, but Princip and Grabež were

passed from farm to farm along the remaining 70 miles to Sarajevo. Eventually, they met at the home of Veljko Čubrilović, a teacher who introduced them to Miško Jovanović in the village of Tuzla. Jovanović agreed to let them store their bombs and pistols in his house as long as they were removed by the following Saturday.

Late Friday night, Danilo Ilič gathered the stored ammunition and transported it back to Sarajevo. Princip was staying with him, so he slid a box containing six revolvers, three grenades, and six capsules of potassium cyanide under Gavrilo's bed. That same evening, Ilić tried to dissuade Princip from carrying out the assassination, but Princip was adamant. "The Archduke is the enemy of the Slav world," he insisted. "I *must* kill him."

Sunday, June 28th, dawned bright and beautiful, a day to warm even the heart of the morose and irascible archduke. Not usually sensitive to beauty, he did, nevertheless, comment to his aide on the lovely day as they stood gazing out over a field in back of his quarters in Ilidža. The archduke had come there, as Inspector General of the Austrian armed forces, to take part in military maneuvers. An ardent sportsman—some said a psychopathic killer of game—he also spent a large portion of each day in Ilidža hunting in the nearby hills. Hunting and inspecting his troops were two of the reasons he had come to Bosnia.

A third reason was that this day was the archduke's 14th wedding anniversary. Doubtless, this last was the reason he was able to enjoy the beauty of the day, for unlike many royal couples Franz Ferdinand and his wife did love each other. Sophie was to meet him in Sarajevo that morning, having come down from Vienna by automobile. She was to join him on the motorcade through the city. He was looking forward to seeing her, although their separation had been very brief.

Archduke Franz Ferdinand had been repeatedly warned by his advisors in Vienna against visiting Bosnia at that time. But he was a stubborn man, determined to take advantage of his official visit by making it also an anniversary celebration and a hunting expedition. Although, according to his country's protocol, his wife (who came from an old but obscure noble Czech family) did not occupy a position of prominence in the hierarchy of things, Franz Ferdinand cherished her. He wanted to use the trip to Bosnia as an opportunity to show his concern and love for her and to award her the honor due her.

"No one in Sarajevo has any reason to harm me," said Franz Ferdinand. "I will not hide from my people. Besides, I am the best friend the Bosnians have." He certainly believed this, for even if he had no regard for his own safety, he would never knowingly put Sophie's life in jeopardy. After all she was actually born a commoner, and she was a Slav, so who would want to harm her?

At 10 a.m. the four-car procession moved away from the railroad station immediately after the archduke's arrival from Ilidža. Crowds lined the street, banners fluttered, and the brassy sounds of a band playing a lively tune could be heard.

There were few smiles in the crowd; there was a feeling of hostility everywhere. This was decidedly the wrong day for a visit by the heir presumptive to the Austrian throne.

For the assembled thousands, this day had significance of quite a different sort. June 28th was the Vidovdan, the Feast of St. Vitus, which marked the great battle of Kossovo in 1389, when the Turks overran the kingdom of Serbia, pillaging the land and making slaves of its Christian subjects. Until Serbia's final victory over the Turks during the Balkan Wars, Vidovdan had for hundreds of years been a day of mourning. Now, it signified freedom from oppression. Archduke Franz Ferdinand was a bitter reminder of Serbia's past, and a hated symbol of present-day control by Austria-Hungary.

The archduke's car was the second of six in line, two additional automobiles having joined the parade two blocks from the railroad station. The archduke and his wife were seated in the rear of an open touring car. They waved and smiled from side to side as the car proceeded along the appointed route.

Just as they moved past the entrance to the Čumurija Bridge, they heard a loud explosion. At first, everybody thought the car behind had blown a tire, but when officers began pouring out of the car, Governor Potiorek, who was riding with the archduke and Sophie, noticed that his aide-de-camp, Lieutenant Erich von Merizzi, was covered with blood. The tire had indeed blown, but it was caused by a bomb that had exploded nearby, narrowly missing the archduke.

Security protection for the archduke was minimal, despite the fact that more than 70,000 soldiers were stationed just a few miles away. Upon determining the source of the explosion, several policemen from the sparse cordon beside the motorcade dove into the crowd after a tall, swarthy youth. At first sight of them, Čabrinović popped a cyanide pill into his mouth, leaped over a low wall running along the quay, and scurried down the rocky embankment to the river below. Moments later, he flung himself into the water. Policemen jumped in and pulled him out, and proceeded to beat him with the flat sides of their sabers. Frightened and sick to his stomach from the cyanide, Čabrinović vomited all over himself—thereby ridding himself of the poison before it had entered the bloodstream.

When the bomb had exploded, the noise was heard all the way up Appel Quay. The three boys whom Ilić had recruited immediately panicked and fled. Grabež, who was stationed only one block from Čabrinović, waited until he saw the Archduke's car move off again, and then he too fled—to his uncle's house. There he stuck his bomb under the toilet seat, and left for his home in nearby Pale.

Princip was unnerved when he saw Čabrinović's bomb detonate, but he did not panic. Thirsty for something to drink, he stepped into a coffee house, calculating—almost correctly—that there would be no more chances.

At the town hall, the fuming archduke upbraided Potiorek for such poor police protection, and interrupted the Mayor during his welcoming address, shouting: "Mr. Mayor, I come to Sarajevo on a mission of goodwill, and I get bombs thrown at me. It is positively outrageous!"

Downstairs in the police station Čabrinović was being interrogated. But, scared as he was, he did not reveal the plot to the police. When the archduke and Sophie left the town hall a few minutes later, neither the police nor they knew that they were headed for a rendežvous with death.

After both were seated once again, in the rear of an open car, the procession continued down Appel Quay. The archduke had insisted on paying a visit to von Merizzi in the hospital, although he had been assured that the officer was only superficially wounded. After that, they would probably cancel the rest of the day's activities.

The governor consented to the hospital visit after some objections, but recommended that they drive as fast as possible so as to thwart any second attempt on the archduke's life.

The trip was uneventful until the lead car reached Radell Street, opposite the Latin Bridge, where it turned to the right. The chauffeur was following the original route to the cathedral; for some reason, the governor had failed to inform the drivers of the change in plans.

"Not that way, you fool!" he shouted from the archduke's automobile at the driver of the first car. "Back up and keep down the Quay!"

The archduke's car was now in a full stop, waiting for the first car to back up. Princip, who moments before had come out of the coffee house, was standing in a doorway of a barbershop on that very corner. Although he was taken by surprise, never expecting to see the archduke, he required but a few seconds to assess the situation. Then he bolted from the doorway, across the sidewalk, and into the street. Holding his Browning automatic straight out in front of him, he pointed it at the archduke who was then less than twelve feet away, and fired as rapidly as he could. Six shots were fired before the whack of a saber knocked him to the pavement. He got up and was raising the gun to his own head when a swarm of dismounted cavalrymen and royal guardsmen leaped upon him and pinned him to the ground. Princip was severely hurt: a rib was broken and one arm so badly mangled that it later required amputation.

The archduke's car, which had begun to turn into Radell Street, now had to back up slightly before continuing along the Quay. When the driver shifted into first gear, the car gave a lurch. It was then that Potiorek realized that his guests were dead or dying, for the archduke now slumped heavily over onto his wife, whose body also gave way. Blood was everywhere.

Princip's first shot had ripped through Franz Ferdinand's chest, severed the jugular vein, and lodged in the upper spine. His second shot struck the duchess in the right side. The other four scattered wildly.

The archduke cried to his wife: "Sophie, don't die; live for our children."

She replied weakly: "Franz, are you dying?" Then she expired.

Potiorek heard the archduke mumble several times, each time more and more faintly: "It is nothing, it is nothing, it is nothing...."

Within minutes Princip's accomplices sent off a telegram to Belgrade: "Excellent sale of both horses."

Due in large part to Danilo Ilić's confession, all of the conspirators were apprehended. Ilić, Veljko Čubrilović, and Miško Jovanović were sentenced to death and were hanged on February 3, 1915. All six of the youthful triggermen were under 20 —Princip by a mere two weeks—and thus escaped capital punishment. Princip, Čabrinović, and Grabež were each sentenced to 20 years in prison; the others received sentences of varying duration. Princip, Čabrinović, and Grabež all died in prison— principally of maltreatment—before the end of the war.

Undernourished, ravaged by tuberculosis, and villified by the guards, Princip remained unrepentent till the day of his death on April 28, 1918. He persisted in proclaiming that he was a South Slav nationalist devoted to terrorism.

Princip's years in Serbia and his reading of anarchistic books combined the concepts of fervent nationalism and raw violence. Young, impressionable, emotionally unstable, and politically naive, Princip "mysticized" Serbian nationalism and romanticized violence. The result was a commitment to terrorism.

Princip's dream of union for the South Slavs is now a reality—although dissatisfaction is occasionally voiced by one of the member states—and Bosnia and Herzegovina, together with Serbia, are parts of Titoist Yugoslavia.

To many Yugoslavs, Princip is a hero. Only *his* name, as the true agent of Slavic destiny, appears on the plaque attached to the museum building on that historic corner in Sarajevo. He is called "The Annunciator of Liberty."

PART III: Hangmen, Henchmen & Mystics

13. Eichmann

"I will jump into my grave laughing because the fact that I have the death of five million Jews on my conscience gives me extraordinary satisfaction!"

These words were uttered by Adolf Eichmann. His friend and subordinate, Dieter von Wisliczeny, so testified at the Nuremberg Trials. When Eichmann reviewed the transcript he made only one correction in Wisliczeny's quotation: He changed "Jews" to "enemies of the Reich." But at his own trial in Israel, more than 15 years later, he admitted that he considered the principal "enemies of the Reich" to be the Jewish people. He would have had a bad conscience, he claimed, if he had *not* ordered the Jews killed, for he was duty-bound to follow the orders of the *Führer*.

Eichmann asserted that he held "nothing personal" against the Jews, that in fact—in the words of the old cliché—some of his "best friends" were Jews. He was indeed carrying out orders. But he did so with an enthusiasm and precision that earned him the appellation of "expert on the Jewish Question."

Eichmann could not tolerate anyone who questioned a superior's orders. After reading about the death throes of the Third Reich in a book by Gerhard Boldt, which states that towards the end SS officers became disrespectful toward their superiors, Eichmann wrote in the margin such words as "ass" and "dumb sow," and recommended that the author be "skinned alive for his vileness." To Eichmann, it was clear that the war had been lost because of a lack of blind obedience to superior authority.

The judges at Eichmann's trial were confronted with a monstrous dilemma. Some of the examining psychiatrists claimed he was completely normal; others, that he was a sadist "obsessed with an insatiable urge to kill." But, aside from the love he may have displayed to family and friends, "normal" meant not being appreciably different from other Nazis. Stated differently, for

Eichmann to have been truly "normal" he would have had to be *abnormal,* and would have had to disapprove of the Nazi regime.

Eichmann was thoroughly abnormal by the standards of contemporary civilized society. Hannah Arendt, in the epilogue to her book about Eichmann's trial, *Eichmann in Jerusalem,* suggests these appropriate closing words to the defendant by the presiding judge:

> Just as you supported and carried out a policy of not wanting to share the earth with the Jewish people and the people of a number of other nations—as though you and your superiors had any right to determine who should and who should not inhabit the world—we find that no one, that is, no member of the human race, can be expected to want to share the earth with you. This is the reason, and the only reason, you must hang.

His trial ended in his being hanged despite all testimony about his high regard for individual Jews, following orders of superior authority, and claims of normalcy.

Eichmann was born on March 19, 1906 in Solingen, Germany—a city in the Ruhr district famed for the manufacture of cutlery. When he was four, Adolf's mother died in childbirth, and within a few months the family left for Linz, Austria to join their relatives. For four years the father remained unmarried, and did his best—with the help of a married sister who lived nearby—to provide for his family. Unskilled, he went from job to job, eking out a living. The children barely had enough to eat and always looked shabby. Adolf swore that one day he would have a better life.

But Adolf was unhappy in Linz for other reasons. Rejected by his playmates, he became withdrawn and moody. He seldom joined in games and picnics with others, and preferred to stay at home where he spent countless hours in loneliness. He was frequently sick, and used his illness as an excuse for avoiding contact with boys and girls of his own age.

Adolf was no more successful in his relations with grown-ups. His father was too preoccupied to spend much time with him, and his stepmother was overbearing and unsympathetic; his teachers considered him lazy and below average. With every passing year Adolf became more introverted.

Adolf's hatred for Jews may very well have begun during these early years. Being slight and dark-complexioned, he fit the stereotype of a Semite. His playmates were quick to notice that they could anger him by simply calling him "the little Jew," and they missed no opportunity to do so. Adolf felt self-conscious about his long nose and would fly into a rage when taunted about it by his schoolmates. They would chant, in a sing-song voice: "Little revolver-snoot, little revolver-snoot . . ." Unable to unburden himself at home to his father or his part-Jewish step-mother, Adolf now became a bundle of intense, disturbed emotions, capable of erupting at the slightest provocation.

Then, as a young teen-ager, he made an abrupt turnabout and began to take pleasure in taunting certain Jewish class-mates in much the same way as others had poked fun at him. He once went so far as to join a gang of youths as they beat another youngster to a pulp. From that time on, he repeatedly partici-pated in sadistic acts of this nature.

Soon, Adolf became the ringleader. During one of their wild sprees a Jewish teen-ager was viciously beaten. The youngster quit school and, in a fit of depression, hanged himself several days later.

Eichmann, himself, quit school after less than two years in a technical high school. He nevertheless fancied himself an engi-neer, and throughout his life listed "engineering" as his profes-sion whenever occupation was asked for, on official documents. Although never one to devote himself to study, he did value titles, rank, and the accompanying status.

Eichmann's first job was as a salesman for the Upper Aus-trian Elektrobau Company. But he spent the next five and a half years—between 1927 and 1932— with the Vacuum Oil Com-pany of Austria. These years were among the most pleasant of his life. His route as a salesman took him through western Aus-tria and parts of eastern Germany. On one of his trips, he en-countered a group of Hitler's Brown Shirts and was immediately attracted to the Nazi movement.

Eichmann joined the movement, and when he was fired from his job, he blamed it on his affiliation with the Austrian Nazi Party. What is more likely is that his heavy drinking and carousing interfered with the performance of his sales duties.

Late in 1932, Eichmann went on active duty with the SS. However, because the party was in disfavor with the govern-ment he was soon threatened with arrest and found it necessary to escape to Germany in February, 1933. He ended up in a training camp in Berlin. After a period of service in Passau, he was sent for further training and indoctrination to a camp in East Prussia. When Eichmann returned, he was completely com-mitted to National Socialism and was determined to make his way to the top. He was greatly assisted in his climb by Ernst Kaltenbrunner, later chief of the Reich Security Office.

Unmarried SS officers were usually passed over for promotion or choice assignments in favor of married men. Since 1931, Eichmann had been dating Veronika Liebl, a native Sudetenlander raised in the vicinity of Salzburg, Austria. He had met her while on a trip for the Vacuum Oil Company. In the spring of 1935, he married Vera, as she was often called, and one year later their first child, a son named Klaus, was born.

At this time, Eichmann was stationed in Berlin doing relatively unimportant clerical work. But he was clever enough to realize that, in order to advance, he needed a specialty. He had heard a great deal of talk about "the Jewish Question" and set out to become an expert on the elimination of Jews from Germany.

He read every book and pamphlet dealing with Jews and Zionism that he could locate—a remarkable undertaking for a person who had always avoided research and study. He even decided to learn Yiddish and Hebrew. As a native of Germany, he obviously had very little difficulty with the Yiddish. But, Hebrew was a different matter. Despite Eichmann's claims to the contrary, the extent of his Hebrew knowledge was limited to a few dozen words. A braggart, he used to belittle Jews who could not speak Hebrew by flaunting the few words he had mastered.

Eichmann's efforts at becoming an expert on Jewish matters did not go unnoticed. Heinrich Himmler considered him so valuable that he appointed him the director of a project which called for the establishment of a Jewish "museum." This was an ominous sign for the Jews. When the Nazis became intent on destroying a group, they often established "museums."

Eichmann warmed to his job immediately. He began to delve into Jewish history and literature, and to deliver anti-Semitic speeches. Dressed to the hilt in a Nazi uniform with shiny, black boots, Eichmann was exhilarated, and strutted about with great pride.

His opportunity for the exercise of the power he so madly longed for came with the German annexation of Austria on March 11, 1938. In Vienna, there was a heavy concentration of Jews, and Eichmann was assigned the task of arranging for their "emigration." However, very soon Reinhard Heydrich, chief of the Vienna Gestapo (secret state police) bureau, accepted Eichmann's suggestion to incorporate all bureaus in Austria dealing with the resettlement of Jews under the roof of one main Gestapo office. Thus, Eichmann placed himself in a position of even greater power, and despite the fact that he had to answer to three superior officers, it was he who was the acknowledged "expert" on Jewish matters.

The Nazis set the scene for carrying out the mass emigration of Jews by creating an atmosphere that left no doubt that "emigration" really meant "expulsion." The dramatic instrument they employed was a pogrom called *Kristallnacht,* or Night of Broken Glass. On November 9, 1938, the fifteenth anniversary of Hitler's 1923 beer hall Putsch, 7,500 Jewish shop windows were smashed. The stores were then looted or burned to the ground. In addition, almost 20,000 Jewish men were rounded up and placed in concentration camps. Is it any wonder that Jews were more than willing to emigrate?

The requirement for emigration was the payment of a so-called "flight tax." However, payment of this tax was tantamount to turning over all of one's property to the Nazis—which meant having to start anew somewhere else with little more than a few personal belongings. Those Jews who were fortunate enough or sufficiently farsighted to have deposited some of their money in Swiss banks were, of course, better off. But many of them felt that, for humane reasons, they should assist the destitute. The German government and the Nazi party made substantial profits from this cruel venture.

Eichmann was among those voicing approval of *Kristallnacht.* And why not? It had made his job that much simpler. Whereas previously he had had to negotiate with Jewish leaders to gain their cooperation in convincing groups to leave the country, the mask had now fallen, and the Jewish people were able to recognize the danger for what it was. Eichmann no longer had to put up a false front.

During the first eight months of his work as head of the Center for the Emigration of Austrian Jews, Eichmann expelled 45,000 people—a record which exceeded the best efforts of his counterpart in Germany where, during the same period, only 19,000 were "resettled." By the end of 1939, Eichmann had rid Austria of 165,000 people, approximately 62 per cent of its Jewish population. He was extremely satisfied with his accomplishment.

After the German occupation of Czechoslovakia on March 15, 1939, Eichmann opened an emigration office in Prague. He was determined to "cleanse" the country of Jews in short order. As in Austria, he began the process of negotiating with Jewish leaders whose job it was to find sufficient money for the flight tax. These leaders experienced difficulty in meeting the goal set for them—mainly because German authorities had already impounded a great deal of Jewish money. When the Jewish leaders protested to Eichmann, he was furious, and he warned them that he would arrest 300 men each day and ship them off to concentration camps if the money was not immediately forthcoming. Miraculously, the money appeared, and thousands of Jews, equipped with phony visas, began to stream out of Czechoslovakia.

The invasion of Poland in September 1939 brought with it an enlargement of the "Jewish problem." There were 3.2 million Jews living in Poland; they had to be removed. Initially, it was proposed that they be resettled in a 400-square-mile area near the Russian frontier, and for a time this proposal was followed. Eichmann was especially efficient and, in the first four months of operation, dispatched 88,000 Jews to Lublin.

But to some Nazi leaders this was not the proper solution. They insisted that the country be completely *judenrein,* "cleansed of Jews." Odilo Globocnik, formerly the Gauleiter of Vienna, and a friend and admirer of Eichmann, had a better idea. Placed in charge of Lublin, in November 1939, he accepted deported Jews for forced labor in some 50 camps that were built between 1939 and 1941. After they had literally been worked to death, Eichmann deported Jews to replace them. The troublesome types—the sick and the young—were done away with in four extermination camps in the same area. This plan became the pattern to be followed by all of Germany and the occupied countries. When expulsion was not feasible, Jews were sent to camps. If they could not be worked to death, they were eliminated by other prompt and efficient means.

During 1940, Eichmann worked assiduously on a plan, approved by Hitler, to send hordes of Jews to Madagascar for permanent resettlement. For a brief time, it was thought that the idea would succeed, but the financial exigencies were such that the scheme had to be abandoned. In its place, Eichmann established a similar center in Theresienstadt, Czechoslovakia, but the plan was never completely successful. The Jews were simply too numerous to be disposed of in a humane fashion. The administration of the center was too complex and costly, and with a new front opening in Russia, the war effort demanded full attention.

In 1941, Eichmann was assigned the responsibility of disposing of the entire Jewish population of Germany and the occupied lands. His new appointment coincided roughly with Hitler's order for the "Final Solution," a euphemism for the destruction of European Jewry.

Eichmann approached his new chore with enthusiasm, and promptly began his merciless program of liquidating Jews. There was to be no more "emigration" or "resettlement." From this time forward there was to be only extermination. Although Eichmann later maintained that he did nothing but follow orders, he was in fact the architect of the plan. Although he later compared himself to an officer supplying bombs and armaments to flyers without knowing the use to which they would be put, history informs us that he was fully aware of the anticipated goals of the procedures he established. To Eichmann, the Jewish people were mere objects, not human beings. Just being Jewish made them instruments of their own destruction. They were the bombs and they were the bombed.

When the regular army moved into a country, it was followed by one or more battalions, called *Einsatzgruppen,* under the command of Eichmann. Their task was to eliminate all "enemies of the state"—hence, the killing of Jews.

A special group of four *Einsatzgruppen* began their work in July 1941. Each commander was a friend of Eichmann and was assigned to head a battalion. Each of the four was a dedicated murderer.

Franz Stahlecker was perhaps the man most devoted to his job. Within three months he had killed 136,000 Jewish men, women and children. Before the year was out he had doubled that number. His method was direct: He shot people through the head.

Arthur Nebe worked more slowly than Stahlecker, but not less enthusiastically or efficiently. In the first three months, he had executed a mere 25,000 Jews. But he had persistence, and maintained this average for three years. And he showed imagination.

In a letter to the SS medical corps, dated June 28, 1944, Nebe recommended that an experiment be carried out on a group of 915 gypsies to determine how long human beings can live on a diet of sea water. The doctors learned little more than what common sense would have taught: People will live a little longer on a diet of sea water alone than on no water at all; and less time than on a diet consisting only of food. Drs. Wirth and Kelmeir read the results of the experiment with more fiendishness than medical curiosity. They were the same pair who, during the middle 1930s, had injected assorted liquids and poisons into the bloodstreams of 75,000 incurably sick, retarded, and insane people. They also supervised the killing and castration of habitual criminals, race-polluters, and *Mischlinge* (half-breeds, that is, half-Jewish and half-Aryan).

Otto Rasch served less than two years as commander of his *Einsatzgruppe*. He was not young when he took over command, and he developed Parkinson's disease in 1943. As a reward for the Jews he did manage to wipe out during his brief career, he received a substantial monetary bonus.

The head of the fourth *Einsatzgruppe,* Otto Ohlendorf, was one of Eichmann's best friends. Although Russian partisans blew Stahlecker's brains out, and the Gestapo executed Nebe for suspected cooperation in the plot to assassinate Hitler in 1944, Ohlendorf was the only one of the four executioners to be tried and hanged.

From the verbal accounts of Ohlendorf, as well as others, the world was able to learn how the mass executions were performed. Trucks were crammed with human beings who had been told they were being "resettled," but were actually being transported to huge ditches. There, the trucks were unloaded, and the people were forced to strip and lay their clothing in neat, little piles. They were then lined up along the trenches, and the force of one bullet was usually sufficient to catapult each body into the ditch. No energy had to be used to move the heavy corpses to the burial places.

When the sides of the ditches were filled to overflowing, the next group of victims was ordered to walk out over the dead bodies to the center. There they, too, were shot.

A variation of this theme required the people to climb down into a trench, stand in a particular spot, and wait for an SS rifleman to shoot them. The scene was so terrifying that even some of the SS men were sickened or driven mad when they witnessed how low and debased their partners in murder had become.

Gassing Jews while still in the transport trucks was another system of annihilation, but the SS men complained about the nuisance of having to direct the unloading of so many bodies. Upwards of 100 persons could be transported in each truck. The trip from the assembly area to the graves took about 15 minutes, time enough for the poison gas to do its work. A Jewish work crew then pulled the bodies out and hosed down the interior of the trucks to clear them of vomit and excrement. They then knocked the gold out of the victims' teeth and sheared their hair off for mattress stuffing.

It is debatable how many actual executions Eichmann witnessed. He reported that he found the executions disturbing at first, but later grew accustomed to them. On one occasion, Eichmann was standing very close to a child being shot by an SS sergeant. The spilled brains and blood had to be washed from his coat. But, several minutes later, he was back to watch the rest of the horror show.

Himmler was convinced that gassing was more humane than shooting, drowning, or burning. He soon ordered that all executions be carried out in this manner, most of them in permanently established gas chambers. It was certainly the most efficient means devised. Nearly 1,000 persons could be crammed into a chamber if they all held their arms over their heads. Eichmann found the method desirable, largely because it spared the SS men the trauma of having to watch so many people die!

As early as 1942, shallow graves became so numerous that a better method of disposing of the bodies had to be found. Crematories at Auschwitz, Buchenwald, Dachau, and elsewhere were already in daily use, but they were too busy to handle additional work. Besides, Himmler wanted to destroy as much evidence as possible in a short time. He therefore ordered Colonel Paul Blobel, an architect, to devise a means of incinerating exposed or recently buried corpses. Blobel engaged the services of chemists who developed a much more highly combustible liquid than gasoline. Trenches were uncovered and the fluid was poured over the exposed bodies. The fluid was then ignited. It sometimes took several days before the bodies were completely reduced to ashes. Blobel reported to Eichmann that he always made sure a ditch glowed bright red at the very bottom before the fueling of the fire was stopped. Eichmann praised Blobel for his work and had him instruct others in his method.

But Eichmann was never satisfied. "Exterminate more, more, more," he demanded as he aimed for an ever higher "production quota." The 184 concentration camps in Germany and occupied countries responded by producing tens of thousands, then hundreds of thousands, then millions of dead bodies. Hannah Arendt has subtitled her book on Eichmann "A Report on the Banality of Evil." Here, banality and evil intersected at a point so distant from reality that only Satan himself can conceive of their magnitude.

Eichmann insisted that he, personally, never killed anyone. The prosecution tried unsuccessfully—and unnecessarily—to prove that he did. It is fitting that the evidence proves that the archkiller and base coward, Adolf Eichmann, murdered just one child. In brief, the story, as told by the witness, a Philadelphia resident, goes like this:

In the 1930's the witness was a rabbi and a businessman in

Prague. He had been introduced to Eichmann as "an important Jew in the community." Years later, in 1943, the two met and the rabbi failed to recognize Eichmann; but Eichmann recognized him, and forced the man to accompany him to his office, where the rabbi witnessed a scene he never forgot.

Eichmann, seated behind a fine mahogany desk under a huge picture of Hitler, ordered five soldiers to bring in some children—a 13-year-old and an eight-year-old boy and a seven-month-old infant. "You will remember me after today," he said to the rabbi. To the SS man he said: "Let's teach these Jews a lesson."

At the time, the rabbi did not understand what Eichmann meant. Later he learned that the boys were being punished for having kicked the SS men in anger over their having struck an old woman over the head with a rifle butt.

The two boys stood in front of Eichmann's desk. Two of the soldiers held the eight-year-old's hand firmly down on the the corner of the desktop while a third calmly touched his burning cigarette to the back of the child's hand. The boy screamed and writhed in pain, but the men held him there. After a few minutes he fainted and was carried off. The rabbi could still smell burning flesh.

Next, an SS man plunged a long needle into the flame of Eichmann's desk lighter and held it there until the shaft was red-hot. Then, without a word, he thrust it into the eyeball of the 13-year-old boy, who was being held immobile by two burly soldiers. The child was dragged out of the room, screaming but conscious.

Eichmann said sarcastically to the rabbi: "Don't be afraid; we won't harm you; you are an important Jew." Leaning closer, he added: "You Jews are the scourge of the earth. The way to destroy you is to kill the young. The old people will kill themselves."

Then Eichmann made a sign to the SS man holding the infant. The soldier stammered something to the effect that he couldn't. Eichmann rose from his desk in a rage and strode toward the soldier. "Report to your captain," he shouted.

But then in the next moment he was calling the soldier back and saying, almost cajolingly: "Wait, I'll teach *you* a lesson. You mustn't be soft. After all, the child is only a Jew."

With that, Eichmann pulled his pistol from its holster and shot the baby through the head. Seeing blood spatters on the gun, he flung it at an SS man and told him also to clean up the mess on the floor.

"Now that's the way to do it," he said to the stunned soldier. "Report to your captain. I'll see that he gives you some duties that will toughen up your nerves."

Turning to the rabbi, he said: "I'll feed this child to my dogs and use what's left for soap and fertilizer."

The rabbi lunged at Eichmann, but Eichmann grabbed up a Luger from his desk and cracked the man soundly over the head. "Take him away," he ordered. "He won't forget me now."

The rabbi didn't forget. He remembered very clearly through his years at Auschwitz and the years between the end of the war and Eichmann's capture. He volunteered to testify at Eichmann's trial.

In 1945, Eichmann pulled a disappearing act. Always the coward, he was going to make sure he saved his own skin. Unlike his hero, Adolf Hitler, he did not have the courage to commit suicide. Disguised as a Luftwaffe corporal and using a fictitious name, he was at first captured by the Americans. But, just as he had figured, they did not pay particular attention to him. He escaped once, but was taken prisoner again. Still, no one really paid much attention to him.

Throughout the next 15 years, his peregrinations took him to different parts of Germany and Austria, to the Middle East, and eventually to South America. When he finally settled in Argentina, he sent for his wife and children. There, after a time, he built a house in a suburb of Buenos Aires and went to work. When he was captured, he was employed under the name of Ricardo Klement as a laborer for a Mercedes-Benz automobile plant. He had done such an excellent job of covering his tracks that only *he* was able to fill in the gaps.

The same methodical ways that he had employed in the extermination of millions of human beings led to his downfall. For some time, Israeli agents had been shadowing Eichmann. They had had an exceedingly difficult job in pursuing him. For a long time they didn't have a photograph of him. For many years Eichmann had avoided being photographed, and what few pictures were around, he had managed to destroy. But, then, one turned up. And information relating to his whereabouts began to trickle in.

Now they had found him and were on the point of grabbing him. They observed that he did the same thing every day: He left home at the same time, took the same bus to work, ate his lunch in the same restaurant, and returned home at the same hour.

The whole operation had been planned with the utmost

care. At five p.m., May 11, 1960, three Israeli agents waited in a car outside the factory. Workers streamed out, but no Eichmann!

Perplexed and panicky, the agents could not understand what had happened to alter Eichmann's usual departure time. One of the men finally went up to a guard at the gate and inquired about the whereabouts of Señor Klement. The man replied immediately and without suspicion that he was attending a workers' meeting till six o'clock.

Relieved, the agents waited. Promptly at six, Eichmann walked out of the factory and boarded a bus. The agents followed it in their car to a point on Liniares Avenue. They watched Eichmann as he dismounted, stepped into a tobacco shop, bought some cigarettes, and emerged to continue on foot in the direction of Coriantes and Dorgunal Avenues at the Buenos Aires city limit. There he always caught a suburban bus which took him to his home in San Fernando.

When Eichmann was 20 paces away from the tobacco shop, a man leaped from the black sedan and hustled him into the back seat of the car. Eichmann received stony silence to his questions: "Who are you? What do you want? Are you Americans?"

As they approached a stop light, the agents saw a policeman standing on the corner. One of the men jabbed a gun in Eichmann's ribs and said in German, "One shout out of you, Eichmann, and you're a dead man."

They took Eichmann to a house on the other side of the city. The question was to the point: "Are you Adolf Eichmann?"

"I have always feared something like this would happen," he mumbled under his breath. "Yes, I am Adolf Eichmann."

The men ordered him to strip. They found his blood type and the insignia of his SS organization tattooed—but now somewhat obliterated—in his left armpit. The tattoo was the trademark of the SS commanders. A doctor entered the room and checked his head and collarbone for evidence of old fractures and compared the outlines with X-rays. Photographs were passed around for everyone to examine so as to confirm his identity. He was ordered to put on an SS hat. When the agents had determined that the hostage was undeniably Adolf Eichmann, he was chained to an iron bed and guarded carefully.

For a week, Eichmann was incarcerated. Then, quite suddenly one night, he was driven to the municipal airport and put aboard an El Al airliner, and flown to Israel.

After a long and exacting trial, Eichmann was sentenced to

die. On Thursday, May 31, 1962, shortly before midnight, he was hanged. His body was immediately cremated, and the ashes were taken aloft in a plane and scattered in Israeli waters.

Eichmann went to the gallows in an uncowardly fashion—erect and without a hood by his own request. But this was just another indication of no more than that same fanaticism and madness of Nazi discipline that had governed his life throughout the years.

"Long live Germany, long live Argentina, long live Austria!" he shouted. "I shall never forget them!"

Nor will the world ever forget mass-murderer Adolf Eichmann!

14. Rasputin

It was one of those bitter cold winter nights in Siberia. Hunched around the big stove in the kitchen of the cart driver, Yefim Andreevich Novykh, six men from the village of Pokrovskoe quietly discussed the misfortune of one of their friends—a poor fellow driver whose horse had been stolen the day before. The animal had disappeared without a trace, and the peasant was now deprived of his means of earning a livelihood.

Suddenly, the child who had been slumbering behind the stove rose from his pallet and leaped upon the massive shoulders of one of the villagers. "*You*, Pyotr Alexandrovich, *you* stole the horse!" he shrieked. An eerie, piercing look passed from the child to Pyotr Alexandrovich, and he then began to pound the big man's chest.

"Grischka, what is the matter with you?" shouted old Yefim. And without waiting for an answer, he covered his embarrassment with an apology. "The boy has been sick," he said. "Very sick."

"Yes, I know," said Pyotr Alexandrovich. "It's all right. He's only playing a game."

At this remark Grischka began to laugh. It was a high-pitched laugh that quickly turned into a rasping cackle. The child grasped at the man's shoulders and dug his knees into the man's back with such force that Pyotr Alexandrovich almost toppled over.

"That's enough!" yelled the father. To the group he said, "Grischka just hasn't been the same since Misha died."

Misha, Grischka's older brother, had recently fallen into the half-frozen Tura River. Twelve-year-old Grischka plunged in to rescue him, but they would have both drowned had a man not come along and pulled them out. Both developed a high fever, and Misha died three days later.

Grischka continued to suffer from the effects of the exposure. His fever rose and fell from day to day, and he had lost a good deal of weight.

Then, his parents noticed that his personality was changing. He was becoming a different child. Before the accident, Grischka had been happy and outgoing; now he was moody and withdrawn, and given to strange outbursts.

Grischka returned to his place behind the stove. The men, shaken and perplexed by the odd scene, got up one by one, said their farewells, and left to trudge home through the snow. As each made his way home, he was puzzled by the boy's accusation. Pyotr Alexandrovich—the richest man in Pokrovskoe—why would he have to steal a horse? Besides, he had been the most vocal of the group in demanding that the culprit be tracked down.

But doubts assailed the men, and one by one they altered their route, turning in the direction of Pyotr Alexandrovich's house. All arrived at the barn at almost the same time, and each hid, watching and waiting.

In a few minutes Pyotr Alexandrovich was seen leading the stolen horse from his barn off into the blackness of a thicket. At the first row of trees, the men caught up with him and beat him senseless. To them, few crimes were more serious than stealing a coachman's horse. But Pyotr Alexandrovich was lucky; they spared his life.

After his guests had left, Yefim Andreevich questioned his son: Why had he made such an accusation? Had he seen anything? Had he heard anything?

No?

Then, why did he think Pyotr Alexandrovich had stolen the horse?

"I just knew it," replied the boy. And his eyes took on that same penetrating quality his father had witnessed earlier. Yefim shuddered. What kind of son did he have who could "just know" without having seen it happen? Was he clairvoyant?

When Grigori (Grischka) Yefimovich (also spelled Efimovich) grew up, he became a coachman like his father. He delivered goods and carried passengers to neighboring villages and to distant towns. His morals were loose and unrestrained and the name "Rasputin," meaning "the dissolute one" was bestowed upon him. During the day he worked like a Trojan, but at night he either chased after women or drank himself into a stupor.

When he was 33, Rasputin's life took a new turn. He was hired by a novice monk to drive him to his monastery at Verkhoture. On the way, the two men talked about religion. The monk was astonished at the breadth of knowledge that Rasputin possessed, and Rasputin, in turn, was fascinated by what he heard about the monastery. For this was no ordinary Orthodox monastery, but the headquarters of the radical Khlysty sect.

Externally, the monks lived according to Orthodox practice, but privately they held a faith that was greatly at variance with conventional Christian doctrine. This faith involved a mystical conviction that only those who had been sinners could be one with Christ here on earth. They believed that Christ was constantly being reincarnated in individuals and that the path to redemption was through sin and subsequent purification. Without having sinned, man could not gain salvation. Once a man was purified, he acquired the supernatural powers associated with Christ, and was then called *starets*, "wise old man" or "man of God." This type of religion appealed greatly to Rasputin.

Rasputin decided to join this order of monks, and he took up residence at the monastery for four months. Upon leaving, he became a *strannik*, a wandering mendicant who preached to the common people and served as their healer. He was very successful, and he quickly became known for his curative powers.

Just at that time—August 12, 1904—a son was born to the Empress. Nicholas and Alexandra already had four children, but they were all girls. The arrival of little Alexis was greeted with great rejoicing throughout Russia. He was the first male heir to be born to a reigning Russian monarch since the 17th century.

But Alexis' parents were worried. They noticed that the czarevich was afflicted with severe bruises and swellings from the simple act of crawling on the floor. Also, at times he would start to bleed for no apparent reason. The doctors sadly informed the czar that his son was a hemophiliac.

At the beginning of the 20th century, there existed no effective medical treatment for hemophilia, and Nicholas and Alexandra were filled with despair over their child's condition. They reacted like most parents of hemophiliacs; they were overprotective of their son.

The czar and czaritza searched anxiously for a cure, and were willing to grasp at any straw. A very devout couple, they prayed often and fervently, hoping against hope that God would intervene and restore their little boy to health. For years their hopes were raised, then shattered, as Alexis' condition improved and declined over and over again. By the time the child had reached four years of age, Alexandra had acquired the psychosomatic symptoms of heart disease, and was confined for a time to a wheelchair. The czar wept often in private, but outwardly kept the optimistic front necessary to maintain the stability of the government. Consequently, the people of Russia had no inkling of the nature of Alexis' illness.

When Rasputin arrived in St. Petersburg, in 1905, his fame had preceded him. The sick and the lame came from near and far to see him and to hear him. They wanted to talk with the *starets,* and to be guided by him.

In time, the aristocracy learned of Rasputin's presence in the city and invited him into their homes and to their social functions. The women found him particularly fascinating. They were attracted to him despite his shabby appearance, crude manners and repulsive body odor.

The empress was among Rasputin's admirers, having been introduced to him in 1907 by Anna Vyrubova, a commoner whose father was director of the Chancellery, and whose husband was an army officer stationed in the court. Anna was Alexandra's closest friend. Completely convinced of Rasputin's heaven-sent powers, Anna urged the empress to seek Rasputin's advice about the care of her son.

The empress accepted the suggestion and invited Rasputin to be her guest at the royal palace. His presence and manner cast an immediate spell over Alexandra. There was something about his sonorous voice, his fierce blue-gray eyes, his heavy, matted beard, his self-assurance and even his rudeness that wove a web of mystery about him. And the mystic spell that Alexandra had succumbed to was never broken—even when incontrovertible proof of Rasputin's profligacy and unorthodoxy was laid before her.

In 1912, when the imperial family was on vacation at their hunting lodge in Poland, Alexis suffered a fall that produced a swelling in his groin. It soon disappeared, much to the relief of the empress. But one day, after the child had taken a bumpy coach ride, it reappeared, looking much worse than before. Alexandra was frantic with worry. The swelling grew and grew until Alexis could no longer straighten out one of his legs. The pain was constant and the boy's terrifying screams for help were more than his mother could bear. Alexandra then acted in a way that was to affect the history of Russia: she telegraphed Rasputin, seeking his advice and urging him to pray for Alexis. The child's doctors had given up all hope, and throughout the country people were entreating Almighty God to save their heir.

The next day Rasputin's answer was received from Siberia. He assured the czaritsa that the Lord had heard her prayers and that Alexis would live. He urged her "not to let the doctors bother Alexis too much."

When Alexandra read the telegram, her heart lightened. As she sat at her son's bedside, she felt confident his health would improve. The very next day, Alexis' bleeding stopped and the swelling in his groin receded. Alexandra was now convinced of Rasputin's powers, and she no longer permitted the court physicians to so much as touch the boy.

To Alexandra, her son's recovery was a miracle, and the miracle worker was Rasputin!

At first, the church leaders were supportive of Rasputin and considered him a true holy man. Later, however, as accounts of his beliefs and stories of his exploits with women came to their attention, they decided that his orthodoxy was in serious question.

When Bishop Hermogen learned that Rasputin had tried to rape a nun, he lost all composure, and beat Rasputin over the head with a three-foot cross, making him take a solemn oath on an icon of the Virgin Mary to cease his philandering. Rasputin had a wife and three children back in Siberia. They were more realistic than the bishop, and had long since given up attempting to reform him.

Complaints against Rasputin became numerous. Alexandra responded by inviting him to the palace less frequently. She refused, however, to end all communication with him. Rumor spread that she was in love with him. Rasputin even boasted that he had kissed her. (From what we know about the close relationship between Alexandra and her husband, the allegation that a love relationship existed between her and Rasputin appears to be groundless. That he had kissed her is probably true-...but such was common practice in the court.)

The rumors persisted, and the new parliament, the Duma, investigated the "Rasputin question." They determined that there was good and sufficient reason to rid Russia of Rasputin. Alexandra vehemently protested, and Rasputin remained.

Russia entered the First World War on August 2, 1914. The populace was jubilant. The chance to fight for Holy Mother Russia and Slavdom excited the masses. Nicholas himself was caught up in the war fever. The czar, for his part, had always loved the pageantry of marching, uniformed troops. He and the military officers looked forward to great battles and ultimate victory.

Rasputin sent a message to the czar advising him against entering any hostilities, and warning him that the war would spell the end of czarism and Russia. Rasputin's advice was ignored, and plans of battle against Germany and Austria-Hungary were formulated.

But the winning of the war was not as easy as Nicholas had

imagined and, by Christmas, Russia had lost an estimated 750,000 men, and another 200,000 had been wounded. The czar decided to visit the front.

Halfway between the Austrian and German fronts, a permanent camp had been set up. The czar, housed aboard his private train, helped Grand Duke Nicholas and his generals in the planning of the attacks. He was elated by the activity and felt very much in his element. He was confident that the war would turn in his favor shortly.

In the fall of 1915, the czarevich was brought to join his father at the front. Not only was the czar lonely, and in want of company; he also thought that it would benefit the boy to get away from his mother and the women at the court.

The morale of the soldiers was instantly lifted when they saw two members of the royal house among them. On occasion, even Alexandra would come to visit. This was especially heartening to the men. Many had felt that the empress was not concerned about them; but now they had proof that Alexandra loved Russia as much as they did.

Alexis was still with his father at the front in the spring of 1916, when, one day, he was stricken with a severe nosebleed. The doctors were powerless to stop the bleeding, and the emperor, thoroughly shaken, took Alexis and rushed home.

When Alexandra saw the state of her child, she panicked and summoned Rasputin. The parents, taking up their watch by the boy's bed, were sure that the end was at hand. But, in the middle of the night, Rasputin appeared in the bedroom without warning and knelt by the child's side. He muttered a prayer, made the sign of the cross, and said to Alexandra: "Don't worry. He'll be all right." In the morning Alexis *was* well, and the czar went back to the front.

Under pressure from his wife, both because of Grand Duke Nicholas's dislike of Rasputin and because of the army's continuing retreats, the czar decided, in 1916, to assume full command of his forces. This was a serious error for two reasons. First, although the czar was militarily knowledgeable, and was willing to take advice from his generals, he was not thoroughly schooled in war tactics. Second, by absenting himself for extended periods from civilian affairs, he left a void at home.

In his absence, anti-czarist forces began to emerge. Alexandra, now in charge, attempted, on the advice of Rasputin, to undertake countermeasures to combat the internal enemy. It soon became clear that she had no idea what she was doing; czarist Russia's doom was sealed.

Alexandra relied entirely on Rasputin's selection of persons for the highest offices in the government. His single criterion for the choice was that the individual "like" him. Otherwise, the person was a "bad" man. After a while, Rasputin started to use the same criterion in recommending military promotions and appointments. He even advised the czar, through Alexandra, of the time and place of attacks. The information, he contended, came to him in dreams.

Even though he consulted regularly with the czaritza, Rasputin lived in a run-down part of St. Petersburg and led his customary immoral life. He was drunk a good deal of the time, and a frequenter of brothels. He was more a degenerate than a holy man. Yet, because he enjoyed the favor of Alexandra, he was able to overcome all criticism, and to maintain his position of power and influence.

The time came, however, when the Duma had had enough, and they called for Rasputin's dismissal. Alexandra ignored the demand, but Prince Felix Felixovich Yussoupov, one of the wealthiest and most influential young men in the country, decided it was up to him to get rid of the czaritza's bearded holy friend.

Yussoupov, not exactly a saint himself, already knew Rasputin, and had even been seen with him on drinking bouts. He didn't think it would be difficult to lure him to a party and poison him. But he needed help.

Yussoupov enlisted the enthusiastic support of four men: Vladimir Purishkevich, an avowed czarist; Lieutenant Suchotin, an army officer; Dr. Lazovert, a Polish physician; and Grand Duke Dmitri, Nicholas's cousin. A fifth man, Minister of the Interior Maklakov, took no active part in the proposed assassination, but fed the group with suggestions and offered them encouragement. At their last meeting he handed Yussoupov a hard-rubber club. "Take it," he said. "It might come in handy."

On the morning of December 18, 1916, Yussoupov telephoned Rasputin. He explained that he wanted to invite him to a small, very private get-together at his house the following evening. Knowing Rasputin's weakness for beautiful women, Yussoupov went on: "My wife Irina has been having terrible headaches lately. She is anxious to meet you, in the hope that you can cure her."

Yussoupov himself was concerned that the invitation might have a phoney ring, but Rasputin took the bait.

"Fine," he said. "What time?"

"It will have to be late—around midnight. Irina doesn't want anyone to know about it."

"Well, pick me up around 11:45."

With that, Rasputin hung up. Yussoupov was trembling. He couldn't believe his good luck. Quickly, he telephoned the others and reported the conversation.

The murder was to take place in a newly renovated cellar below the prince's apartment in the Yussoupov Palace. All morning long, servants brought down pieces of furniture, spread out a rug, and placed various decorative items about the room. When Yussoupov came home for the noonday meal, he instructed his staff to be sure to light a fire that afternoon, so that the room would be warm by evening. He also left orders for sliced meat, cakes, six bottles of red wine, and a steaming samovar with six glasses to be brought downstairs.

The prince did not return to the room until nearly 11 o'clock that night, having been out to dinner. It wasn't long before the other conspirators knocked at the door at the top of the stairs. Yussoupov admitted them and immediately asked Dr. Lazovert: "Where is the poison? Do you have it?"

"Yes, here," he said. He took out a small cardboard box and opened it for all to see. It was filled with cyanide crystals.

"There's enough poison in here to kill six men," Lazovert volunteered.

"Let's get busy," Yussoupov urged from the other side of the room. He was standing next to a long table on which the servants had laid out the food.

Lazovert strode over to the table, and started to take the tops off three slices of cake, exposing the creamy filling. "This will do fine," he said and smiled.

Donning rubber gloves, he began to pulverize the cyanide crystals with a little pestle he took from his pocket. Rapidly, he poured a small amount of the poison onto each piece of cake and then replaced the top carefully, so that it looked the same as before.

"Any one of these three slices will kill him," said the doctor. "He loves chocolate cake, they say. But just in case he isn't hungry, let's give him a dose in the wine, too. We've got plenty of poison."

Yussoupov uncorked two bottles of wine, and Lazovert poured in the rest of the cyanide. He whistled. "Either one of those bottles would kill a horse!" He tossed the empty box into the fire, where it crumpled and turned to ash.

"Did you find a suitable dumping spot for the body?" asked Yussoupov. His question was directed to the grand duke, whose task that day had been to find a break in the ice on the river.

"Right by the Petropavlovsk Bridge," he answered. "There was still a big hole when I came by a little while ago."

Yussoupov moved the furniture around and scattered some glasses and ashtrays about to give the impression that a party had just broken up.

"All is in readiness," he said. "Let's go."

Yussoupov and Lazovert, who was disguised as a chauffeur, drove off to fetch Rasputin. Purishkevich, Grand Duke Dmitri, and Lieutenant Suchotin went upstairs to wait in the prince's study.

When Yussoupov and Lazovert returned with Rasputin, music was heard coming from the second floor.

"What's that?" inquired Rasputin.

"It seems that my wife's guests are still here," said the prince. "I'm sure they'll be gone shortly, and Irina will come right down. Come on in and have something to eat and drink."

Actually, Irina was at the Yussoupovs' country home. The conspirators had put on a record to produce the proper effect.

Rasputin was satisfied, and descended the stairs with his host. Lazovert sneaked up the back stairs to join Purishkevich and the others. They began what they thought would be a short wait.

Rasputin looked around the cozy room, fingering objects here and there, and opening and shutting cabinet doors. It made Yussoupov nervous.

"Won't you sit down, Father Grigori, and have a glass of tea?"

The tea was the only thing not poisoned. Felix had a glass, too.

"Have some cake with your tea."

Yussoupov's hand shook as he picked up the tray and held it for the monk.

Rasputin reached for a wedge and consumed it in a flash. He called for another. "Very good," he said, "but a little too sweet."

Yussoupov sat down opposite Rasputin and watched him. 'How long will it take?' he wondered. 'Surely no more than a few minutes.'

They were chatting about all sorts of things and people. Felix found it hard to concentrate. He looked at his watch. Twenty minutes had passed, yet the victim seemed fine.

Rasputin got up and stepped over to the table with the food and popped the third piece of cake in his mouth.

Felix almost fainted. In desperation, he stammered: "How about a glass of wine? It's our own—from the Crimea."

"Yes—please—my throat is a little dry," said Rasputin. He finished the glass in two gulps. Yussoupov poured him another. Rasputin sat back and said, "Sing me a song."

By this time Felix was so unnerved that he had no idea whether or not he would be able to sing, let alone accompany himself on the guitar. He took the instrument down from the wall, and as he turned around, he saw Rasputin pouring himself a third drink. 'My God, it's not possible,' he thought.

He sat down opposite Rasputin and began to pluck at the guitar, but his fingers were shaking so violently that what he played hardly sounded like a tune.

Yussoupov looked up. Rasputin stared straight at him. It seemed to Felix that the mad monk had suddenly comprehended the purpose of the evening. Rasputin's eyes turned from their normal blue-gray, to green. He sat glued to his chair, his limbs drained of all strength, his mind unable to think. Suddenly, Rasputin's gaze shifted slightly and his eyes clouded over.

"Have some more wine, Father Grigori. Then I'll sing for you."

Rasputin held out his glass, and Felix poured. The monk swallowed the wine. "Well, sing then!" he shouted.

Felix started to sing, his voice quavering. His guitar playing was no better. But what did it matter? Rasputin *had* to collapse any minute now. According to Lazovert's calculations, Rasputin should be filled with enough poison to kill six men and half a horse.

At that moment there was some thumping on the ceiling from the room above. The conspirators were becoming restless and curious.

"What's that?" demanded Rasputin, suddenly fully conscious.

"Must be my wife's friends finally leaving," said Felix. "I'll just go take a quick look."

Before Rasputin could object, Felix was bounding up the steps. On the way he looked at his watch. It was 2:30! Two and one-half hours of eating and drinking poison, and the man was still alive! It was incredible.

Just inside his study Felix found the others crowded together at the door, their revolvers in their hands.

"The poison's not working," Yussoupov bellowed. "The swine has eaten all the cake and drunk wine till it's coming out of his ears, and he's still fine!" Felix was close to hysteria, and his accomplices were too astonished to reply.

Without another word, Felix grabbed Dmitri's gun and

bolted back down the stairs. He would put an end to this business!

When he re-entered the cellar room, Felix saw that the monk had slumped over. It's over, he thought.

But no. Rasputin looked up as Felix approached.

"What's the matter, Grigori Yefimovich? Don't you feel well?" Yussoupov asked.

"No," he said. "My stomach's burning a little." He helped himself to another glass of wine and downed it in two seconds flat.

Yussoupov walked over to a cabinet in a far corner. There was a large cross on top. He studied it deliberately while fingering the pistol in his pocket.

Suddenly, Felix became aware of Rasputin, who was standing behind him. His blood ran cold. He screamed: "Father Grigori, you'd better say a prayer before this cross!"

Felix turned and faced the monk, pistol in hand. Rasputin looked surprised at first, then gentle. Felix fired at Rasputin's chest. With a roar the monk toppled forward and fell to the floor.

Hearing the shot, the men upstairs dashed down to the cellar and huddled around Rasputin's prone form. The front of his white peasant blouse was stained red, but his heart was still pumping blood. His fists were clenched, and his eyes were tightly closed.

"He's still alive!" someone said.

Dr. Lazovert was searching for a pulse. After five minutes, he straightened up and announced: "He's done for."

Back upstairs, the men poured themselves some strong drinks and talked about how they were to dispose of the corpse. Worried that someone may have seen Rasputin enter the grounds, they decided to make it appear that he was leaving. Suchotin, who was closest in size and build to Rasputin, put on the monk's coat and fur hat and, with Lazovert acting as his "chauffeur," walked outside. Dmitri followed. They planned to drive around for a while and return.

Purishkevich and Yussoupov sat together and smoked. After a time Felix was seized by a desire to see the body again. He had a driving urge to return to the scene of the crime. He invited Purishkevich to come along, but the latter said that he had seen quite enough of Rasputin.

Felix opened the door to the cellar room, switched on a light, and looked around. There lay Rasputin, on the edge of the carpet where they had dragged him. Felix knew he was being ridiculous. Nevertheless, he felt relieved to find Rasputin.

Then, without any clear understanding of why he was doing it, Yussoupov leaned over and grasped the body by both arms and shook it violently. When he let go, the body fell back on the floor like a ton of lead.

He stared at Rasputin's face. What in God's name was happening? First one eye, then the other, opened and gazed at him. The facial muscles began to work, giving the appearance of one who was chewing. Felix was rooted to the spot. His hair felt like it was standing on end. His throat was so constricted that he could not utter a sound.

Then the impossible happened. Rasputin pulled himself to his feet and lunged at Yussoupov. He was foaming at the mouth, and his hands looked like grappling hooks as he tried to get at Yussoupov's throat.

Felix felt his knees buckle. He staggered backward, and Rasputin caught hold of him and held him in a viselike grip. With a mighty effort, Felix pulled himself free and headed for the steps.

Rasputin was behind him. Like a beast he crawled up the stairs on all fours, covered with blood.

Yussoupov ran into the study and shrieked at Purishkevich: "He's still alive! He tried to choke me!"

Purishkevich, who up to this time had been the steadiest of the lot, turned white.

"Give me your pistol!" screamed Felix.

Purishkevich started to unpack the weapon, which he had just finished putting back into his holster, when he heard a loud noise. Rasputin had ripped open the locked door leading to the outside.

Purishkevich ran down the back stairs and saw Rasputin staggering across the snow. Yussoupov stood motionless in his study, his heart pounding wildly.

Two shots rang out. Awakened from his transfixed state, Felix hurried out the front way and ran around to the rear courtyard in time to hear two more shots and see Rasputin tumble into the snow. Purishkevich was standing several feet from the doorway with the pistol still in his hand. Then he turned and went back into the house.

At that moment a policeman ran up to Yussoupov and inquired about the shots. Yussoupov replied that it was nothing, some drunken guests had been taking pot shots at a dog. The policeman did not appear to be fully convinced. He looked around for a while, but, seeing nothing suspicious, left the scene. The massive body had fallen behind a huge mound of snow, and was out of view.

When Felix stepped around the mound to check the body, he found two of his servants standing over it. They helped Yussoupov carry the corpse back down into the cellar room, promising that they would not utter a word about the incident.

Dismissing the servants, Yussoupov and Purishkevich looked in wonderment at the beaten, battered, and bullet-ridden body on the flagstones. Felix was holding the rubber truncheon Maklakov had given him earlier, and which he had grabbed before rushing out into the yard. Suddenly, he was overcome by a surge of anger. In a frenzy, he beat the corpse about the head unceasingly, until Purishkevich forcibly pulled him away.

When the others returned and saw the state of the body, they were aghast. They quickly tied the hands and feet—no one wanted to take any more chances—and wrapped the corpse in several muslin sheets. Dr. Lazovert sent Yussoupov to bed. The other three then lugged the body out to the car and drove off with it in the direction of the Petropavlovsk Bridge. There they pushed it out, and it plunged into the black waters below. Everyone breathed a sigh of relief as Rasputin disappeared under the ice. Dr. Lazovert assured everyone that by the time the spring thaw came, the body would be gone forever.

The next day, the police interrogated Yussoupov again, and he repeated the dog story. The empress was not satisfied, and ordered a thorough investigation. When the police found one of Rasputin's overshoes on the Petropavlovsk Bridge, they sent divers into the river. The body was retrieved. Upon examination, it was discovered that the lungs were filled with water, and that Rasputin had freed one arm from his bonds!

Alexandra wanted the conspirators executed, but the czar, in whose hands the matter ultimately lay, was content to banish Yussoupov to his estate in Tursk, and the grand duke to Persia. Because of the lack of evidence, the others were not prosecuted.

True to Grigori Yefimovich's prediction, czarism came to an end in less than two years. The czar and his entire family were shot and bludgeoned to death by the revolutionaries. Then their bodies were hacked into pieces and burned. What was left of them was dumped into an abandoned mine shaft outside far-off Ekaterinburg, not far from Rasputin's home.

15. Quantrill

"Kansas should be laid waste at once! Meet the torch with the torch, pillage with pillage, slaughter with slaughter, subjugation with extermination!"

This, and more, was what William Clarke Quantrill said to the Confederate Secretary of War as he sought promotion from captain to colonel, and the authority to raise a regiment of Partisan Rangers. He didn't receive either, but that didn't stop him from carrying out his brutal plans.

What did Quantrill have against Kansas? Part of the answer lay in the slavery question, and in the border wars between Kansas and Missouri. But above and beyond these issues, it was Quantrill's uncontrolled sadistic tendencies that created his unbridled hatred.

Quantrill's father, Tom, was born in Maryland in 1813. A tinker and tinner by trade, he met his future wife while working in Chambersburg, Pennsylvania. They were married on October 11, 1836 and, upon the advice of relatives, left immediately for Canal Dover, Ohio, where they had heard a tinker was needed. William was born there on July 31, 1837.

Father Quantrill set up shop and did a good business from the start. He became so expert at this occupation that he wrote a book on tinning. The book was published with funds from the local school board—of which Quantrill was a trustee—without authorization. When a fellow trustee, Harmon V. Beeson, discovered the questionable use to which the board's money had been put, he exposed Quantrill's action to the citizens of Canal Dover. Quantrill was furious and swore that he would kill Beeson.

Shortly thereafter, Quantrill appeared at Beeson's house with a cocked pistol in his hand. Beeson was in the process of making himself a cup of sillabub. When he saw wild-eyed Tom Quantrill approaching him, he took the hot poker he was about to plunge into the cider, and cracked Quantrill across the head, knocking him senseless and leaving a nasty scar.

In spite of this incident, Quantrill became assistant principal of the Canal Dover Union School in 1850. In 1851 he was appointed principal and held that position until 1854, when he died of tuberculosis.

After the death of her husband, Mrs. Quantrill found it hard to provide for her family and she hurried her oldest child, William Clarke, out into the workaday world. She had counted on his contribution to the family income, but soon enough discovered that William was lazy and irresponsible. Except for a six-month term of teaching in Kansas, he was never gainfully employed for more than several months.

Her other seven children were, for the most part, equally unenergetic. Thomson, seven years younger than William, was a worthless tramp and horse thief. The other four boys were petty thieves who made no contribution to the household, let alone to society. Franklin and Mary were cripples. Of Cornelia, the other girl, we know little. All of these children died before they reached middle age.

Young William was cruel. His greatest pleasure was hiking off by himself into the woods and shooting at animals. He was a crack shot, and he delighted in crippling small creatures and then watching them suffer and die. He would often stand at the pigsty, shoot pigs through the tip of the ear, and laugh uproariously when they ran about squealing in pain. He thought it great fun to catch snakes and nail them to trees. At times, while walking along a corral or a fenced-in meadow, he would ram his knife into a horse or cow. It is hardly surprising that other boys avoided him.

William was a treacherous character to associate with. All friends and acquaintances were potential enemies. He would not hesitate to attack them if there was an advantage to be gained. Kindness was unknown to him; he did not show it, nor did he expect it from others. If, however, he was wronged, he would never forget the deed, and would seek ways of retaliating.

Aside from these serious defects of character—to which might have been added: defiance, malice, ingratitude, and depravity—William did possess one positive attribute. He was extremely adept at the power of persuasion, an attribute that made him a most effective leader.

Quantrill did well academically, but he was obstreperous in the classroom. When he made things difficult for his teachers, they sent for his father, the principal. The old man was more than willing to set his son straight by offering a full measure of corporal punishment. He would flail his son with a heavy stick or pound him with his fists until the boy "saw the error of his ways."

William Quantrill despised his father, but he was fond of his mother. She doted on him, and never quite comprehended the extent of his mean streak. Even at the height of his notoriety, she made excuses for him. He rewarded her love with a few letters and the promise of money—which he never sent.

In the spring of 1857, Harmon Beeson, his son Richard, Colonel Henry Torrey, and William Quantrill set out for Kansas. Beeson and Torrey were in debt in Canal Dover, and decided it would be to their financial advantage to start a new life out west. They were honest men and had intentions of paying off their debts owing in Ohio.

Beeson and Torrey did not take their families with them, but Richard and William were friends, and Richard asked that William be allowed to join them. Mrs. Quantrill was especially keen on William's going; she hoped that he would find a farm where they all might settle. Neither Torrey nor the elder Beeson was enthusiastic about William's presence, but they consented to take him because of their friendship with his mother. They also hoped that William might be induced to give up his idle ways, learn an occupation, and make his home in Kansas.

The travelers bought claims near Stanton, in Lykins County, and set up rough housekeeping in an old log cabin on Torrey's land. Normally, the two boys slept together on blankets in front of the fire. The men slept in the rear of the cabin, on a raised platform. One night Mr. Beeson awakened suddenly, and found Quantrill standing over him with Torrey's 12-inch Mexican dagger in hand, ready to plunge it into his chest. When Quantrill hesitated momentarily, Beeson jumped up, awakening Torrey. Shaking with fear and anger, Beeson went outside and picked up a stick with which he beat Quantrill until the boy screamed for mercy. Not even Quantrill could explain what had come over him. After that, one of the men always slept with Quantrill—endeavoring to discourage his violent ways.

For nearly a year Quantrill lived—off and on—at the Torrey cabin. When he wasn't there, he was roaming about the countryside stealing cattle and goods. He even stole from Beeson.

During this period he also came in contact with anti-slavery elements and became what was then known as a "border-ruffian" in Missouri, or a "Jayhawker" in Kansas. His duplicity stood him then, as later, in good stead. He would help to steal slaves, acting as an abolitionist guerilla soldier, and then return the slaves to their masters for the reward. He was a thief and robber and, on occasion, a murderer. He was feared in every border town and known for his violent temper, quick draw, and conniving ways.

In Kansas, from 1858 to 1860, Quantrill called himself Charley Hart. Exactly why he adopted an alias is unknown. He may have done so to protect the family name—upon which he had already brought much scandal. In Missouri, he was known as Charles William Quantrill or Charley Quantrill. Sometimes he spelled his name Quan*trell*. His father had done the same years before. The use of aliases often caused confusion—but history has left no doubt that all the dastardly deeds associated with "Hart" may be imputed to Quantrill.

Except for a period of time in 1858 when he served as a cook for some soldiers in Utah, Quantrill spent the years 1858 to 1861 largely in and around Lawrence, Kansas as a slave-stealer, blackmailer, kidnapper, and robber. Although, for the sake of his own safety, he acted mainly as an abolitionist, he continued his practice of capturing runaway slaves and reselling them. When the law finally chased him out of Kansas and into Missouri in 1861, Qauntrill realized that he could no longer continue his double-dealing. The Civil War had begun, and he decided to support the guerilla activities of the South.

Up until the early months of 1862, the band of guerillas with whom Quantrill had cast his lot was nothing more than a mob. The nominal head was Upton Hays, a kind of mobile "Partisan Ranger Chief." His territory was broad, stretching all the way from the Missouri to the Osage River in western Missouri. Quantrill recognized that even a troop of bushwhackers needed a modicum of discipline and direction, and, upon the departure of Colonel Hays, he assumed command. Quantrill had a flair for psychology and he gave his men a sense of pride by equipping them with long, outer-shirts of brown homespun material with bright trimmings.

Included in this force of cutthroats and bandits were a number of former border-ruffians: people like Quantrill. Some were deserters from the Union army, and some were Missourians who believed in the Southern cause, but could not take the step of joining the Confederate army. It was a motley group. What they had in common was an innate desire to plunder and kill.

In March 1862, Major General H. W. Halleck officially declared Quantrill and his raiders outlaws; they were subject to being hanged or shot on sight by federal officers. Quantrill read the order to his men and immediately set out to look for some Union soldiers he had learned were in the vicinity of Independence, Missouri. At Blue Bridge, near Pitcher's Mill, an advance scouting party captured a Union sergeant and disarmed him. Quantrill rode up with a large body of men. Wanting to impress his followers with his disdain for Halleck's order, Quantrill drew his pistol and shot the sergeant at point-blank range. Turning to his men, he said, "Boys, Halleck issued the order, but we drew the first blood!"

At that very moment, a man and his young son were crossing Blue Bridge on their way out of town. Quantrill had the man seized, and accused him of spying. The man protested the trumped-up charge, but to no avail. Quantrill gunned him down on the spot, burned the bridge, and rode off with his bushwhackers. The youngster was left on the side of the road, crying over his father's dead body.

On August 15, 1862, Quantrill was commissioned a captain in the Confederate army. One hundred and fifty men were placed under his command. Quantrill was inordinately proud of his commission and he displayed it frequently. It provided him with status—and with a license to loot and murder.

Federal forces tried desperately to break up Quantrill's band, but every time they thought they had the guerillas cornered, Quantrill would attack another town or company of Union troops. After an assault on Palmyra, Missouri, in September 1862, in which an elderly Unionist by the name of Andrew Allsman was abducted, U.S. Army Colonel W. R. Strachan delivered a strong ultimatum to Quantrill. If he did not return Allsman to Palmyra within 24 hours, Strachan would seek authorization from his commanding general to shoot 10 Confederate prisoners being held at Palmyra.

It is not known whether Quantrill ever received Strachan's message. But, good as his word, Strachan requested and obtained permission to execute the prisoners.

The men were picked at random and lined up before a firing squad. The soldiers ordered to carry out the execution found the work distasteful. They were so nervous and upset that only three of the hostages were killed with one bullet. The other seven had to be shot at again and again at close range.

When a relative came to claim one of the bodies, Strachan said to him: "Take the whole goddamned bunch, if you like. They're not good for anything but fertilizer."

Many people throughout the country, both in the North as well as the South, were enraged over this unfair and senseless act, and demanded that Strachan be court-martialed. He was sentenced to a year at hard labor, but was never imprisoned—so intense was the disdain in the military against Quantrill's raiders.

But the executions did not deter Quantrill. On October 17th

he marched toward the village of Shawneetown, Kansas. On the outskirts, he and his men encountered a wagon train guarded by an escort of federal troops. The soldiers were asleep. The raiders didn't disturb their peaceful slumber—but proceeded methodically to knife and bludgeon 15 of them before any awakened. The others fled in panic.

Still hungry for blood, the raiders tore into Shawneetown and shot the first seven people they saw on the street. Every building was then set ablaze and the town leveled to the ground.

When Quantrill returned from Richmond, Virginia in the fall of 1862, after having talked with the secretary of war about his promotion to colonel and the formation of a new regiment, he was crestfallen. He was not wined and dined as a hero; in fact, he was hardly known to anyone. The few military men and senators who had heard of Quantrill criticized his wantonness. They talked about his disregard for the amenities and rules of war—concepts unknown to Quantrill and many others in the West.

Quantrill's return route took him through Vicksburg, Mississippi, where he ran into General Sterling Price. Price admired Quantrill, and was concerned about his dejected state. It has been reported that Price *may* have commissioned Quantrill a colonel. (This practice was not uncommon in the 1860s.) Quantrill purchased a colonel's uniform and from then on called himself "colonel." When pressed to prove the validity of his claim, however, he was never able to produce legitimate documentation.

Of all the heinous deeds carried out by Quantrill, the most notable is the Lawrence Massacre. Quantrill, himself, harbored personal feelings of animosity toward the town, and the raiders felt a similar deep-seated hatred because of the town's liberal abolitionist attitude. Since its founding, Lawrence had been in the forefront of those western towns urging freedom for all slaves, in addition to liberty for all. It was clear to the South that if slaves were freed in Lawrence and then throughout Kansas, the slave-freeing fever would soon spread throughout the country. Quantrill's solution was simple: Wipe Lawrence off the face of the earth.

On August 21, 1863, Quantrill and his men rode into Lawrence and attacked the small, white Union army camp, killing 18 young recruits. They then headed immediately for the Second Colored Regiment billeted across town. But, by the time they reached the camp, the soldiers had escaped. Filled with fury, Quantrill's raiders turned upon the civilian population and, with gun, knife, and sword, murdered 150 men. After allowing the women and children to leave, they put the town to the torch and destroyed nearly 200 buildings.

In retaliation, General Thomas Ewing, Jr., Union commanding officer of eastern Kansas and western Missouri, instituted a "scorched earth" policy four days later. The citizens of four counties in western Missouri, known to contain many Southern sympathizers, were given two weeks in which to evacuate. On September 9th, Union soldiers burned every home and farm building over a 2000 square-mile area—but not before they had stolen everything of value left by the evacuees. This wasteland was long after known as the "Missouri Burnt District," and inspired the famous painting, "Order No. 11," by George Caleb Bingham. Quantrill's raiders no longer had a place in which to hide and fled northward and eastward for temporary refuge.

Instead of discouraging Quantrill and forcing him to discontinue his activities, Ewing's measures merely served to infuriate him. He headed back into Kansas. By the first of October, Quantrill was well on his way to Baxter Springs in Cherokee County, in far southeastern Kansas. There, he carried out his second famous massacre.

At about noon on October 6, 1863, Quantrill charged the little log fort outside Baxter Springs. But his efforts were repulsed, and the guerillas rode out aimlessly onto the prairie to the northeast. Then, quite by accident, they encountered General James G. Blunt, a Union Civil War hero on his way to a new assignment at Fort Gibson. Accompanied by two companies of soldiers and a military band, and riding in a carriage with the pretty, 22-year-old wife of Chester Thomas, an army contractor, Blunt cut a figure of pure vanity. His vanity was to be short-lived.

When Quantrill and his men appeared suddenly, riding from the direction of the fort, Blunt, in his conceit, naturally thought it was a welcoming party. However, when the raiders came closer and lined up in battle formation opposite Blunt's lead company on the east side of the Fort Gibson Road, the general knew something was terribly wrong.

Before the order to attack was given, two of Blunt's men broke ranks and fled. Major Curtis ran them down personally, and sent them back just as eight more turned tail. Quantrill was observing all this from 200 yards' distance. Sensing weakness, he charged. All of Company A panicked and scattered, and Blunt was left with Company I of the Third Wisconsin Cavalry. The Wisconsin troops made the mistake of waiting too long to flee, and Quantrill's raiders cut down 29 of the 40 men—23 of them were dead when they hit the ground, and six were left wounded.

The escaping Union soldiers headed west, where they unfortunately encountered a deep ravine less than a quarter of a mile away. Many were trapped, and soon they were at Quantrill's mercy. It was like a turkey shoot!

Meanwhile, Blunt had realized that it was Quantrill who was decimating his ranks, and he looked about desperately for a way to escape and to reach the fort. Leaping out of the buggy and pulling Mrs. Thomas with him, he grabbed the first two saddle horses he could lay his hands on. With total disregard for decorum, he hoisted Mrs. Thomas up on one of the animals, jamming her feet in the straps without bothering to shorten the stirrups. Off she dashed, minus one boot and with her skirt blowing over her head. Blunt and Cyrus Leland, the father of Lieutenant Cyrus Leland, Jr., Union hero at the Lawrence Massacre, mounted and caught up with Mrs. Thomas. The party of three arrived at the fort, safe but frightened. Blunt was immensely embarrassed. It was the worst defeat of his entire military career, and he never lived it down.

Not too long after the Baxter Springs Massacre; Quantrill's band began to disintegrate. Much dissension had arisen over the leadership of the group. George Todd very much wanted to be in command. Unlike Quantrill, whose guerilla activity had always been selfishly motivated, Todd was devoted to the cause of the South. In comparison with Quantrill, he was an ineffective commander, and Quantrill still had the confidence and support of the men.

Seeing that the South was losing the war—and being one who had not entered the battle out of principle—Quantrill decided to relinquish command. He and Todd finally severed their relationship in the spring of 1864. Todd was left in command. Quantrill took eight of his most trusted men, and rode off for Howard County, Missouri, where he spent the summer. From this time on he was no longer a factor in the war.

When Todd and his second-in-command, Bill Anderson, were killed in October 1864, Quantrill thought briefly about making a comeback. He formulated a plan to gather together as many of his old band as possible and set out for Washington. There they would assassinate Lincoln. With Lincoln assassinated, the Northerners would be so disheartened they would surrender immediately. The plan seemed so outrageous to his men that he was unable to persuade anyone to accompany him.

But Quantrill did convince 33 of his men to travel with him to Kentucky—for an unknown purpose. Disguised as Union soldiers they made their way down across Missouri into Arkansas and Tennessee before arriving in Hartford, Kentucky on January 22, 1865. They succeeded in deceiving the Federals stationed in Hartford into thinking that they were a detachment of the Fourth Missouri Cavalry.

Murder and robbery became Quantrill's way of life once again. Almost continuously, he plundered villages and towns throughout southwestern Kentucky. Contrary to his earlier practice of sparing women and children, he took to beating and killing them too. Every community lived in fear of his sudden appearance.

On the night of April 16, 1865, Quantrill and his band were at a drunken party at the home of Jonathan Davis, a judge of Spencer County, Kentucky, who had befriended them. Quantrill abruptly interrupted the festivities to announce that he had heard Lincoln had died the day before. A toast was raised: "To the death of Abraham Lincoln, hoping that his bones may serve in hell as a gridiron to fry Yankees on!" Quantrill laughed so hard he choked.

But he soon would have a premonition of his own death. It came in a strange way.

His horse, Charley, had carried him faithfully throughout his career without injury. It was said that the horse had been with Quantrill so long it had absorbed his personality. Mean as a snake, it would bite and kick anyone who approached him— but never Quantrill. Shoeing the horse was an especially difficult task.

On one occasion Jack Graham, a guerilla, had old Charley tied hard and fast preparatory to shoeing him. In using a buttress—an old-fashioned device for paring the hooves—Graham, in his effort to keep the horse from struggling, pushed too hard on the buttress and disabled Charley. When Quantrill learned that his horse could no longer perform, he turned white: "That means that my work is done. My career is run. Death is coming, and my end is near."

His instincts were correct. Astride a new horse that was not accustomed to him or the smell of gunpowder, Quantrill found it difficult to outdistance and outsmart his pursuers. Headquartered temporarily in the southern part of Spencer County on the Wakefield farm, Quantrill was asleep in the hayloft when cavalry Captain Edwin Terrill rode up on May 10, 1865 with a contingent of battle-seasoned men.

Hearing the soldiers descending the slope behind the barn, Quantrill rolled out of his blanket, skittered down the ladder, and tried to mount his horse. But the beast reared crazily and kicked wildly at Quantrill. Now desperate, Quantrill dashed out of the barn, and chased after his men who had already mounted their horses and were riding off.

At the orchard, just outside the lot, Quantrill caught up with Dick Glasscock, who tried to pull his chief up onto his horse. At that moment Glasscock's mare took a rifle ball in the hip and went wild. Quantrill kept on running until he caught up with Clark Hockensmith, who was threading his way through the trees. As he reached for the rump of Hockensmith's horse, a bullet tore through his back, striking the spine and paralyzing him from the arms down. Another ball lopped off his right index finger.

Two Federalists passed by, but no more shots were fired. Instead, they pulled off his boots and rummaged through his pockets. Finding nothing of value, they left with a curse.

Quantrill was carried up to the Wakefield house where his men tried to make him comfortable. Terrill came along and, with his lieutenant, began to plunder the house. But when Wakefield offered them some money and whiskey and praised them for the valuable service they had rendered in shooting Quantrill, they ceased their thieving. Quantrill gave Terrill his watch and $500—in return for leaving him unmoved. A doctor was summoned: He expected Quantrill to be dead by morning.

But when Captain Terrill returned to the Wakefield farm on the morning of May 12th, Quantrill was still alive. Thinking there was some hope, Quantrill consented to be transported to the army prison hospital in Louisville. There he lived, to the surprise of all, until the afternoon of June 6, 1865.

Thus did the end come to William Clarke Quantrill— border-ruffian, bandit, Jayhawker, guerilla, and madman of the West.

16. Turner

Just before daylight, on Monday, August 22, 1831, a courier astride a lathered horse delivered a message to the mayor of Richmond who, minutes later, personally placed it into the hands of Governor John Floyd. The notice came from James Trezevant, Justice of the Peace of Southampton County, and it told of a slave insurrection that had begun in the early hours of the same day. Already several families had been massacred, and the people of southeastern Virginia were shocked and frightened.

The instigator of the rebellion was Nat Turner, a slave employed on the farm of Joseph Travis. His act led to the death of 61 white people and nearly twice as many blacks. To the minds of some, the vicious events instigated by Turner were bold strikes against slavery. Many black Americans, today, look upon Nat Turner as a hero.

Nat was very much a product of his environment. Like all the other plantation blacks, he experienced the oppression of slavery intimately, and if Nat was mad, it was the idiocy of the institution of slavery that was, in large measure, responsible for it. Nat Turner found a place in the pages of history because of his desire to secure freedom for his people. Sadly, his concern was coupled with murder, and that was unfortunate.

The immediate result of the Southampton 1831 uprising hurt the black community. Black preachers were denied the right to preach, beatings were increased, and suspicion and fear heightened. But in the long run, the effect was to provide black Americans with a sense of history and unity.

Nat Turner was born in Southampton County on October 2, 1800 to parents of unmixed African descent, and was the "property" of Benjamin Turner. Little is known of his childhood, but one fact is certain: He acquired his rebelliousness from his parents.

When Nat was a baby, his mother attempted to kill him; she could not bear the thought of him growing up in servitude. During his formative years, his mother and father implanted in him a love of freedom and a high regard for self. Nat's father escaped from the Turner farm and fled to Liberia when Nat was still very young. The incident made a deep impression on the boy, for, in a very real sense, all blacks were peers—even parents and children.

Over the years Nat's resentment towards slavery grew. Once, he was caught away from the plantation without a pass. Two district patrollers beat him severely and returned him to his master. Nat was angry. On another occasion, he enlisted the assistance of two boys from a neighboring farm and, together, they strung a piece of clothesline across a road regularly travelled by the patrollers. Nat tricked the men into a chase that resulted in their tripping over the rope and landing face down on the ground. One of the men broke his wrist; the other dislocated his shoulder. Both had badly scarred faces and knees from the "accident."

Today, a snowfall is a fairly infrequent occurrence in southeastern Virginia. When it does fall, the children rush out to take advantage of the opportunity to engage in snowball fights. It was no different in the early 19th century—except that then black children were always on the receiving end, and were never expected to retaliate when pummeled by white children. Nat was so annoyed by this that on one occasion, he waited till nightfall, and threw rocks at a gang of whites. He had been sure to pull his hat down over his face so as to avoid recognition.

Nat's resentment expressed itself in another way. Having been continually reminded by his mother and grandmother that he was too smart to be a slave, Nat began to develop a feeling of superiority over other slave children with whom he lived. Treated like every other black slave by the whites, he found it ego-bolstering to assert himself over his own people.

As a youngster, Nat would gain attention by telling about incidents that had taken place before his birth. Since they were all events which his family could verify, he had probably obtained the information by overhearing his parents as they reminisced. His ability to embellish these incidents with verifiable facts led his mother, who had no idea where he could have learned about them, to believe that her son possessed a sixth sense.

When he began to prophesy, she was positive that there was something extraordinary about him. She had often told Nat that he was put on this earth to achieve some higher purpose. She had had this intuition, she claimed, ever since she had noticed the little bumps on his head and chest. This was a sign which many slaves looked for, for it identified an exceptional person—possibly a savior.

It would be unfair to say that Nat's original intention was to deceive; there was an element of religious sincerity underlying his early actions. All the people around him, even his master, were religious. They believed in God, read the Bible, and attended church and camp meetings. The Bible, worship, and prayer were all integral parts of Nat's upbringing.

But the strange way in which he capitalized on them—the fervor with which he employed them—leads one to conclude that he was either fanatical or devious. He may have been both, because religion to a slave was an avenue of spiritual and social escape. It was a force that could inspire rebellion. Its blend of African, American Indian, and local practices was employed by Nat to create an unusual aura about him.

Fanatically devout as a child, he withdrew from the company of other children and shrouded himself in mystery. Discerning that this withdrawal made others view him with awe, he added to the mystery by reporting visions and making prophecies. After a time, he himself began to take his own religious visions and soothsaying abilities very seriously.

He would slip into the woods and drip blood on the leaves of a particular tree. At a later time, he would return to the site with some of his peers, and would "predict" that they would find certain leaves covered with blood. The slave children would rush to examine the leaves and find that it was indeed the truth.

As a teenager he often bragged of his ability to spit blood at will. When challenged to do so, he immediately obliged—to the amazement of everyone. Of course, it wasn't blood that he spit. It was logwood coloring matter which he had stolen from his master's dye pots!

Nat learned the alphabet as a child, but, as he often insisted in later years, he held no recollection of when or how—except to say that one day he was shown a book and was able to spell the names of the objects pictured in it. There is no doubt that his parents taught him, but Nat probably learned it at such an early age that he really didn't remember. The blacks were astonished at his ability, and Nat lost no time or opportunity in putting this talent to work for him.

By the time he had reached adulthood, Nat had had extensive exposure to religion. Like others of fundamentalist stripe, he felt confident in interpreting individual Bible verses, in or out of context. Among his favorite passages as a young man was, "Seek ye [first] the kingdom of Heaven and all things shall be added unto you." While praying as he plowed in the field one day, a Spirit spoke this verse to him. For two years thereafter, Nat prayed for the meaning of this verse. When the Spirit spoke the verse again, Nat knew it meant that he was "ordained for some great purpose in the hands of the Almighty."

As the years passed, Nat became more and more confirmed in this belief. He saw that he was able to impress and manipulate black people more and more—not by "conjuring," but through "the communion of the Spirit and the wisdom of God."

About this time Nat was assigned to work for a most disagreeable overseer. We don't know what he did for the man. He was probably not a slave driver, although he had the ability and status. A slave driver would hoe, but never plow—and we know that Nat spent most of his time in the field plowing. At the first opportunity, Nat ran away. But after 30 days in the woods he returned of his own free will—much to the amazement of the Negroes on the plantation.

By way of explanation, Nat claimed that the Spirit had appeared to him and warned him that in contemplating escape he had fixed his mind on earthly things, when he should have been seeking the Kingdom of Heaven. The Spirit, he continued, had advised him to return to the service of his earthly master, for "he who knoweth his Master's will, and doeth it not, shall be beaten with many stripes, and thus have I chastened you." The plantation blacks felt that if they were as smart as Nat, they wouldn't serve *any* master.

For a long while Nat avoided his fellow blacks and spent all his spare time praying for guidance. One day, he had a startling vision. He saw white and black spirits fighting each other in the sky. The sky became dark, he heard roaring thunder and saw blood flowing. Then a voice said: "Such is your luck; such you are called to see; and let it come rough or smooth, you must surely bare [*sic*] it."

He prayed fervently for a revelation, and the Spirit imparted to him "knowledge of the elements, the revolution of the planets, the operation of tides, and changes of the seasons." The year was 1825, and from this moment on Nat felt that he had been made "perfect."

In his confession (published under the title *The Confessions of Nat Turner*) made to Thomas R. Gray, a local white lawyer, during the first three days after his capture, in November 1831, Nat painted a vivid picture of other aspects of this religious experience, which, in his mind, had formed the basis for his act of rebellion:

> The Holy Ghost was with me and said, "Behold me as I

stand in the Heavens"—and I looked and saw the forms of men in different attitudes—and there were lights in the sky to which the children of darkness gave other names than what they really were—for they were the lights of the Savior's hands, stretched forth from east to west, even as they were extended on the cross on Calvary for the redemption of sinners. And I wondered greatly at these miracles, and prayed to be informed of a certainty of the meaning thereof—and shortly afterwards, while laboring in the field, I discovered drops of blood on the corn, as though it were dew from heaven—and I communicated it to many, both white and black in the neighborhood—and I then found on the leaves in the woods hieroglyphic characters, and numbers, with the forms of men in different attitudes, portrayed in blood, and representing the figures I had seen before in the heavens. And now the Holy Ghost had revealed itself to me, and made plain the miracles it had shown me. For, as the blood of Christ had been shed on this earth, and had ascended to heaven for the salvation of sinners, and was now returning to earth again in the form of dew; and as the leaves on the trees bore the impression of the figures I had seen in the heavens, it was plain to me that the Savior was about to lay down the yoke he had borne for the sins of men, and the great day of judgment was at hand.

When he shared his experience originally with a white man, Etheldred T. Brantley, Nat reported that the man stopped his wicked ways, but immediately suffered from boils over his body. Blood oozed from them, but after nine days of prayer and fasting, he was cured. Soon after, the Spirit again appeared to Nat and told him that he and the black people should be baptized. He therefore gathered together a group, and led them down to the river where he baptized himself, Brantley, and the blacks. Because he had promised that a dove would fly down and light on his shoulder, the curious as well as the devout came along. They all sang, and rejoiced, and gave thanks to God.

Everybody recognized Nat as the "preacher." Even though he was not conventionally ordained, his ability to prophesy had set him apart from the other blacks. With this status, the stage was set for a religious drama in which Nat assumed the role of spiritual leader of his people.

On May 12, 1828, Nat heard a loud noise in the sky. He looked up and saw the Spirit descending. The Spirit said that the Serpent had been loosed, and that Nat should take on Christ's yoke for the sins of man, and "fight against the Serpent, for the time was fast approaching when the first should be last and the last should be first." To Nat, this was a sign that he should exercise his leadership by rebelling against the white man. Religion was one way through which the world could be changed. Thus, persuaded by his own reasoning, by visions of heavenly forces and by the response of his peers, Nat was convinced that he was a messiah sent to deliver the slaves from oppression and misery.

When Nat's master, Benjamin Turner, died, Thomas Moore became his new owner. But Moore did not live long, and his infant son, Putnam, legally inherited Nat. In 1830 Moore's widow married Joseph Travis, and Nat went to work for Travis. Travis was kind to his slaves; in fact, as Nat later reported, he was "too indulgent" and this was one of the reasons he (Nat) killed him. Weakness begets attack.

Almost three years had passed since the Spirit had instructed Nat to fight against the Serpent. On February 12, 1831, Nat received another sign—this time in the form of an eclipse of the sun. It meant to him that he should now tell others about the work he was to do. He chose four slaves in whom he placed the utmost confidence. They were Henry, Hark, Nelson and Sam. They agreed that July 4, 1831 would be the day of murder and rebellion.

But when July 4th came, Nat was sick. The group waited. Nat looked for another sign. It appeared on August 13th.

When the sun rose, it had a strange, greenish cast, which shortly became bluish. Late in the afternoon many people discerned a large black spot moving across the surface of the sun. Nat knew right away that this represented black people trampling on white people. He said, "As the black spot passed over the sun, so shall the blacks pass over the earth." He made plans for the group to meet one week later: Sunday, August 21st, in a swamp on the Travis place.

Jack and Will Artist, two free men of color, now joined the group. Hark had brought a pig for barbecuing; Nelson, some sweet potatoes; Sam, bread; and Henry, a bottle of brandy.

When Nat arrived—rather late in the afternoon—a feast was in progress. He refused to eat. Instead, he fasted and prayed. Playing the role of the chosen one—the messiah—he made his entrance late, and chose not to eat, symbolically denying his total identity with the group. When Henry offered Nat a swig of brandy, he turned it down contemptuously, reminding his friend that he had "never sworn an oath or taken a drink."

In the next breath Nat told the assembled slaves that he had purposely kept the size of the group small; he didn't want any information to leak out. His intention was that their "march of destruction and murder should be the first news of the insurrection."

Nat would not use a swear word or take a sip of brandy, but he was willing—even anxious—to murder!

No record exists of the plans formulated at the meeting that day. The objectives of the planned massacre are not clear either. Nat may have explained their task as an exalted one, with deliverance from slavery as the result. He may also have said that God had selected him as the leader of the movement, and told him to slay all white people they might encounter without regard to sex, age, or condition of health. But he may have *felt* somewhat differently—mostly revengeful. For one thing, Nat was once severely whipped for saying the blacks ought to be free. For another, he was married to a young slave girl belonging to another master who greatly restricted Nat's association with her.

What we do know is that Nat expected that ever increasing numbers of slaves would join the group as it went from farm to farm. There is some indication they were to reach Jerusalem (now Courtland, Virginia) as quickly as possible, and from there they would hike to the Dismal Swamp in North Carolina, some 35 miles distant. Although a young Negro girl later testified (at Nat's trial) that she had heard the slaves discussing the conspiracy for a year and a half, it is more likely that the specific plan of action was very vague, and that the group only made a decision regarding the first two or three farms and left the rest of the route more or less to chance. Despite his talent for leadership, Nat was no tactician.

In those days, church services were interminable, sometimes lasting all day and on into the night, including a picnic in the afternoon. After the picnic meal, the congregants would troop back into the church for an evening service and some singing. It was, therefore, almost midnight when the Travis family returned to their farm on that fateful Sunday. Exhausted from the long day, they prepared for bed and fell sound asleep almost immediately. They had no idea that at 1:00 o'clock in the morning Nat was crawling through an upstairs window.

Stealthily, Nat moved through the upstairs hall, made his way to the staircase and tiptoed down the steps to the front door. He unlatched the door—and in streamed the group Helping

themselves to the weapons on Travis's rack, they climbed upstairs without uttering a word. Hark was carrying an axe, and
Nat a hatchet, both of which they had picked up in an outbuild-
ing before entering the house. Everybody was liquored up except
Nat. Not only had they been drinking brandy until 9:00 o'clock,
but they had gotten into the Travis cider press as well. In spite
of his acknowledged command position, Nat could not maintain
discipline.

Hark had wanted to chop the front door down, but Nat had
restrained him and told him it would be better for them to
murder the people in their beds. He stated that he was willing
to spill the first blood.

Nat and Will entered the master's bedroom and stood by the
bed for a moment or so trying to make out the figures lying
there in the pitch-black darkness. Nat raised his hatchet and,
with a sudden jerk, brought it down on Travis's head—but instead of severing his head, the blow glanced off. Stunned, Travis
leaped out of bed with a scream, but Will dealt him a murderous
blow with his axe. Turning to Mrs. Travis, Will then brutally
split her in two.

While this was going on in the master bedroom, the other
men searched out the rest of the family. One by one, each was
slaughtered. When the murderers had left the Travis house and
realized that they had neglected to kill an infant who lay asleep
in his crib, Nat sent Henry and Will to end that young life as
well.

The job now complete, Nat lined up the members of the
band in front of the barn and drilled them in military fashion.
He liked to fancy himself a soldier; some people called him General Cargill or General Nat. But Nat was no Napoleon.

After about 15 minutes of marching, Nat led his followers
off in the direction of Salathiel Francis's house, some 600 yards
away. Sam and Will pounded on the front door. Mr. Francis
called out from inside, his bewildered voice asking who was
there. Sam quickly identified himself, and said he had a letter
for Mr. Francis. As Francis opened the door, Turner's men
grabbed him, dragged him onto the porch and beat him to death.
Next destination: Mrs. Reese's house up the road.

Doing away with Mrs. Reese was a very simple task; she
had not even locked her door. One of the men entered the house,
walked upstairs, and, axe in hand, entered her bedroom and
slashed her to death.

The sun was just coming up when the party reached Mrs.
Turner's place. Henry, Sam, and Austin headed straight for the

still and shot Mr. Hartwell Peebles, who worked on the farm, and helped themselves to some corn liquor. The rest of the group moved toward the house.

Nat and Will tried the front door, but it wouldn't give. It was bolted tight. Will whacked at it with his axe, and it swung open. In the living room, huddled together and trembling with fear, were Mrs. Elizabeth Turner and Mrs. Sarah Newsome. Will laid his axe into Mrs. Turner's chest; she died instantly. Nat drew Mrs. Newsome over to him by the hand. Using his dull-edged sword, he brutally slashed at her head. Will finished her off with his rusty axe.

One wonders what the relationship between the two men was. Was Nat the theoretician and Will the tactician? The rebellion was Nat's idea, but his sword was rusty and dull, and Will's axe sharp and sure. In comparison with Will, Nat avoided becoming personally involved in killing. Why was Nat the leader and not Will? Will was big and strong and a free Negro. The only answer seems to be the one Nat himself promoted—namely, that he was imbued with "the Spirit."

At the conclusion of each murderous spree, Turner's men would roam through house and property, destroying anything and everything that struck their fancy. They picked up all guns, axes, swords, scythes, and the like, and distributed them to the growing number of slaves that had joined the original band. The group had grown to 21 men on foot and nine on horseback.

Nat dispatched six of his group to Mr. Henry Bryant's house. He instructed everyone else to head for Mrs. Catherine Whitehead's residence where all were to meet in an hour and a half.

As they approached the Whitehead place, Richard Whitehead was spotted at work in the cotton patch. Nat ordered him to step over to the fence by the road. When he did, Will laid him low with his axe.

Approaching the house, Turner saw somebody in the garden. The chase began, but Nat soon discovered that it was only a slave girl. Disappointed, he went back toward the house. He was informed by one of his men that the group had managed to kill everybody except Mrs. Whitehead and her daughter, Margaret. As he neared the front door, Will was dragging Mrs. Whitehead out by the hair. Will flung her down on the porch at the top of the steps, and struck her such a fierce blow with his axe that she was almost decapitated. To Nat it appeared as if Will was splitting kindling on a chopping block.

Nat circled the house and found Miss Margaret crouched in

a corner where the outside cellar door made an angle with the house. The moment she saw him she struggled to her feet and attempted to flee. But she was easily caught. Once again, Nat whammed away with his sword. But the dullness of the blade frustrated him. He cast it to the ground in disgust and, instead, ripped a rail from a fence and proceeded to, literally, beat Miss Margaret's brains out.

The six men who had gone to the Bryant place soon joined their comrades at the Whitehead home and filed their report of death and destruction. They had carried out their assignment so well that Nat decided that this method of operation—functioning in separate groups—would be continued. Accordingly, they split up again, one group heading for Mr. Richard Porter's farm, the other for Mr. Howell Harris's. When Nat reached the Porters' place, he learned that the alarm had been spread, so he doubled back to warn the others. But as he approached farm after farm, he found dead bodies strewn everywhere. His men had already been there.

Nat finally caught up with the group—now numbering upwards of 40—at Captain Newit Harris's. Shouts of "hurrah" could be heard as he rode up. Some of the men were loading their guns; others were drinking and getting more and more drunk. Occasionally, one would take a lick of gunpowder along with a slug of whiskey so as to become still "more excited." The Harris family had escaped, but no matter—the men had taken out their vengeance on property, destroying and looting. Nat looked with disdain at his drunken army, but with satisfaction at the havoc they had wrought.

It was now mid-morning on Monday. Nat ordered his men to strike out for Levi Waller's, three miles away. He usually brought up the rear, and was thus spared having to participate (with two exceptions) in the murders themselves. But, by his own admission, he took enormous pleasure in viewing the maimed and mangled bodies. He was not disappointed when he reached the Waller place. The dead Mrs. Waller and her 10 children were piled up in a heap. Mr. Waller happened to have been away at the time.

Turner next ordered his men to go to a nearby school. There they flailed into a knot of huddled children, killing several of them and horribly mutilating others.

On and on the group went—to William Williams's house, to Jacob Williams's, and to Mrs. Rebecca Vaughan's. By now the entire mob was mounted and consisted of nearly 60 bloodthirsty slaves. Nat was anxious to get to Jerusalem. It was at this point that he made a grave error.

Some of the band members wanted to stop off at the Parkers' to kill the whites and pick up some more slave support. Part of the group went to the Parker house while the others waited at the gate half a mile away. When his men did not return after a long time, Turner rode up to the house to see what had happened. There he discovered the slaves comfortably lying around swilling Mr. Parker's apple brandy which they had found in the cellar. At that very moment those slaves guarding the gate were attacked by a group of 18 whites, whom they successfully drove off. But the whites soon regrouped and were reinforced by other whites. Before Nat and his group could come to the aid of their comrades, the blacks were thoroughly routed, and for all intents and purposes the rebellion was over.

But Nat did not give up. He spent the rest of the day and night recruiting more slaves and searching in vain for more whites.

The following morning his group appeared at the house of Dr. Simon Blunt, but they were repulsed by Blunt, his sons and a number of their slaves. It was particularly odious to Nat that his own people were no longer his supporters.

By this time, militia units, vigilante groups, and federal forces were converging on Southampton County and indiscriminately killing all black people in their path. The carnage was almost as frightful as that perpetrated by the insurrectionists.

By August 31st, all the insurgents, except for Turner, were rounded up and presented for trial. Most were sentenced to death, but some were sent to the Richmond penitentiary—and later to slave markets in the deep south. In all, there were 50 separate trials, extending from August 31st to November 21st, 1831.

Nat had left instructions with two of his men to rally a new group and to meet at the same spot where the planners had met the previous Sunday. But no one ever showed up. Left alone, Nat stole some provisions from Mr. Travis's house and set out Thursday night of the same week. This time his destination was unknown. His mind was totally confused. As he walked, he came upon a pile of fence posts stacked up in a field. There, under the rails, he dug a hole and crawled in.

He stayed in the cave for six weeks, emerging only at night to drink water from the nearby stream. No doubt, he would have remained there indefinitely had it not been for a passing dog. The animal, smelling the man and the food under the fence rails, barked so loudly that Nat stuck his head out to quiet him.

When he did so, he saw two black men standing at the entrance to his refuge and staring down in fear and amazement. When they suddenly began to run in the direction of the Travis farm, Nat knew they were going to betray him.

Hastily, he crawled out of his hole and ran in search of another hiding place. Less than a mile away he discovered a fallen tree. He began to dig, and in an hour he had made himself another cave. He remained there—about 12 miles from Jerusalem—until noon on Sunday, October 30th—for about two more weeks—when a certain Benjamin Phipps located him.

Nat surrendered without offering any resistance. He was a pitiful sight. Half-starved, he was well under his normal weight of 150 pounds, and he seemed shorter than his five feet six inches. He was barefoot, and wore a battered, old hat pierced with buckshot holes received in the fracas in Parker's cornfield. At his side was the dull sword he had used against Miss Whitehead and others.

Phipps did not harm his prisoner, for he wanted to be sure to collect the $1,100 bounty that was posted. The next day he turned Nat over to Deputy Sheriff Edward Butts in Jerusalem and obtained a receipt.

Nat Turner was tried and convicted on November 5, 1831 and sentenced to hang on the 11th. He faced death quietly, with dignity, at 1:00 o'clock in the afternoon. He had predicted that the sun would shine no more after his death. And although it is true that the sky became dark and a storm arose on the day of his execution, it did turn bright again before nightfall.

17. Mishima

The *samurai* spirit can best be explained as aspiring towards a perfect balance between action and the arts. The title of Ruth Benedict's famous book, *The Chrysanthemum and the Sword,* is a metaphorical statement of that ideal, but also an assertion of a basic dichotomy in Japanese history.

For nearly 30 years of his life, Yukio Mishima, internationally renowned author and actor, was the embodiment of the chyrsanthemum. His attempt to strike a balance with the sword, both figuratively and literally, by committing public *hara-kiri,* did not inspire, but shocked the world.

His act has been explained as arising out of insanity, sexual perversion, or grotesque aestheticism. In a man as complex as Mishima, all three explanations apply. His insanity was also the cause and result of his genius.

Yukio Mishima was a pseudonym used by Kimitake Hiraoka, adopted upon the advice of his teacher, when Kimitake published his first work at age 16. It was a remarkably mature work, called *Hanazakari no Mori* ("The Forest in Full Bloom"), published in installments in the nationalistic literary journal, *Bungei Bunka,* and dealing with the lives of aristocrats from various periods of Japanese history. The language of the book was of such incredibly high quality that the editor felt it necessary to keep the author's real name and age secret.

Kimitake himself chose the name Mishima after a town near Mt. Fujiyama from which one had a perfect view of the top of the mountain. Yukio is a derivative of the Japanese word for "snow." It was fitting and predictive that a name representing a point of distinction in Japanese geography be chosen by a writer who was to become a distinguished literary success. The name Mishima became so much a part of Kimitake Hiraoka that for most of his life he was never called by his real name—even by his closest associates.

Mishima was born in Tokyo on January 14, 1925, the son of upper middle-class parents. His father was a government official of some stature, and his mother came from a fine family For the first ten years of Mishima's life, he and his family, which later included a younger sister and brother, lived at the home of his paternal grandparents. This was a typical Japanese family arrangement, but it was to have special consequences for Mishima.

By tradition, the Japanese mother-in-law exercises very strict control over her son's wife. Natsuko, Mishima's grandmother, made use of this right to an extreme degree. Filled with disdain for her husband, who lacked the *samurai* outlook of her forebears, and excessively critical of her son, whose position in the government she considered insignificant, she staked everything on her grandson. To make sure that her hopes were fulfilled, she insisted upon raising the child herself.

It was a virtual kidnapping. When Mishima was not quite two months old, Natsuko took him from his parents' apartment upstairs, and moved him into her room. She told her daughter-in-law that it was unsafe for a child to live on the second floor. Shizue, Mishima's mother, was heartsick, but did not protest greatly. It would have done her no good if she had, for Natsuko was a domineering woman who controlled the entire family with an iron hand. Besides, she had tradition on her side.

Natsuko was physically and emotionally sick. Crippled by gout, tormented by chronic neuralgia, and afflicted with syphillis contracted from her husband as a result of his youthful indiscretions, she spent most of her life in her bedroom complaining about her lot. It was in this room, redolent of illness and age, and permeated by an atmosphere of hatred, that the little boy spent his formative years.

Natsuko justified her overprotectiveness of Mishima on the grounds that the child was delicate. For fear that he would catch cold or fall prey to other children's germs, she was careful to see that he spent little time outside. He was never permitted to play with "dangerous" toys or with little boys who were "too rough." Mishima's playmates were, therefore, always girls. The old woman had, unknowingly, laid the foundation for Mishima's homosexuality.

She also taught him to revere pride, rigidity, and aloofness —qualities she considered to be the essence of his family's and Japan's venerable *samurai* spirit. Mishima developed these attributes to a fine degree, but he added to them an innate sense of humor and irony, as well as a sensitive nature. In another age, Mishima would have been the ideal *samurai*; in the mid-20th century, he was an anachronism.

When Mishima was almost four, he came down with an illness diagnosed as *jikachudoku*, which, literally translated, means "auto-intoxication." The major symptoms were dark vomit and renal failure. For a while the family feared for Mishima's life, but, after injections of camphor and glucose, the child rallied. The attacks occurred periodically for one year thereafter, apparently being triggered each time by the grandmother's angry or peevish moods. It is a reasonable conjecture that his sickness was psychosomatic in origin. Living with Natsuko in her sick room was like living in a prison infirmary with the warden.

It is not surprising that a child deprived of playmates and left so much to his own devices should turn to the world of fantasy for his pleasures. Mishima enjoyed reading fairy tales. His favorite stories were those of warriors and princes facing great danger. Living as he did, in the midst of sickness, and being told at every turn that he himself was frail and sickly, he developed a morbid fascination with death. Nothing stimulated him so much as the sight of suffering and death—the more dramatic and gory, the more exciting to him.

When Mishima had just turned six, his grandmother took him to visit two female cousins of his same age. He sensed (correctly) that in this household he was expected to act like a boy, and could give free rein to his play inclinations. Accordingly, he and the little girls played a game of war in which Mishima shouted and ran around loudly imitating the sound of gunfire. He imagined himself the victim, and tumbled down upon the floor, writhing and groaning. In his *Kamen no Kokuhaku* ("Confessions of a Mask"), he tells us: "I was enraptured with the vision of my own form lying there, twisted and fallen. There was an unspeakable delight in having been shot and being at the point of death. It seemed to me that since it was I, even if actually struck by a bullet, there would surely be no pain." This incident signaled the beginning of a lifelong masquerade. The mask he wore for the next 39 years belied his homosexuality and his death wish. All that was normal about him was abnormal.

In 1935 the family followed the custom of *inkyo*, according to which the grandparents and parents took up separate residences. Mishima was finally allowed to live with his parents and sister and brother, but he had to promise to visit his grandmother overnight at least once a week. If for any reason he was late or could not come, the old lady would be "seized by a paroxysm."

Over the remaining four years of her life, Natsuko often took Mishima to the theater and introduced him to *kabuki* and *no* drama. It was on these occasions that he came to know the meaning of *hara-kiri*, that ritual suicide by disembowelment usually called *seppuku*—an artful act practiced by aristocratic Japanese to avoid execution or disgrace. The sensitive youth concluded that death was beautiful, a thing to be desired more than life; and that death by *hara-kiri* was ultimate beauty.

Alone at home, Mishima reveled in looking at pictures of people undergoing horrible deaths or in drawing others to suit his own fancy: people with skulls split open; *samurai* warriors slitting their bellies; soldiers being blown apart. He was developing an aestheticism that combined death and darkness and blood, and he was joining it to an eroticism based on violence. He had his first ejaculation while viewing a reproduction in a book of Guido Reni's painting, *St. Sebastian*. This painting depicts a nearly naked youth bound to a tree with two arrows sunk into his sides and a third penetrating the left armpit. A quarter of a century later Mishima was photographed in the same pose.

For Mishima, being at home with his mother was little different from the years spent with Natsuko. His mother was so starved for his company that she lavished excessive affection and attention on him. She even referred to him as her "lover." Mishima returned her adoration with a full-blown Oedipus complex.

Clashes with his father often centered around Mishima's literary efforts. Azusa made light of his son's writings and scolded him for not working for a career in government service, as was proper for a boy with his upbringing. Shizue would then take the part of her son and praise his writings. Azusa, not being a forceful man, would always give in and retreat into silence.

In praising her son's talent, Shizue was not just opposing her husband. She came from an intellectual family. She, herself, had long wanted to write, and often had worthwhile advice to offer. Mishima read all his earlier works to her, and derived immeasurable benefit from her criticism and encouragement.

When war broke out with the United States in December of 1941, Mishima was a student at the Gakushuin, a school principally attended by children of the aristocracy. It was not the best school academically, but it was chosen by his grandparents because they considered themselves to be among the higher strata of society. During the first part of 1942, Mishima was promoted to the senior division of the school, where he excelled in all subjects. He even received an "A" in athletics. And, even though he was not particularly robust, he no longer suffered ill health.

But Mishima did suffer. He suffered from pessimism and stoicism, as did so many among the student body of that day who could only foresee a dismal future of military service and war and death.

In a short time, Mishima came under the influence of a group of writers—among them the classics scholar, Zenmei Hasuda. Hasuda spoke of the war as a "holy war," and espoused the view that it was noble to die young. Mishima also read widely from the works of the *Roman-ha,* the romantic writers—in the tradition of 19th-century German Romanticism. What he found particularly fascinating in these writings was the stress laid upon self-destruction, and a credo of reincarnation which involved the special powers of the emperor.

While still a student at the Gakushuin, in the spring of 1944, Mishima passed his military service exam at Shikata—his grandfather's official place of residence. (Mishima's father had chosen Shikata instead of Tokyo as his son's place of registration in the hope of postponing his induction.) In July, Mishima was sent on maneuvers to a base on the coast of the Sea of Japan, but after two weeks he was released, for an indefinite period, until his call-up to active duty.

In September, Mishima graduated at the top of his class at the Gakusuin and, in October, entered law school at Tokyo University. Almost immediately, he and other students were compelled to work in a factory to help the war effort. The university had, for all intents and purposes, shut down its regular operations by this time. However, having being accepted, Mishima had the privilege of returning to study there once the emergency was reduced or the war was over.

Azusa had forced his son to choose law as a career because he felt it was the perfect ingress into upper bureaucratic circles. Tokyo University had long been *the* institution of higher education. Mishima was glad he had followed his father's advice. He found the university stimulating and the study of law a challenge to his intellect. Azusa had a practical goal in mind for his son, but Mishima discovered much more.

In February of 1945, Mishima was called to active duty and underwent another physical exam at Shikata. He had a fever when he arrived, and the deliberately misleading answers he gave to the examining physician's questions convinced the doctor that Mishima had a light case of tuberculosis. He was rejected for service and sent back home that same day. This rejection—even though he had planned to obtain it—had a lastng effect on Mishima. It was the stimulus for the body-building program to which he dedicated himself in later years, and it made him subconsciously indebted to the armed forces. It may, in great measure, account for the establishment of his own private army, the Tatenokai.

The end of World War II brought bitter disappointments, disillusionments, and sorrow to young Mishima. No longer were people especially interested in him as a boy literary genius; they were more interested in rebuilding their cities and their shattered lives. The emperor disavowed his divinity. Hundreds of military officers committed suicide in disgrace at having failed the emperor. Zenmei Hasuda shot himself in the head after murdering his commanding officer for making critical public remarks about the emperor. Even some civilians disemboweled themselves over Japan's having lost the war. And, in October 1945, his sister, Mitsuko, died of typhoid. With all that had transpired, it was a wonder that Mishima could address himself to his law studies once again; but he did apply himself, and, at the end of 1947, graduated and obtained a good position in the Ministry of Finance.

His father was very pleased. Mishima was not displeased, but all his spare time was devoted to writing. By September 1948, he had succeeded in having his works published, and he decided to leave the Ministry and to devote himself entirely to writing. In November, he began work on *Confessions of a Mask,* his famous novelistic autobiography in which he describes his nihilism, his sado-masochism, his narcissism, and his homosexuality. It is not a pretty picture, but it is an honest one.

At the end of the book, there is a famous scene which points all too clearly to Mishima's final act in life and to the eroticism attached to his act of *hara-kiri.* The narrator observes a young man among a gang of thugs sitting in a disreputable dance hall. The youth gets up and removes his shirt and begins to wind a dirty bellyband around his middle. The narrator reports that the youth is suntanned and sweaty and has hairy armpits. For Mishima this is a picture of supreme eroticism. The sun is warm and sensuous—something denied him as a child. Sweat and body hair were two of his fetishes. The bellyband highlights the abdominal area. In his imagination he sees the youth walking out into the street half-naked and getting into a fight with other youths He imagines him being stabbed in the stomach and the bellyband becoming soaked with blood.

In many of Mishima's works violent death is the focus, and in most instances it is death by suicide.

It was important to him that the victim be young and virile. In an article he wrote in 1962, Mishima, then 37 years old, expressed his distaste for a long life. People who live much past

40, he thought, must necessarily have an ugly death. To die beautifully, one must die young. He cites the Bronze Age and Roman times as periods furnishing Heaven with beautiful youths of 18 and 20. Medical care had prolonged life to such an extent that to Mishima Heaven was a place populated by ugly, old people.

Mishima felt that it was especially desirable that death be agonizing. One of the most painful ways to die was by *hara-kiri.* It is so excruciatingly painful that the victim often selects someone to finish him off by *kaishaku,* beheading with a sword.

By treating *hara-kiri* as ultimate beauty, Mishima was equating violent death with ecstasy. *Hara-kiri* would, then, presuppose an obsession with intense emotional excitement accompanied by pain. It would be related to rapture in producing a state of emotional exaltation. It was similar to a trance in rendering the victim oblivious to his surroundings. It would approach ultimate or maximum beauty by affording great sensory pleasure or by producing a subjective awareness of moral exaltation.

If pain and pleasure are opposite sides of the same coin, or if they can be conceived of as meeting at some point on a circle, then, presumably, that which causes the highest degree of pain can produce the highest degree of pleasure. Mishima's literary effort, *Honba* ("Runaway Horses"), ends with this confirming, descriptive passage: "Isao drew in a deep breath and shut his eyes as he ran his left hand caressingly over his stomach. Grasping the knife with his right hand, he pressed its point against his body, and guided it to the correct place with the fingertips of his left hand. Then, with a powerful thrust of his arm, he plunged the knife into his stomach. The instant that the blade tore open his flesh, the bright disk of the sun soared up and exploded behind his eyelids."

By 1955 Mishima had published 30 works and established himself firmly in the literary firmament. He now turned to the development of his body.

Deprived of vigorous exercise and sunshine as a child, Mishima had developed a disdain for his body. On board ship, in 1951, on one of his numerous overseas trips, he lay on deck, sunbathing, and discovered for the first time the strength-giving warmth of the sun. In the beginning, he found this pleasurable and satisfying. But later, he saw it as a necessary discipline for the development of a strong body. A strong mind and a strong body, sound literary accomplishments and well-toned muscles— these were the true ingredients of the *samurai* tradition.

Just under five feet four inches tall, Mishima undertook a rigorous body-building program that resulted in a physique that was powerful and well-sprung, but not muscle-bound. He had himself photographed on many occasions—to the delight of some, and to the amusement or amazement of others. He boxed, jogged, fenced, and performed as an actor. Always the showman, people wondered who the real Mishima was.

In one photograph, he posed nude on his back with a rose in his teeth. In another, he stood half-naked, a grim look on his face, with a *hachimaki* (headband) around his head, and a sword in his hands. In others, he knelt in the snow, holding a sword and wearing only a *fundoshi* (loincloth); or he lay on the street like a bloody traffic fatality. In still others, he pretended to be drowning in mud, to have a hatchet sunk in his head, or to be committing *hara-kiri*.

In a film of his own short story, *Yukoku* ("Patriotism"), he played the lead part of the lieutenant who disemboweled himself. Mishima's body had become a display item. Only days before his death, he chose many of these pictures to be exhibited in a Tokyo department store, as a photographic biography of his life.

But another ingredient was essential to the *samurai* tradition—martial action. In 1967, Mishima began to train with the Jieitai (Japanese Self-Defense Force), a volunteer army of some 250,000 men. Shortly thereafter, he tried to recruit students at Tokyo's Waseda University for his private army, the Tatenokai (Shield Society). Its purpose was to protect the emperor and to support the Jieitai through guerrilla action in time of emergency—and thus restore the *samurai* tradition. The students expressed more amusement than interest.

Mishima insisted that the Jieitai was unconstitutional. Article 9 of the Peace Constitution of 1947, drawn up by the Allies, forbade Japan to maintain a national army. In October 1969, it was decreed that the Jieitai would protect and safeguard the constitution. Mishima saw a contradiction in the Jieitai, officially just a police force, protecting the very constitution that denied its existence. He urged that the Jieitai assert itself by rebelling and re-establishing itself outside the direct control of the Western powers. His nationalism is all the more strange in view of his own wide travels and Western habits.

Failing to attract the left-wing students at Waseda, Mishima turned his attention to a small, conservative group that was responsible for the publication of an insignificant magazine called the *Ronso Journal*. They were interested in his ideas, and agreed to swear an oath to imperial Japan.

The ceremony was held at the Journal headquarters and consisted of cutting one's finger and dripping blood into a cup, and then signing the oath in blood. After everyone had signed the oath, Mishima drank from the cup and passed it around, a red smile on his face. He seemed to relish drinking the blood— he even added a dash of salt—but most of the group found the experience revolting. One boy hurried out of the room and vomited in the hall.

Mishima made arrangements with the Jieitai, in the spring of 1968, to train his militia at Camp Fuji. The Jieitai furnished trucks and other equipment, the students paid their own travel expenses, and Mishima provided everything else. Some of the original group had by now dropped out for various reasons, so Mishima sought to replace them by appealing once again to the students at Waseda. A few did show up, among them, Masakatsu Morita, a young man who was to figure most prominently in the activities of the Tatenokai.

Morita was a round-faced but attractive 21-year-old boy who had been orphaned as a baby and raised by an older brother. He received his elementary and secondary education at a Roman Catholic mission. Morita and Mishima felt an immediate attraction for one another. It may, in fact, have been a homosexual relationship, but there is no proof that such was the case.

Morita shared Mishima's imperialist views and was invaluable in encouraging the interest of the Waseda students in the group. In a very short time, he was Mishima's acknowledged second-in-command. His loyalty was absolute.

The Tatenokai were a strange little band. The members received no pay, enjoyed no rank, and were often the laughing stock of the public. Yet, they undoubtedly found something satisfying in the leadership of a famous man, in their colorful uniforms, flag, slogans, meetings, and military exercises. The army decided to accept up to 100 men, a limit which was never quite reached. The fact that there was a limit to membership afforded the group an aura of exclusivity.

For over two years Mishima directed the curious and spasmodic activities of his militia, all the while hoping to find an activity that would arouse public attention. In the spring of 1970, he chose Morita and two other Tatenokai members, Masayoshi Koga, known as Chibi-Koga, and Masahiro Ogawa, as a secret nucleus within the Tatenokai. During the summer he added one more member—Hiroyasu Koga, usually called Furu-Koga, to distinguish him from the other Koga. All these young men swore allegiance to Mishima "to the very end"—without knowing what that end might be. Morita is a possible exception here; he may have known Mishima's total plan from the start.

What was the plan?

It changed several times—from staging a putsch and take-over of parliament with the help of the Jieitai, to *attacking* the Jieitai; from kidnapping one senior officer to holding another hostage. Eventually, a decision was reached to take General Kanetoshi Mashita hostage. After his capture, Mashita was to be compelled to assemble the troops at his garrison at Ichigaya in central Tokyo. Mishima planned to make a speech before them, urging them to join the Tatenokai in bringing about a revision of the constitution. He and Morita would commit then commit *hara-kiri*. The two Kogas and Ogawa would prevent the general from possibly committing suicide himself.

Mishima sought death in an effort to become a tragic hero. It was his thesis, in his long essay *Taiyo to Tetsu* ("Sun and Steel"), that "one who dabbles in words can create tragedy, but cannot participate in it." He also insisted that tragedy requires "an anti-tragic vitality," but above all it demands "a certain 'inappropriateness.'"

Mishima made his final arrangements. He wrote several letters, made some phone calls, invited two reporters to be present at his speech, severed connections with his publishers, and completed the last installment of his *Hojo no Umi* ("The Sea of Fertility").

The day of the "inappropriate" incident, November 25, 1970, was at hand. Mishima, in Tatenokai uniform and carrying a briefcase containing various papers and two daggers, was wearing a 17th-century Magoroku sword as he stepped out of his house at approximately 10:15 a.m. and strode toward a waiting car. In it sat his four Tatenokai co-plotters.

Mishima sat down in the front seat, and passed out envelopes containing a letter in which he took the blame for the "incident." The envelopes also contained money for eventual legal fees. Mishima seemed to be in fine spirits and joked and sang all the way to Ichigaya.

The group was waved through the gate at 10:50 and went directly to General Mashita's office. The general was most cordial and invited everyone to have a seat. He had been expecting them.

The students took chairs along one wall, but Mishima remained standing in the center of the room in front of General Mashita's desk. He introduced the young men, explaining that he had very much wanted them to meet the general. He also said that the Tatenokai were having their monthly meeting there at the base that day, and these men were to receive commendations for their helpfulness to their injured comrades while on a recent maneuver.

The general expressed his congratulations, and then commented on the sword which Mishima had just removed from his person, and propped up against a chair. He said he was doubtful that it was legal to wear such a weapon, but that he admired it very much. At that remark, Mishima withdrew the sword from its scabbard and held it up for the general to see, calling at the same time for a handkerchief. This was a prearranged signal at which Chibi-Koga stepped in back of the general, choked him into submission, and gagged him with the handkerchief. The handkerchief was actually a *tennugui,* the towel used to wipe the grease and smudge from a sword. The others helped tie Mashita to his chair.

Unknown to Mishima and his boys, Major Sawamoto, the general's aide, was in the hall, and was watching what was happening through one of the opaque glass side-door panels. Not understanding, but sensing that something was amiss, he summoned his superior, Colonel Hara. Together they sought out General Yamazaki in the office next door.

In a few minutes groups of five to seven officers and men started to come into Mashita's office through the two side doors connecting the adjoining rooms. Mishima and his group had clumsily secured the doors with wire and piled furniture up against them, but the barriers only served to slow up the angry soldiers. When they stepped over the furniture into the room, Mishima wounded several of them with his sword, and threatened to kill Mashita if the men did not leave immediately. They saw that he was deadly serious.

He demanded that the troops be assembled on the parade ground before 12:00 noon so that he might address them. At first, the officers refused to comply, but when Mishima again threatened Mashita's life, the general ordered Colonel Yoshimatsu to carry out the order. Yoshimatsu did so, but he also called the police.

In the meantime, Mishima and his students donned their *hachimaki* with the rising sun and the slogan *Shichisho Hokoku* ("Serve the Nation for Seven Lives") and waited for the crowd to gather. Mishima calmly smoked a cigarette and kept an eye on the soldiers watching him through a broken glass panel.

At exactly 12 o'clock, Mishima and Morita climbed out of

one of the windows at the end of the room leading onto a balcony on top of the portico which stretched over the main entrance to headquarters. Morita slung two long, white banners containing statements of their objectives over the parapet, and fastened them.

He then flung copies of their manifesto to the ever-increasing crowd of soldiers and curiosity-seekers below. Mishima jumped up on the parapet and, legs apart and arms akimbo, began his speech—a rambling summary of the manifesto. He was wearing white gloves, another fetish of his. They were blood-stained.

The shouts and jeers drowned him out after the first sentence. Mishima called for silence and tried to be heard again, but the crowd was in a nasty mood. Individual remarks could occasionally be heard soaring upward: "Stop trying to be a hero!" "Asshole!" "*Bakayaro* (a filthy invective)!" "Madman!"

Mishima gave up after just seven minutes. He had planned to speak for half an hour, but was thoroughly unnerved by his total rejection. Suddenly, in mid-sentence he stopped his speech, and shouted three times in defiance of the crowd: "*Tenno Heika Banzai*" ("Long live his imperial majesty"). He then sprang down from the parapet, walked quickly across the balcony, and re-entered Mashita's office through the still open window. Morita was close behind him.

"I don't think they even heard me," he muttered morosely.

Already he was unbuttoning his tunic. He was not wearing an undershirt. He threw off his shoes, let his trousers drop to his knees, exposing his white loincloth, and took a seat cross-legged on the floor not more than ten feet from General Mashita.

Grabbing up his *yoroidoshi,* a 12-inch dagger, he caressed his belly with his left hand, inhaled and exhaled several times, gave a cheer for the emperor, set the point of the knife on his skin, and plunged the dagger deep into his abdomen. His face went deathly white, blood ran from the wound down between his legs, staining the loincloth. As he began to slice to the right, his hand started to tremble violently. Gripping his right hand with his left, he shoved the knife across his stomach for a distance of half a foot.

Morita was standing in back of Mishima with a raised sword. Mishima was groaning terribly and muttered a signal to Morita. But just as Morita swung to decapitate him, Mishima toppled over onto the carpet and Morita's swipe only cleaved his back as the blade struck the floor.

"Again!" screamed Furu-Koga.

Morita brought down the sword, but missed the neck, hacking Mishima's body instead. Mishima was in dreadful agony. His intestines spilled onto the rug.

"Again!" the students shouted.

This time Morita hit the neck, but his hands were shaking, and the blow was not sufficient to sever the head from the body.

At this point, Furu-Koga seized the sword and completed the task. Mishima's head rolled away, and blood spurted from his torso. The body jumped and twitched like that of a chicken whose neck had just been wrung.

Morita said: "Pray for him." With tears running down their cheeks, the students bowed toward the bloody mess and prayed.

In a moment, Morita had removed his tunic. Taking the *yoroidoshi* from his master's dead hand, he attempted to drive it home, but the blade did not penetrate very far, and made only a superficial wound. Furu-Koga was standing behind him with upraised sword. Upon a nod from Morita, he gave a mighty whack, lifting Morita's head from his body. With a thump it hit the floor and rolled toward Mishima's stump.

Once again the remaining students said a Buddhist prayer for their comrade, with the general joining in. He begged them to stop the bloodshed.

But it was all over. They told him that Mishima had instructed them to live and speak out at the trial.

The students covered Mishima's and Morita's torsos and placed their heads upright nearby. Together with the general, they walked to the door and submitted to arrest.

The world was shocked at this abominable deed. Why had so successful a man done this heinous thing? Author of 40 novels and more than 60 other shorter works, nominated three times for the Nobel Prize for Literature, actor, philosopher, sportsman, father of two young children, husband—it did not make sense.

The 17th-century writer-philosopher Matsuo Basho once said: "The white chyrsanthemum, even when lifted to the eye, remains immaculate." Mishima would not have agreed. It had to be stained with blood.

In Japan, white is the appropriate color for a funeral. When on the day following Mishima's death a friend brought white roses to the house, Shizue gently chided her, and told her she should have brought red ones for a celebration, for Kimitake had for once acted out of his own free will. For Mishima, blood was life, vitality.

His last note read: "Human life is limited, but I would like to live forever."

18. Torquemada

The Inquisition is an integral part of the development of the Christian religion. It is not an admirable chapter in the history of the church.

The Grand Inquisitor, the man who headed the Inquisition during its most infamous period, Tomás de Torquemada, represented in the abstract much that was retrogressive among many religious leaders.

History has provided us with grudgingly little information about Torquemada's personal background, but in the institution which he fostered, it is possible to see a clear reflection of the man and his times. In most ways, modern man has moved well beyond the institutional cruelties of the 15th century, although it is evident from recent wars, and particularly from the persecution inflicted upon the Jews by Hitler and his henchmen, that what Christianity calls man's "innate sinfulness" has not disappeared.

Torquemada was born in 1420 in the north central Spanish city of Valladolid. He was the son of Pedro Fernández de Torquemada and the nephew of Cardinal Juan de Torquemada. His basic education was acquired at San Pablo Dominican convent in Valladolid, where the Dominicans implanted in young Tomás an intense fervor that was to manifest itself in his later years and fully emerge when he assumed the role of Grand Inquisitor.

The formal history of the Inquisition begins with Domingo de Guzmán, better known as St. Dominic. He was the first Inquisitor, and founder of the Dominican order. Like his contemporary, Francesco Bernardone, later canonized St. Francis of Assisi, St. Dominic strove to help the lowly and the poor who were trapped and largely forgotten in a church led by aristocrats catering primarily to the needs of aristocrats. Both men subscribed to Jesus's example of renunciation of worldly wealth. This must not have been easy for either of them, for Domingo came from a noble family and Francesco's father was a well-to-do merchant of Assisi.

Despite the similarities of vows, and the sincerity of purpose, there were distinct differences between the two men. St.

Francis, perhaps the favorite saint of all times, is remembered particularly for his gentleness toward animals. St. Dominic, though also popular, is recognized primarily for his learning and his zeal.

Where it was a matter of the propagation of the faith, Domingo's ardor was unexcelled. On a trip to southern France, in the company of the Bishop of Osma, he preached fervently and eloquently to the heretics at Toulouse, converting many. He rejoiced in the bloody victories of the French crusader, Simon de Montfort, over the heretical Albigensian sect.

Encouraged by his oratorical successes, Domingo requested that Pope Innocent III found an order of mendicant preachers whose mission it would be to bring heretics back into the true fold. The Pope looked favorably upon Domingo's request, but he was unable to grant it. A Lateran Council had forbidden the establishment of any more monastic orders, so numerous had they become. The solution reached in 1215 was to establish a brotherhood attached to the order of St. Augustine. At the same time, the Franciscans were also made affiliates of St. Augustine.

The aim of the Dominicans was twofold. Not only did they seek, through the spoken word, to convince those who had "strayed" to admit the error of their belief and return to orthodoxy, but they spurred the faithful to employ all means—even terror—to assist them in their task. It was, therefore, natural for the Dominicans, in 1233, to form, with the support of Pope Gregory IX, the governmental and executionary foundation of a tribunal for the protection of faith and morals. This tribunal was called the Holy Office and was a euphemism for the Inquisition. In short order, the persuasion of the spoken word was replaced by "tongues of fire," and some of the most ingenious torture techniques ever devised by the mind of man were introduced.

St. Dominic was the first Inquisitor and Torquemada was his successor. Each went about his job with equal fervor and zeal, but where in the case of St. Dominic it led to canonization, in Torquemada's case it led to madness, and placed a stain on the history of Christianity for all time. To later generations of Christians and non-Christians, the Inquisition was an enigma. It was incomprehensible, for it was part of a religion that proclaimed brotherly love and forgiveness as two of its most basic tenets.

When Torquemada was graduated in theology from San Pablo, he was named as prior to the Santa Cruz (Holy Cross) convent in Segovia in 1452. He also became the confessor to the royal treasurer, Hernán Núñez. This latter honor and responsibility earned for him the confidence of the royal family, and, upon their accession to the throne in 1474, Queen Isabella I and King Ferdinand V appointed him their official confessor.

Like most noble families, the Torquemadas had Jews in their line. One can only speculate whether that fact made Tomás all the more ardent in his condemnation both of religious Jews and even of those Jews who had converted to Christianity whether of their own free will or forcibly, some of whom later reverted to Jewish religious practices in secret. He was instrumental in persuading Ferdinand and Isabella to investigate the activities of crypto-Jews, and, in 1478, he headed the first official inquisition.

In 1483, upon the urging of the king and queen, Torquemada was made the Grand Inquisitor by Pope Sixtus IV. This action unified the entire inquisitional office for Castile and Aragon.

Torquemada warmed to his task immediately and set up five regional courts, reserving himself as the final appeal in all cases. Every procedure was explicitly stated and followed for the next 300 years. Remnants of the Inquisition persisted until the middle of the 19th century.

The sovereigns had made an excellent choice in Torquemada. His zeal was unbounded, and he carried out his task with originality, enthusiasm, and perseverance. Not waiting to receive information about suspects, he ordered his inquisitors out into the field to track down apostates, witches, necromancers, soothsayers, sorcerers, and lapsed Christians.

Popes and kings alike praised his tireless efforts, for he wielded a sword which was both spiritual and temporal. His object was to create a nation—and, eventually, a world—united in the Christian belief and not sullied by Jews, Moors, or those whom he believed to be in league with the Devil and other evil spirits. His ruthless fanaticism pointed ahead to the Hitlers and Stalins of a much later day

Acquittal before the Inquisition was a rarity. Soon after taking charge as Grand Inquisitor, Torquemada was angered to learn that his territorial tribunal at Medina had acquitted some persons accused of heresy

Although this court was fully empowered to investigate cases and hand down sentences, Torquemada ordered that the persons be tried again in the presence of his *visitador*, Licentiate Villalpando. Several months later, Villalpando attended their second trial, at which several were again acquitted. Furious that anyone should be let go Torquemada ordered the unfortunate souls to be brought to Valladolid, where they were tried for a third time and burned at the stake. Not only was there double jeopardy, there was often triple or multiple jeopardy under Torquemada's Inquisition.

Torquemada's methods were those of a secret police agency, his courts Kafkaesque and kangaroo-like, and his sentences harsh beyond belief. It is particularly in the means of punishment that the viciousness of the man and his institution become clear.

From 1483 on, Torquemada executed more than 2,000 persons and tortured thousands of others in ways beyond comprehension. Even for their times, Torquemada and his inquisitors were excessively cruel. It is difficult, if not impossible, to imagine that the Inquisition was in any way related to a religion whose founder had preached brotherly love and forgiveness.

The best known public exhibition of punishment of heretics was the *auto-da-fé*, meaning "act of faith," a ceremony which accompanied the pronouncement of judgment by the Inquisition. It involved torture or death officially dispensed by secular authority. Announced two weeks or more in advance, great crowds gathered to witness the ghastly show. There were great similarities of ceremony and symbolism to the torch-lit parades and cross-burnings of the Ku Klux Klan during the early part of the 20th century in America.

Leading the procession was a crucifer who carried the white cross of St. Dominic, or the green cross of the Inquisition shrouded in black crepe. He was followed by a group of solemn men dressed in robes of black, with white crosses emblazoned on the front. These were representatives of the Confraternity of St. Peter the Martyr, the familiars or lay servants of the Holy Office. Behind them trudged the penitents and accused, usually bareheaded, barefooted, and stripped to the waist—regardless of the weather. They often carried unlighted green candles to signify that they had lost the faith. Bringing up the rear were the inquisitors and their various attendants, a number of Dominican priests, the secular officers of justice, and numerous bearers of effigies of those heretics not yet snared.

Typically, the procession wound slowly through the main streets of the city until it reached the cathedral. There, before being ushered inside, clergy at the door made the sign of the cross on the forehead of each accused person and proclaimed: "Receive the sign of the cross which you denied, and which, being deluded, you lost."

Erected in the church for the occasion were two raised platforms. On one an altar had been built, and on the other sat the inquisitors. The accused watched as Mass was celebrated. A sermon on the evil of heresy was always preached.

When Mass was over, the names of the accused were read aloud, together with each person's particular offense. Punishment or penance was then announced. The lucky ones were whipped in procession over a number of successive Fridays. Usually, they were also forced to fast on those and certain other days. Often they were barred for life from holding all public office. If they ever again lapsed into heresy, they were turned over to secular authority and burned summarily at the stake. "Mercy" was extended to those who confessed their Judaizing, or other heresies, before being fed to the flames; they were first strangled from behind.

There were variations in autos-da-fé, but the foregoing was the general procedure. The ceremony might occasionally take place in a city square instead of a church; there might be only 25 accused instead of hundreds; all might be burned that same day, or all might be penanced. The heretics might be wearing yellow penitential sackcloth, with a red St. Andrew's cross in front and back, called a *sanbenito,* or they might be provided with a black garment painted with red images of flames, dragons and devils. A noose was placed around the neck of each accused, and his hands were tied fast. For many people, the shame of being on public display was the most severe punishment of all.

Actually, the punishment and the humiliation were worse than death itself. Even burning at the stake was not the "simple" act of burning. The victims were often first roasted over a slow fire—and then burned. Sometimes fat was rubbed on the soles of their feet so they would sizzle a while. The Church claimed it desirable to proceed in such grave matters with stately leisure!

Other leisurely means of carrying out executions included starvation in a dank dungeon; stretching on the rack; binding with cords that cut through the skin and muscle down to the bone; flailing at specified intervals with whips studded with knots or small sharp blades; pulling out fingernails and toenails one by one, and breaking legs and arms with blows of the mallet; covering the victims with steel helmets containing screws which would be tightened one at a time in order to crush noses or break eardrums. Just showing the torture machines to the accused frequently was sufficient to get a confession—sincere or otherwise. All of this in the name of Christ!

The Inquisition bred fear and suspicion in every quarter. No one was safe—not laity, not clergy, not royalty. Only the Grand Inquisitor, his immediate subordinates, and the Pope had any claim on security. Neighbor was pitted against neighbor, daughter against mother, father against son, and so on. Anyone suspected of disloyalty to the church was a legitimate target.

"Send me more heretics," Torquemada demanded of his inquisitors, "and I will unify Holy Mother Church." They obliged. Often, an accusation against an individual was exaggerated or totally untrue, but the more zealous one was in bringing outrageous charges against others, the less the likelihood of his own conduct being scrutinized by the inquisitors.

When Sixtus IV was succeeded in 1484 by Pope Innocent VIII, many powerful Spaniards tried to unseat Torquemada by arguing that inasmuch as he had been appointed by Sixtus, his term expired with Sixtus's death.

They did not reckon with Torquemada's influence. Not only did Innocent quickly reconfirm Torquemada as Grand Inquisitor, he even extended Torquemada's control beyond Castile and Aragon to include all the Spains. Innocent went so far as to order all Catholic princes to apprehend and turn over to Torquemada all individuals requested by him for whatever reason—particularly Jews.

Many so-called New-Christians, those Jews who converted to Christianity officially, but continued practicing Jewish rites secretly, were appalled at the prospect of submitting to an auto-da-fé in order to be reconciled to the faith, for this demanded the "shame" of marching half-naked through the streets of one's city and then doing public penance. They, therefore, applied directly to the Pope for secret absolution. Since the requests were accompanied by large sums of money, they were invariably granted. After all, the Pontiff was accomplishing two very fine objectives at the same time. He was converting souls and enriching the treasury of the Church.

This practice greatly displeased both Torquemada and King Ferdinand—the former because he wished to reconcile, penance, or punish the Jews himself, the latter because it irked him that Rome should be milking any of his subjects of the gold which, he felt, belonged to him. Rome reacted to Torquemada's fierce complaint by simply canceling the absolutions already granted. The money that had been pocketed was kept.

Jews looked upon these shenanigans as nothing more than a colossal swindle—which, in fact, it was. They justifiably complained to the Pope that absolution cannot be canceled, and that one cannot be tried for heresy while in a state of grace.

What they did not count on was the power of the Inquisition to take action even against the dead (and his estate), if it were discovered that he was guilty of an offense which had not been dealt with according to the rules of the Inquisition. In short, the Inquisition had to grant a temporal absolution—the other absolution being only one of conscience. The price for complete absolution was confiscation of all property, infamy for the family, and life imprisonment for the reconciled. The king's and Torquemada's coffers filled up rapidly.

In complete fairness, it must be noted that the collected wealth was not enjoyed by Torquemada personally, or by members of his family. In fact, his way of life had not changed one iota from the way he lived when he was the simple Prior of Holy Cross of Segovia. He still slept on a board, clad himself only in the coarse garments of his order, and ate no meat. His asceticism did no more than reinforce his fanaticism.

The wealth derived from the victims of Torquemada's policies was used to continue the activities of the Inquisition and for the enlargement and beautification of the religious edifices—churches and convents—which he adored. A good deal of the funds went to support the increased number of inquisitors, as well as the instruments of torture that were added to increase efficiency.

In 1492, the money that had been collected reached an all-time high. By governmental decree, initiated and supported by Torquemada, all Spanish Jews refusing baptism were given a three-month period, from May till the end of July, in which to leave the country. The penalty for not complying with the law, or for subsequently returning, was death. Most Jews found the idea of denying their God—the God of Israel—repugnant. Yet, it was equally hard to leave their native land.

Given such a short time in which to sell their property and settle other affairs, the king and Torquemada once again profited greatly by buying up the homes and land of the Jews at substantially reduced prices. Toward the end of July, when the deadline was reached, they simply confiscated the unsold property of all remaining Jews.

What was the reasoning behind Torquemada's fierce treatment of the Jews? After all, liberty was officially granted to members of the Jewish and Moslem faiths. What made him pursue his policy to the point of madness?

The presence of such large numbers of unconverted Jews frightened Torquemada more than all else. They were, he felt, a corruptive influence on the New-Christians—the *conversos*—and this thought drove him mad. He accused the Jews of perverting Christians, and of desecrating churches and objects of Christian reverence. To him, therefore, the best and only solution was to banish them from the country—and in the process, to reap a huge profit by confiscating their wealth.

It would be folly to assume that Torquemada, despite his religious and ascetic personal life, did not revel in the power he commanded. Who could wield such power over so many and not lose his humility?

In the same year that Torquemada contrived to throw the Jews out of Spain, Rodrigo Borgia became Pope Alexander VI. No one was surprised when Torquemada was once again confirmed in his position as Grand Inquisitor. What did surprise some was that it was Alexander, of all people, who exercised a tighter rein over Torquemada, and that it was this tainted pope who was responsible for his retirement.

Throughout Spain, Torquemada's enemies were becoming more and more numerous. Torquemada appeared oblivious to the fact that he was being assailed from all sides; in fact, he considered himself a living martyr—the person who had effected the unification of the Spanish church. Despite his apparent lack of awareness of a rising opposition, Torquemada was careful, even when he took a very short trip, to be accompanied by armed guards. And when he dined, a magical horn was always close at hand to drive away any poison that may have been placed in his food.

There was much resentment among the magistrates when Torquemada began to assume many functions of the civil courts. Resistance to Torquemada's incursions resulted in the magistrates' questioning by the Inquisition and the subsequent imposition of penances. When they presented their complaint to the king, they received no satisfaction; he, too, was powerless in the face of the zealous old madman. The only recourse left to the magistrates was to appeal to Pope Alexander.

The appeal to Alexander was made by two well-known and most respected bishops, Juan Arias Davila of Segovia and Pedro de Aranda of Calahorra. They were well received in Rome, and the Pope seemed sympathetic to their accounts of the situation back home.

Torquemada was enraged when he learned that Alexander had betrayed him. He was now determined to undermine the two bishops. The *modus operandi* was the same as always—find a Jew in the bishops' ancestry, or convict them of heresy.

Bishop Davila's grandfather had been an important member

of the court of Henry IV, but a baptized Jew. Torquemada, therefore, attempted to taint Davila's position with the accusation that his grandfather had been Judaizing before his death. The proceedings instituted against Bishop Davila produced a scandal, but one of minor proportions, for the Pope instructed Torquemada to cease and desist from his persecution of Davila. This was the first time Torquemada's activities had ever been curtailed or even questioned.

Bishop Aranda was not as lucky as Davila, and although the sentence was some years in coming, he was imprisoned for heresy. In looking over the accomplishments of his life, it seems incredible that Aranda could have been accused of heresy. In examining the actual charges, it becomes obvious that they were formulated by a crazy man.

From this time forward, more and more complaints reached Alexander. He clearly saw that action had to be taken. To remove Torquemada summarily from office was too drastic a step, he reasoned. He decided, instead, to appoint four assistants, all inquisitors themselves, and all granted the same authority held by Torquemada. In a letter to the old Grand Inquisitor, the Pope explained the reason for his actions: He wanted to relieve Torquemada of some of his responsibilities because of the latter's failing health. He assured Torquemada, devious diplomat that he was, that he "cherished him in the very bowels of affection for his great labors in the exaltation of the faith."

Four months later, the Pope appointed Don Francisco Sanchez de la Fuente, the Bishop of Avila, the final judge of appeal, thus placing him—at least nominally—above Torquemada and the other assistants.

But abuses continued and, in fact, increased under the multiple leadership of the Inquisition. At last, the king himself appealed to Alexander to curb the excesses. The Pope's answer was the appointment of the so-called Richelieu of Spain, the former barefoot friar, Francisco Ximenes de Cisneros, as the Primate of Spain. Ximenes was empowered to take all measures necessary to bring the inquisitors in line with a more moderate policy.

In 1496, Torquemada retired from his position of eminence and entered the monastery at Avila. Sick in the body, but well of mind, he continued to watch with interest and to advise on activities of the Inquisition. It never once occurred to him that his cold, uncompromising zeal had not been completely in the service of his Master.

Despite the horrible deaths he had brought to thousands of his fellow human beings, he had a peaceful departure from this life in the year 1498. For him, a quiet death must have seemed the reward for a job well done. In the nearly five centuries since his death some have revered him, but most have seen him as a fiend. The historian W.H. Prescott tries not so much to defend him as to explain him when he maintains that "Torquemada's zeal was of so extraordinary a character that it may almost shelter itself under the name of insanity."